Advance Praise for *Rethinking Free Speech*

"This timely, important, and accessible book offers both a scholarly overview of and a close critical engagement with freedom of expression, in a way that helps readers move past naïve, monolithic and dogmatic accounts. Ives pays particular attention to social media and the internet, and to differences between Canada and the US, making the book essential reading for Canadians in the digital age. It is also highly readable. Pick this book up, and you won't put it down until you're done!"

— DR. SHANNON DEA, dean of arts and professor, University of Regina

"Ives delivers a master class on academic freedom and free speech — a must read for scholars and activists of all political stripes!"

— AJAY PARASRAM, associate professor, Dalhousie University, and author of *Frequently Asked White Questions*

"In light of the weaponized ways in which the concept of freedom of speech is often used today to silence minoritized groups and promote the spreading of disinformation, this historically informed and level-headed intervention into the current debates couldn't be more timely or necessary. Ives clarifies and disambiguates the concept of freedom of speech from that of academic freedom, showing how they have been consistently confused and misinterpreted, including by universities themselves. His analysis of how freedom of speech is thwarted on social media — not because of the curtailing of hate speech but because of the mutation of public interests by commercial ones — is particularly revealing. *Rethinking Free Speech* provides readers, especially those outside the United States, with the perspectives required to identify sloppy or downright incorrect uses of this key concept, as well as insightful ideas about where the debate can go from here."

— ZOE DRUICK, professor, Simon Fraser University

"This is the book we need right now as debates on free speech and academic freedom become increasingly prominent in our society. Peter Ives has found a way to make the complex philosophical and political terrain of these debates both in Canada and the US comprehensible and compelling for all readers with an interest in these topics. This book provides insight into the growing polarization around academic freedom and free speech debates online, on campuses and beyond. It is exactly what we need to read in order to effectively address these questions today and into the future. Read this book now."

— EVE HAQUE, professor, York University

RETHINKING FREE SPEECH

RETHINKING FREE SPEECH

by **Peter Ives**

Fernwood Publishing
Halifax & Winnipeg

Copyright 2024 © Peter Ives

All rights reserved. No part of this book may be reproduced or transmitted in any form by any means without permission in writing from the publisher, except by a reviewer, who may quote brief passages in a review.

Copyediting: Karen May Clark
Development editing: Fiona Jeffries
Cover design: Evan Marnoch
Text design: Lauren Jeanneau
Printed and bound in the UK

Published by Fernwood Publishing
Halifax and Winnipeg
2970 Oxford Street, Halifax, Nova Scotia, B3L 2W4
www.fernwoodpublishing.ca

Fernwood Publishing Company Limited gratefully acknowledges the financial support of the Government of Canada through the Canada Book Fund and the Canada Council for the Arts. We acknowledge the Province of Manitoba for support through the Manitoba Publishers Marketing Assistance Program and the Book Publishing Tax Credit. We acknowledge the Nova Scotia Department of Communities, Culture and Heritage for support through the Publishers Assistance Fund.

Library and Archives Canada Cataloguing in Publication
Title: Rethinking free speech / Peter Ives.
Names: Ives, Peter, 1968- author
Description: Includes bibliographical references and index.
Identifiers: Canadiana (print) 20240432029 | Canadiana (ebook) 20240437780 | ISBN 9781773636979
(softcover) | ISBN 9781773637068 (EPUB) | ISBN 9781773637051 (PDF)
Subjects: LCSH: Freedom of speech—Political aspects. | LCSH: Freedom of speech—Philosophy. | LCSH:
Freedom of expression. | LCSH: Academic freedom. | LCSH: Social media.
Classification: LCC JC591 .I94 2024 | DDC 323.44/3—dc23

CONTENTS

Acknowledgements viii

Preface 1

Introduction 7

1 | Philosophical Justifications 27

2 | Constitutional Protections 49

3 | Academic Freedom Is Not Free Speech 69

4 | Social Media 97

Conclusion 130

Notes 150

Bibliography 180

Index 197

ACKNOWLEDGEMENTS

Despite my skepticism about social media, one impetus for *Rethinking Free Speech* came from Jill McConkey who responded to my various posts about free speech and academic freedom with a comment, something like, "Is there a book here?" Her subsequent input has been invaluable. Eve Haque was also instrumental in her continuous encouragement that I write this book, providing important feedback. To both I owe much gratitude. I presented earlier versions of what became Chapter Three at "Within and Against Academic Freedom," hosted by the University of Toronto's Ontario Institute for Studies in Education (OISE), in 2018, and the public lecture series, "Il Foro," hosted by the Centro Caboto Centre at the Italian Canadian Centre in Winnipeg in 2021. I was very fortunate to workshop various sections of this work in the "Writers' Café," organized by the Centre for Research in Cultural Studies (CRICS). Thanks to Angela Failler and Lauren Bosc for running it and my colleagues who provided thoughtful feedback. Thanks to Noah Schulz who helped me work through some of these ideas in relation to our op-ed concerning transphobia and to the other members of the "Building Trans Solidarity" crew.

I would also like to thank those who read drafts of the manuscript or parts of it in various phases: Sean Carleton, Zöe Druick, Alan Sears, Sam Popowich, Julia Smith, Hillary Pimlott, and three anonymous reviewers. Fiona Jeffries and everyone at Fernwood Publishing have been so wonderful to work with and I highly recommend them to any authors. I would like to thank my students over the years who have heard and responded to many of these points in different forms, particularly my Fall 2021 students in "Special Topics: Free Speech."

Thanks also to Adele Perry, Theo Ives Perry, and Nell Ives Perry who had to put up with too many arcane discussions about free speech. I dedicate *Rethinking Free Speech* to my mum, Pauline A.H. Ives, who passed away as I was writing it. Her sarcastic, Yorkshire wit instilled in me the knowledge of how much power and humour even a few words can have.

PREFACE

COMMENTATORS HAVE SUGGESTED THAT THE FREE SPEECH TABLES HAVE turned (once again) since Hamas' attacks on 7 October 2023, and Israel's massive and fierce response. Now, so the argument goes, it is the left advocating free speech and decrying the censorship of pro-Palestinian protestors, and the right that declares the need for students, especially Jewish students, to feel safe and comfortable on university campuses. Those who previously offered more absolutist free speech positions — where all speech should be permitted — are suddenly outraged and calling for suppression of slogans like, "From the River to the Sea, Palestine Will be Free," and the utterance of the word "intifada." This book was substantially written before the fall of 2023 and these events have clearly changed the terrain of free speech debates, even leading to the resignation of the presidents at Harvard University and the University of Pennsylvania.[1] But this idea that freedom of expression is so simple and dichotomous — one is either for or against it — is what this book aims to rethink. The changing of the terrain of free speech debates convinces me that the analysis offered in this book and my plea that we need to re-evaluate the differing rationales for free speech is even more crucial.

For example, I insist that we need to recognize importance differences between free speech in Canada and the US. This point was confirmed by a letter sent on 13 December 2023 by five prominent Liberal MPs to twenty-five Canadian university presidents. Drawing heavily on US congressional hearings involving three prominent presidents of American universities, the MPs' first demand was that each president respond to the question of whether a call for genocide of the Jewish people was against their university's code of conduct.[2] Neither the letter nor the major news coverage pointed out that, unlike in the US where the First Amendment protects hate speech, including calls for genocide, Canada's hate speech laws specifically outlaw the promotion or advocation of genocide. In essence, this letter asked university presidents if their university policies accepted speech that is, in fact, illegal in Canada.[3] As I argue in this work, Canadian politicians, journalists, and the general public require a far greater ability to situate and disambiguate differing principles often conflated in the concept of free speech.

One of the many problems of simplistic approaches to free expression, that we are currently seeing, is that it leads people to equate demands for decent, humanitarian treatment of innocent Palestinians with the types of harmful speech — antisemitic, misogynist, white supremacist — that many of those critical of free speech absolutism find intolerable. It is no wonder many have lost patience with any invocations of the freedom of speech. But I do not think we can afford to abandon careful consideration of this terrain, especially as the changing landscapes of communication through social media and technological developments become ever more inescapable.

This book was initially prompted by my astonishment at the public discussion over free speech and academic freedom following the situation at Wilfrid Laurier University in the fall of 2017. The incident involved a teaching assistant, Lindsay Shepherd, attempting to enliven a tutorial on grammar in essay writing by showing a video clip of Jordan Peterson, the controversial psychology professor and conservative commentator. He argued that he should not have to address others with their preferred pronouns and that the bill under discussion in Parliament adding "gender identity or expression" to the Canadian Human Rights Act and Criminal Code would force him to do this. Later, Shepherd was called into a meeting with the course professor and two others and told that showing the video to her class was inappropriate and made some students uncomfortable. In the future, she would be required to submit her lesson plans and the professor may attend her tutorials. Shepherd secretly recorded this meeting and after she released the recording to the media, a national outcry ensued. Commentary in the media deemed this situation to be indicative of how universities were no longer allowing free speech. I was surprised that almost everyone, including university administrators, framed this incident as an issue of free speech rather than academic freedom. As I explain in Chapter Three, academic freedom is a distinct concept concerned with one's right to pursue knowledge and education in a university setting, whereas free speech is a right of individuals to express themselves in public. While there are similarities between free speech and academic freedom, they are not the same, and if we confuse them and allow students (and instructors) in classrooms to have free speech in the robust sense that Canada's Charter of Rights and Freedoms protects, it will be difficult to teach effectively. Perhaps more troubling, if we understand free speech as that expression allowed in classrooms or other workplaces, we necessarily diminish its scope and meaning. Reading the outpouring of reactions concerning Shepherd's situation, I became deeply concerned about the implications for the future of the university. As a professor, I worry about the prospect of my classroom being reduced to a glorified arena where yelling matches resembling social media exchanges occur — but worse because of the hefty price tag of tuition included — all in the name of free speech.

At a deeper level, I have been thinking through issues of language politics and free speech for most of my adult life. Born in the US and raised there in the 1970s and 80s, I, like many Americans, absorbed the idea that the First Amendment is what defines free speech and is central to democracy and a vibrant, open society. The years prior to moving to Toronto for graduate school in 1991, I was living in Portland, Oregon, attending Reed College — one of several free speech crisis zones in recent years.[4] Along with many people in Portland, I was deeply distressed by the rise of white-supremacist and skinhead activity, including the brutal murder of a 28-year-old Ethiopian man, Mulugeta Seraw. In November 1988, Seraw was attacked outside his apartment by members of the White Aryan Resistance (WAR) and East Side White Pride, another white-supremacist group. Ken Mieske, Kyle Brewster, and Steven Strasser confessed that they attacked Seraw because he was Black and that they were involved in white-supremacist organizations. This use of violence was part of WAR's strategy, along with handing out hate propaganda and recruiting other young skinheads. Indeed, Tom Metzger, the founder and leader of WAR, stated afterwards that these skinheads had done their "civic duty," although he added — presumably to try to hide his own involvement — that "they didn't even realize it."[5]

Metzger was incriminated in a civil trial launched by Morris Dees of the Southern Poverty Law Center on behalf of Seraw's now-orphaned son and Seraw's father. In the trial, Dees and his co-council, Elden Rosenthal, presented evidence that Metzger and his son, John, had sent their up-and-coming recruiter Dave Mazzella from California to Portland specifically to tutor the East Side White Pride skinhead group in racist violence and the organizing techniques of WAR, which included targeting youth who were ignorant and full of resentment.

I remember being appalled by Metzger, representing himself, who told the jury that his words could not be put on trial because of the First Amendment and thus he held no responsibility for the murder.[6] I was disappointed but not surprised that the Oregon chapter of the American Civil Liberties Union (ACLU) expressed concerns about how findings against Metzger could diminish the First Amendment right to free speech. This idea that words — used in this case to organize ignorant racist youth to partake in a white-supremacist murder — were protected by the First Amendment as long as they were not deemed to be *action* struck me as deeply problematic. I take up this question about the line between speech and action in Chapters One and Two. As Chapter Two discusses, Canadian law has a different understanding of this speech/action distinction, as evidenced in its enactment of hate speech laws, laws that are considered to be violations of the First Amendment in the US.

Not only did the jury convict Metzger, but they awarded unexpectedly high damages of $12.5 million, despite the fact that Metzger and WAR's assets amounted to much less.[7] Anti-racists and progressives were understandably delighted: the verdict effectively shut down the organization financially.[8] As a 21-year-old at the time, I remember thinking that while this outcome was positive in practical terms, there was something deeply disappointing about Metzger's guilt being a matter of civil rather than criminal law. Not only did it mean Metzger would not go to jail, but it seemed to me a blow against justice. The terrible harm done was deemed one confined to Seraw's family and not acknowledged as a crime against society itself — a damage to everyone, not just these victims. If, as a white man, I felt that Metzger's speech and actions were harming my society, it most certainly was far, far worse for racialized people subject to white supremacy in Oregon.

A couple of years later, having settled in Toronto, I heard the news that Tom and John Metzger had been arrested and deported from Canada under a Canadian law by which anyone *likely* to incite racial hatred may be barred from entering the country. They had been invited to attend a rally organized by the Heritage Front, a white supremacist group.[9] I was glad to be living in a country with laws against hate speech, especially when it's used to organize white supremacists. Such anti-hate speech laws are not possible in the US because of how the courts have interpreted the First Amendment. I had little time for those who argued that giving space to hate-mongers like the Metzgers was preferable to censoring them, the rationale being that allowing their ideas to be expressed in the public realm meant they could be rebutted and thus made ineffective. As I discuss in Chapter Two, this position is often portrayed as "more speech" rather than "enforced silence," and is attributed to US Supreme Court Justice Louis Brandeis. Whenever I hear such arguments, I think of Seraw and all the other victims of hate crimes, especially those perpetrated by organized hate groups. Seraw's death and so many others seem to me ample evidence against the use of the First Amendment to incite disaffected youth to perpetuate racist violence. Canadian hate speech legislation is no panacea for white supremacy, but those events — and the notable differences between the US and Canadian legal and political contexts — have stuck with me. Notably, as I was writing this book, Kyle Brewster, one of the three men found guilty of Seraw's murder, was out protesting in Salem, Oregon, on 6 January 2021, in support of the insurrection attempt by Donald Trump's white-supremacist followers.[10]

In the intervening years, we have witnessed the massive expansion of the internet, which now constitutes the site of so much public discussion and debate, as well as white-supremacist organizing and the dissemination of hatred, especially against women, Indigenous peoples, trans people, Jewish people, and people of colour. The early days of optimism that the internet would promote greater democracy, equality, and participation have been eclipsed by social media inundated with political polarization, disinformation, hate, racism, misogyny, transphobia, antisemitism, and crime. In many ways, social media raises new issues for freedom of expression and open, critical discussion, but some of the age-old issues persist. In Chapter Four, I explore the emergence of the internet as one of the most actualized experiments in the possibility of unrestricted discussion that can help us determine if such technology indeed leads to the ideal goals of free speech that influential thinkers like John Stuart Mill, Alexander Meiklejohn, and Justice Oliver Wendell Holmes envisaged.

Language and speech are very complex, as is their relationship to politics and democracy. In various ways, my academic research has explored the politics involved in language use, language policy, and specifically the rise of global English since the middle of the twentieth century. This work always considers speech within the larger context of the structures of language and communication, never as an individual act that can be understood on its own.

As a settler living on Treaty 1 Territory in Winnipeg, Manitoba, whose parents are from England and settled on Turtle Island just over a decade prior to my birth, I am striving to learn more about the importance of language in its connection to the land and about treaty relations from Cree, Anishinaabe, Métis, and other Indigenous thinkers. It is ironic that current free speech discussions claim to value openness and diversity, but almost never include Indigenous values of dialogue.

Rethinking Free Speech is aimed at a general readership, including the interested public and students, as well as university administrators, journalists, and other policy-makers. It is also written for academic specialists from various disciplines who can benefit from returning to key arguments about why free expression is important and what its various goals are. It summarizes some classic positions but also makes several original arguments — most importantly, that by paying attention to different goals of free speech, we can be in a better position to be open to truly new, diverse, and challenging ideas.

INTRODUCTION

EVERY TIME DEBATES AROUND FREE SPEECH ERUPT, WHICH IS OFTEN these days, the sides seem to harden into opposing camps. On one side are those who proclaim the ultimate importance of defending all speech, especially speech expressing ideas they ostensibly reject. On the other side are those who find the particular speech under consideration to be harmful and indefensible. Whether it is anti-vaccine misinformation, the use of the N-word, Holocaust denial, criticism of Israel, or hateful rhetoric targeting women, Indigenous peoples, people of colour, immigrants, queer or transgender people, debates concerning free speech abound in both new and traditional media, in university classrooms, on street corners, and around kitchen tables. Some claim that in the wake of the re-emergence of the Israel-Palestine conflict, their opponents are being hypocritical in their free speech principles. This seems to apply both to those who think "cancel culture" promoted by those on the left (or so the argument goes) is now being applied to pro-Palestinian protests by those on the right; or whether it is those who were formerly in favour of free speech absolutism, where "counter-speech" is the only response to "objectionable speech," who are now outraged that the chant "From the River to the Sea" is permitted on university campuses or that Israel's actions are compared to Nazi Germany and to South Africa's apartheid system. All such debates and accusations hinge on simplistic understandings of free expression as a "for-or-against" argument, or on naïve assessments of where to draw the line. In all these controversies, the role of social media in enabling immediate and widespread communication — yet mediated through algorithms — has greatly exacerbated these tensions.

These debates often blur many boundaries that could otherwise help us navigate such complex minefields. The Canadian Charter of Rights and Freedoms and the US First Amendment allow individuals to express many ideas, even if they are false and could have adverse effects. But this specific situation of free speech is different from many of the other situations we contemplate when we talk about free speech, especially when evaluating public discussion. For instance, it is a different question when we consider whether medical associations that accredit doctors need to give the same unrestricted berth of free speech to their members, some who may deny the existence of COVID-19 or the safety of vaccines.[1] In Ontario and Alberta, premiers Doug Ford and Jason Kenney castigated universities for allowing a "crisis of free speech" and threatened to withdraw funding if universities in those provinces failed to adopt policies fostering "free expression" in accordance with standards devised at the University of Chicago, often referred to as the Chicago Principles (see Chapter Three for further discussion).[2] In June 2022, the Quebec government passed a law defining "academic freedom" as a right that everyone has, regardless of their position or qualification.[3] Commentators have compared Facebook's Oversight Board — set up to adjudicate whether any of its billions of users have violated its policy of acceptable speech — to the Supreme Court (presumably of the US) as if Facebook (recently rebranded Meta) were not a private company but a part of the legal oversight of a sovereign democratic country.[4] Political discussions quickly become embroiled in accusations of "cancel culture," "de-platforming," "doxing," and "trolling." Though free speech debates are at least as old as modern democracy, we seem to be in more turbulent waters than ever before. It is difficult to separate the current terrain of free expression from the advent of social media, the resurgence of nationalist populism, and the backlash against anti-racism, feminism, and LGBTQ+ identities. Before addressing the complexity of such issues, I argue that we need first to be clear on some basic concepts and distinctions.

Free speech debates often boil down to: *Where do we draw the line?* And *Who gets to decide where to draw the line?* While communications scholar Stephen A. Smith insists that these are the "key questions,"[5] this book demonstrates that such thinking is too simplistic and contributes to the intractable controversies about free speech. One reason for the disagreements is that the principles of free speech get lost in subjective debates caught between the extremes: free speech absolutism and tyrannical censorship. I illustrate how this myopia of focusing on where *the line* is to be drawn and arguing as to who draws it is reductive and often unhelpful. While in important cases a line will need to be drawn, I argue that there are many different dimensions that determine different lines and grey areas, depending on what we take to be the goals of free speech and the arenas in which they play out. Governments, for instance, have a line that restricts them from intervening too much in the rights of those subject to their laws. Individuals wishing to create and participate in productive discussions need to think about where their own lines are, taking into consideration the types of statements that, if made, may result in some discussants being less likely to be open and willing to participate in the dialogue. Protestors, or those wishing to express their political ideals, face legal lines, but they also face other types of lines on free speech that limit their goals of spreading their beliefs, educating potential supporters, and mobilizing activists. At universities, there are still other lines and these are created by academic freedom, which is related to, but distinct from, free speech. This is because the goals of academia are education and knowledge production which rely on such elements as peer review, disciplinary methods, and ethical responsibility. Differing forms of social media also require their own lines, some of which depend on their business model, need for profit, and relation to government regulation. To ask all of these diverse situations to adhere to *a single line* is to invite a superficial understanding of free speech. It also obscures how free speech impacts different people differently. It ensures that free speech controversies will merely repeat themselves, endlessly mired in confusion and conflict.

Another approach to free speech posits that there should be no line separating speech that can be banned from that which is allowed: speech should be absolutely free. However, even the most ardent free speech absolutists cannot escape some limits to speech. They are forced to admit that some speech must be prohibited, whether by the government or the public.[6] In the tradition of the US Supreme Court and John Stuart Mill, limits are warranted when speech becomes action, a distinction epitomized by US Supreme Court Justice Oliver Wendell Holmes's example of a person falsely yelling "fire" in a crowded theatre. Holmes's point, in a 1919 court decision, *Schenck v. United States,* was that speech that provokes harmful action is not protected by the First Amendment (see Chapters One and Two where I discuss this further). Of course, even the US, despite having one of the strongest free speech traditions, has implemented laws, including those against libel, slander, defamation, and copyright infringement.

Rejecting free speech absolutism, other approaches offer a balancing one, where free speech is imperative but must be weighed against other rights, such as equality, security, justice, or freedom of assembly or religion. Pluralists like Isaiah Berlin or Robert Dahl — however different their approaches to the study of politics may be — hold that different people have differing values, that these values will come into conflict, and that no single value can or should be absolute. In this context, free speech absolutism means that in relation to these other values, free speech should always take priority. So, we need to be clear what we mean by free speech absolutism, a term often invoked but rarely clarified: Does it mean that no speech should ever be curtailed? Or does it mean that free speech has a value that is higher than all others, yet still has limits?

Such confusion is evident on right-wing social media platforms that present themselves as free speech absolutist sites with no censorship. These platforms, such as Parler, GETTR, and Truth Social, denounce Facebook and what was then Twitter (especially before Elon Musk acquired it and rebranded it "X") for their regulation of content and for banning former president Donald Trump. Yet their "Terms of Use" policies are similar to those they decry and go well beyond prohibiting only content that is illegal. For example, they all prohibit hardcore pornography, including legal pornography involving consenting adults. Without such restrictions, these sites could end up dominated by pornography, which is not the intent of their owners and would make it hard for them to attract and sell advertising.[7] The illusion that any social media platform can be a forum for absolute free speech is also disrupted in discussions of "content moderation." Parler CEO George Farmer, for instance, has engaged in lengthy exchanges about moderating the platform's content but still declares that he runs a free speech site with no censorship.[8] As is common these days, he does not define what he means by "content moderation," or "censorship." Censorship is a hot-button word that may seem to be more draconian than content moderation, but without clear definitions these concepts are vague and unhelpful. "Censorship" derives from the Latin *censēre,* meaning "to judge or assess," and is arguably very similar to moderating content. It could even be understood as more transparent and potentially less intrusive. Whereas censoring is usually understood as a straightforward and explicit ban, "moderating" — from the Latin *moderatus,* meaning "to mitigate or restrain," or "to make less violent, intense, rigorous" — could involve manipulating and obscuring how the content has been changed or shaped. As Chapter Four discusses in detail, *all* social media platforms structure how speech is expressed, whether it is X's 280-character limit, Facebook's news feed algorithms, or Snapchat's time limitation on all posts. More profound is the way these structures are inherent in the social media platforms' business models that enable them to generate such massive profits.[9] Chapter Four shifts the debate about censorship and content moderation to focus on how different goals of free speech and public discussion might be truly fostered in the digital realm of social media.

The simplistic approach to free speech that focuses on a single line to determine what should be allowed and what should not collapses different arguments for free speech and limits the goals that it is supposed to achieve. Many scholars acknowledge that there are different aims and rationales for free speech, but most view them as complementary. The Canadian legal scholar Richard Moon explains: "There are many arguments for protecting freedom of expression, but all seem to focus on one or a combination of three values: truth, democracy, and individual autonomy."[10] That is, free speech allows individuals and the public to strive for new knowledge and contest orthodox truths; it is also essential for curtailing too much government power, while still fostering a deliberative public process because a well-functioning, modern democracy depends upon voters and elected officials knowing what others think; and lastly, it allows citizens to express themselves and thus be autonomous.

British historian and social commentator Timothy Garton Ash uses the initialism STGD to summarize *four* main reasons why speech should be free: Self, Truth, Government, Diversity. This rendition adds "diversity" to Moon's triptych, but more explicitly than Moon, Garton Ash maintains these reasons to value free speech are complementary elements of a single conception of free speech.[11] That the differences among these rationales matter, let alone the possibility of tension or even incommensurability among them, is neglected in the scholarship, as well as in public discussions of free speech, is noteworthy. In this book, I challenge this assumption and illustrate why it is important to place greater focus on the differing reasons for — and goals of — free speech. I follow the legal scholar Frederick Schauer's position, that "One of the problems of theorizing about freedom of speech is that there has been too much distillation and not enough distinction."[12] I then distinguish venues, specifically universities and social media sites, where issues of free speech need to be understood in their specificities. Universities need to be able to educate and produce new knowledge; social media platforms, as they currently exist, are driven by the needs of private companies.

Other scholars never explicitly address the underlying reasons for their advocacy of free speech. For instance, Danish lawyer, commentator, and free speech expert Jacob Mchangama pulls illustrations of what he labels "free speech examples" from spans of history and continents. His illustrative cases are as diverse as mothers protesting against the disappearance of their sons in Buenos Aires in the 1970s; the young Karl Marx's critique of press censorship; and ancient Athenian notions of *parrhēsia* (meaning "bold speech" or "telling all").[13] He sometimes describes these diverse events as the struggle against oppression or sometimes against the concentration or abuse of power; at other times, as obstacles to the freedom of religion.[14] Despite his rich, historical accounts of struggles over free speech, Mchangama provides no definition of free speech nor much insight into any of the underlying foundations or tension that may exist among these very different circumstances. Like many who engage in free speech discussions, he proceeds as if it were self-evident what free speech is and why it is important.[15] This fits Schauer's description of freedom of speech positions presented decades ago as "a weak assembly of platitudes."[16] My approach here challenges both the notion that free speech is a self-evident, single good; and that the questions about free speech revolve around the issue of where the line is to be drawn for legitimately curtailing speech.

The irony is that I agree with the free speech absolutists however they may define themselves — or fail to. Like them, I believe that our ability to express ourselves is centrally important. But this is not because speech cannot hurt us, as Chapter Two will demonstrate. Indeed, I will show how problematic it is to hold the position that "sticks and stones may break my bones, but words will never hurt me." On the contrary, we live in language. It is naïve to try to separate the realm of speech and language from that of violence and harm. This is one reason why we cannot ignore free speech controversies: they impact all our lives.

Beyond the Line of Free Speech

Rethinking Free Speech covers many of the issues raised by people who invoke this supposed *line* to define free speech. It shows how we need to go beyond such linear metaphors. I argue that the line is symptomatic of how such important debates are conducted in dangerously simplistic ways. They feed into the increasing political polarization that is especially evident in the US, but increasingly on display in Canada too. My analysis shows that for the concept of free speech not to become a mere weapon, we need to disentangle the fundamentally different reasons why unencumbered speech and a variety of diverse viewpoints are important. I illustrate how many of the underlying principles that render free expression vital are not only different from each other but often in tension, leading to quite different applications in practice. I do not expect that I will convince all readers to agree with me about all free speech issues. But this is not my aim. My goal is to provide some tools and distinctions for readers that will hopefully enrich the debates around these issues, especially in the Canadian context, which, I emphasize, differs from the American one.

While this book contains many criticisms of specific free speech arguments, I repeat: I am not anti-free speech. Quite the opposite. My position is that there are many crucially important reasons why free expression is fundamental to democracy, equality, freedom, the pursuit of knowledge, human life, and just social interaction. The problem is that most free speech advocates do not interrogate their own reasons for supporting free expression nor distinguish the many different reasons why it is important. This ultimately results in debates in which some take free speech to be merely the absence of government censorship, others think it is a more general attitude toward what constitutes a good discussion, others hold an underlying faith that it will lead to something they regard as progress, and still others see it as an essential feature of being human.

Underlying my analysis is the idea that speech can never be considered alone. It is always a part of language, communication-creating processes, and politics and this makes it impossible to simply attach the adjective "free" to the activity of "speech." It is in this sense that *Rethinking Free Speech* aims to trouble and re-think the concept of free speech. This involves emphasizing the key principles for which free expression is often, but not always nor is consistently, used as shorthand for: the critical interrogation of a variety of differing viewpoints, analyses, claims, moral positions, and empirical assessments based on differing life experiences.

My stance is different from that of journalist and critic P.E. Moskowitz, for example, who argues that "free speech as a concept is meaningless." Moskowitz sees the term "free speech" as an "empty" or "hollow signifier," a "mask" for the "unsettled history of racism," or a cover for inequality, misogyny, and homophobia.[17] I agree that free speech is a malleable concept and that it is often used to cover over issues of inequality, especially racism, colonialism, antisemitism, white supremacy, misogyny, homophobia, and transphobia. And I commend Moskowitz for demonstrating in broad strokes and with convincing empirical examples how free speech has been used to justify these hate-induced positions. But the principles of free speech are not only that. Thus, while I agree with much of Moskowitz's analysis, I do not hold its overall negative assessment of free expression.

Nor do I follow literary critic and legal scholar Stanley Fish's pragmatic approach to free speech, although I will draw on many of his arguments. For Fish, free speech is a "political prize," merely the "name we give to verbal behavior that serves the substantive agenda we wish to advance."[18] From this pragmatist perspective, Fish rarely calls for any changes to the status quo in the US. He ends up rejecting hate speech legislation. He argues that universities should aim to support "the maintenance of a way of life — the life of disinterested contemplation," rather than improving our state of knowledge and society. In other words, for Fish, the university does not have a central role to play in progress (whatever you take "progress" to mean), and ultimately, he holds that free speech controversies come down to particular distinctions for which no formulas or generalities can be made.[19] This seems to me a futile position.

Rather, my approach comes from a different angle than that of Moskowitz, Fish, and other critics of free speech. I unpack the diverse values and goals that underlie the different uses of freedom of expression and the different spheres in which it appears. Where others see free speech as empty and endlessly malleable, I see it as *too full*, overdetermined, if you will. Free expression means *too much*. We are asking it to do too much work, often the work of distinct concepts that are much better at articulating clear principles, concepts such as critical, inclusive, diverse, public discussion and academic freedom (even though academic freedom itself is riddled with complexity).

Tools of Free Speech

Instead of focusing on some line that determines what expression should be acceptable and what expression is too harmful, egregious, or dangerous, I demonstrate that we require a *collection* of concepts and distinctions, especially in the context of the twenty-first century. I think of this collection as a metaphorical toolbox with various helpful tools inside. Both a hammer and a screwdriver help us build things. But there are obviously important differences in how a hammer and nail hold things together versus a screwdriver and screw, even if the general goal is similar. Moreover, some screwdrivers are flatheads, others are Phillips. While a flathead screwdriver can sometimes get a Phillips screw in or out, it can be disastrous to use a Phillips screwdriver on a flathead screw, potentially stripping it so that it is irremovable. This metaphor of tools, I think, captures the relationship between free speech and academic freedom: sometimes they seem synonymous, but other times, one ends up in a mess if they are confused. Adding to the complexity of the toolkit is the fact that Canadians have Robertson screws and screwdrivers, with square-shaped sockets and screw heads, and Americans do not. So the key to an articulate debate about free expression and critical inquiry is knowing which tool or concept to use in which circumstance. For instance, one should not try to use a Phillips screwdriver on a Robertson screw. Even if one is in awe of America (thinking they do things better over there), if the screw is a Robertson, one needs to drive it in with a Robertson screwdriver. This metaphor is an apt one in thinking about how the First Amendment applies to public universities in the US, whereas Canada's Charter of Rights and Freedoms generally not being applicable to Canadian universities, as will be examined in Chapter Three. Thus, it does not matter if one personally favours the First Amendment if they are living in Canada; it is the Charter that is the rule of law in Canada. One needs to use the right tool for the job and the tools that are actually available in one's toolkit.

Unfortunately, many controversies over free speech seem to proceed by someone yelling for a tool without specifying which particular tool they need or hoping that whichever one they have around or that they prefer will get the job done.[20] The goal of having a serious discussion about free expression is not only to determine what speech should be allowed and which curtailed, but also to understand what is at stake for the individuals involved, as well as society as a whole. For me, as for many, free expression includes trying to foster a truly democratic and open society where all can participate in public deliberation. But such a goal, I argue, cannot be achieved merely by removing constraints from all speakers.

To expand and overcome the common linear framing of free expression and to provide a set of useful tools, I present three different dimensions or questions often raised in free speech debates. These are: (1) *What type of freedom?* That is, freedom from what? Who or what is impeding the expression — the government or the public, an individual or a corporation? From the legal perspective, one of the main reasons for the right to the freedom of expression as protected by the Canadian Charter of Rights and Freedoms or the US First Amendment is to curtail *government* infringement on those who must follow its laws — that is, citizens, residents, and visitors to the country. One main goal here is to prevent government from having too much power over the expression of those whom it governs.

This central legal or constitutional idea is distinguishable from the next, more general dimension or question: (2) *What is required for a society to have open, critical public discussion that is inclusive of all members and encourages a diverse array of perspectives?* For some, the main goal of this public discussion is to enable democratic participation. Others assert that such open, public debate fosters truth or new knowledge or allows for new, innovative ways of living to emerge — in other words, it brings about progress. Still others place greater emphasis on the need for humans to be able to express themselves to the entire community, regardless of the outcome. Chapter One investigates these diverse perspectives by looking at key historical thinkers who offer systematic articulations of such positions, illustrating their differences and the tensions among them.

The final dimension or question is: (3) *What is the realm for such free expression?* For instance, can the internet be governed by the same rules as the public square? Does one have the same rights of free expression when one is at work, school, or university, and what about when a person is on their "free" time in their personal life? Are universities public spaces, workspaces, or something else? Are courtrooms — where guilt or innocence is determined — places where free speech should reign, or does the integrity of the legal process require rules of evidence, legal requirements to tell the truth, and a judge to conduct highly structured proceedings? This book argues that to address these questions, we need more than a line — we need a set of distinctions and tools.

This first dimension or question concerning legal restrictions on the actions of government brings us to what is often described as a "negative right," a right not to be interfered with, whereas the second question or dimension — concerning what is required to bring about a productive, critical, and inclusive discussion — is associated with a "positive right," a right that only really has meaning if there exists the ability to use it. Both involve equality, but very different types of equality. Legal principles restricting government censorship of free expression are equal if they are applied equally and do not discriminate. Political theorists call this "formal equality" and often distinguish it from "substantive equality." This formal equality means that individuals may not be constrained by the government from expressing themselves based on any of their individual characteristics, including religion, gender, class, ethnicity, or political ideology. This principle of free speech is a freedom of opportunity that one may or may not choose to exercise, depending on whether they have the resources to do so. It does not include the government providing the capacity for people to express themselves, or asking why certain groups may not be participating, or ensuring that no group is being ignored. The second principle, positive rights to free expression, supports a more idealistic value of open, critical debate, where discussion requires more than the constitutionally protected equality of opportunity. Truly open discussion demands a forum that includes a diversity of people with differing views to participate effectively, an inclusivity that often requires substantive effort, especially given the historical and political divides that frame our experiences and interactions.[21]

My point here is that for truly marginalized and heterodox ideas to be available and to be listened to, formal equality is rarely sufficient. A hostile environment in which some speakers insult or debase others is unlikely to facilitate an open, inclusive, and diverse exchange of ideas. Furthermore, traditions and approaches to free speech emanating from outside the European Enlightenment may hold important insight but are rarely considered, as will be addressed in the concluding chapter, using examples drawn from various North American Indigenous approaches.

Governments may opt to take on positive rights to create resources and venues which may support truly diverse and critical expression, everything from public education to ensure a literate population to infrastructure like roads that enable newspapers and so many other goods to be transported. Even the literal "public square" and many of its metaphorical cousins require government to create it. While we are moving towards wireless communication (often using private satellites), the internet could not have developed as it has without the fibre-optic backbone initially built by the US government and extended by other governments. However, now social media is provided by corporations whose objective is to maximize profits.

These first two underlying dimensions — legal or constitutional protections of free expression and ideals of inclusive discussion — are often confused or combined in an undifferentiated way that threatens to undermine the goals of both. An example of this is Donald Trump's lawsuit against Facebook, Twitter, and Google for suspending his accounts in the wake of the insurrection on the US Capitol building in 2021. Trump based his lawsuit on First Amendment principles.[22] As will be discussed at length in Chapter Two, the First Amendment states that "Congress shall make no law … abridging the freedom of speech," and thus, it clearly does not apply to private companies such as Facebook, Twitter, or Google. Similarly, Senator Josh Hawley claimed on Twitter that Simon & Schuster breached his First Amendment right to freedom of speech when they cancelled his book contract because of his role in the January 6 attack. Like Trump, he confuses the obvious distinction between a private company, this time a book publisher, and the US government.[23] While commentators have deemed these gambits of Trump and Hawley to be mere publicity stunts and fundraising ploys, I argue in Chapters One and Four that there is more at stake to such confusion and misunderstanding and that they undermine both the First Amendment and the principle of open, critical discussion.[24]

This second dimension of free speech as a necessary component of a free society can be, and historically has been, formulated in quite distinct ways. As an idealistic aspiration more than a definable rule, free speech compels society to grapple with and consider nuanced questions regarding whose voices are prevalent in public debate. It is unsurprising that such ideals are even harder to agree on than the constitutional dimension of freedom of speech. Such aspirations must also confront how free speech for some imposes silence on others. Key contributions to Western[25] political philosophy of public discussion, from Immanuel

Kant, John Stuart Mill, Alexander Meiklejohn, and C. Edwin Baker, show that the differing rationales for any specific concept of free speech provide a different set of criteria for how the principle of free speech is applied. The value of each of these thinkers, and others surveyed in Chapter One, is that they offer influential rationales for free speech, its parameters and protections, and do not take it as an assumed good or self-evident right. As this book is aimed at analyzing contemporary discussions of free speech, I draw on the dominant ideas drawn from a specific line of thinking, often problematically dubbed the "Western tradition." As I will address in Chapter One and the Conclusion, my position is that this tradition has been too dominant and too often separated from alternative understandings of open, critical, inclusive, and diverse discussion. There is an irony that the free speech tradition of the West — from Kant and Mill onwards — has not engaged successfully with North American Indigenous traditions of open and public debate, nor with other traditions. My focus on the "great thinkers" of the European-American tradition of political theory does not mean to absolve nor obscure its exclusionary history based on race, gender, and colonial categories. Rather this work is based on immanent critique, on dissecting the tensions and contradictions that exist in even the dominant understandings of free speech, in order to open up the concept to the greater diversity evident in Indigenous, African, and Asian traditions that are beyond the scope of *Rethinking Free Speech*.

To illustrate this basic distinction between free speech as a constitutional protection against government suppression of expression, on the one hand, and free speech as a plea for open, critical and inclusive discussion (or what some call "discourse ethics"), on the other, let me present two examples of discussions of free speech. Together, they also illustrate how these two different meanings of free speech are often confused in public controversies. I will begin with the second principle, that of critical and inclusive public discussion. In July 2020, *Harper's Magazine* published a "Letter on Justice and Open Debate," signed by more than 150 writers, scholars, and media figures, including Noam Chomsky, Salman Rushdie, Margaret Atwood, Cornel West, David Frum, J.K. Rowling, Gloria Steinem, and Wynton Marsalis. I view this *Harper's* Letter as an encapsulation of broader sentiments and will use it as indicative of this second dimension of how free speech is understood today to mean critical and inclusive discussion. The Letter denounces "a new set of moral attitudes and political commitments that tend to weaken our norms of open debate and toleration of differences in favor of ideological conformity." Significantly, the Letter argues that, "While we have come to expect this on the radical right, censoriousness is also spreading more widely in our culture." The Letter is clearly critical of the culture of public discussion, though it never actually uses the terms "free speech," "freedom of speech," or "freedom of expression," nor does it explain why its authors wrote it at this particular moment. The nearest it comes to addressing explicitly free speech is when it uses the language of the "free exchange of information and ideas," calls for "exposure, argument, and persuasion," and notes it "uphold[s] robust and even caustic counter-speech from all quarters."[26] Notably absent is any reference to governmental activity or any legal principles of freedom of expression. Nevertheless, it roughly paraphrases the famous argument of US Supreme Court Justice Louis Brandeis regarding First Amendment protections from government sanction, that the best response to "evil speech" is "more speech, not enforced silence"[27] (which will be discussed at length in Chapter Two). Much of the commentary that ensued framed the Letter as a defence of free speech.

Even with the Letter's focus on critical and inclusive discussion, the question raised but not addressed by it, nor by so much of the ink spilled in the name of free speech or the transgression of it, is: *Why do we value such public discussion?* One signatory, Jeet Heer, the Canadian editor of *The Nation*, described the Letter as "an anodyne enough statement of liberal truisms."[28] Others agreed that the Letter was vague and wished it had supported its position with more rigour.[29] My interest is how the Letter frames the desire for critical and inclusive debate. Its thesis statement — "We uphold the value of robust and even caustic counter-speech from all quarters" — implies a distinction between speech that is to be *tolerated*, despite being caustic, and speech that is *action*, and thus should not be encouraged or permitted. "Caustic" literally means corrosive, a specific version of harm that erodes the integrity of the body it acts upon.[30] As such, the Letter seems to rest on a key distinction between speech and action that I will discuss in Chapter One in relationship to Mill's rationale. But the Letter is not endorsing caustic action. It is not written from the perspective of an anarchist or a free speech absolutist. While the Letter does not cite Mill, it suggests that even "caustic-counter speech" can improve public discourse as we evaluate what is true or valuable. The readers of the Letter must take it upon themselves to presume what the advantages of such "open debate" are and why they should outweigh the potential harms done. As I explore in Chapter One, the authors of the Letter could be assuming the rationale of Mill, or Kant, or Meiklejohn, or Baker. And depending on which one it is, then the Letter actually calls for different ideals for public discussion, with each ideal having differing ramifications, as we shall see.

In early 2022, there was another free speech controversy but this time the debate involved both dimensions: critical and inclusive discussion, as well as what I have been calling the constitutional protections of the freedom of speech. The situation involved the musician Neil Young, the streaming service Spotify, and controversial podcast host Joe Rogan. Accusing Spotify's flagship podcast *The Joe Rogan Experience* of "spreading fake information about vaccines — potentially causing death to those who believe the disinformation," Young threatened to remove his music from the site. He presented Spotify with an ultimatum: their catalogue could include either Young or Rogan, but not both. Predictably, the controversy was met by right-wing pundits who declared that Young and others joining his protest were attacking or undermining Rogan's right to free speech. Young was accused of being hypocritical to his 1960s counter-cultural roots and the ethos of his 2006 "Freedom of Speech" tour.[31]

Young's response was quite clear:

> I support free speech. I have never been in favor of censorship. Private companies have the right to choose what they profit from, just as I can choose not to have my music support a platform that disseminates harmful information. I am happy and proud to stand in solidarity with the front line health care workers who risk their lives every day to help others.[32]

It is an open question as to whether the signatories of the *Harper's* Letter would see Young's protest as part of the "new moral attitudes" that they decry for undermining the "free exchange of information and ideas." Would they join free speech advocates like Zaid Jilani who claimed that Young was weakening the norms of public discourse by trying (unsuccessfully) to "cancel" Rogan?[33] Is the misinformation disseminated on Rogan's podcast the type of "caustic" speech that the Letter insists we need to tolerate even if we disagree with it? As is the case in many of these controversies, even if Spotify had opted to remove *The*

Joe Rogan Experience instead of Young's music, Rogan and guests still would not have been "silenced" in any meaningful sense of the word. Rogan was reported to be the most popular podcast host in the world, and there were other outlets for whatever ideas he wanted to broadcast. As a private company, Spotify can determine the content it hosts within the bounds of the law. It is not obliged to provide a forum for public discourse, nor is it bound by First Amendment strictures against government infringement on freedom of speech.

Young's position clearly delineated the boundary between these two aspects of free speech. He did not call for Rogan to be censured by any government; he asked a media corporation to revisit their editorial decision to pay $100 million for exclusive rights to carry *The Joe Rogan Experience*. He gave Spotify an ethical choice: his music or Rogan's podcast. The more nuanced question as to whether or not his attempt to remove Rogan from Spotify dampens critical and inclusive discussions on vaccines is immediately complicated by the counterpoint: What about Young's free speech? Young and his defenders have maintained that it is Young's right of free expression both to critique Rogan's show as dangerous and potentially deadly and to set terms for the licence to distribute his music.[34] But these distinctions were generally lost in the controversy as those on either side talked past each other, using the term "free speech" to mean different things. Brené Brown, a podcaster and academic who joined Young and Joni Mitchell in pulling their material from Spotify, reported the backlash she received on Twitter, which included comments like, "I'm cancelling you for cancelling people."[35] Ironically, given Spotify's reach, removing their content from the platform more effectively "cancelled" their ability to connect with millions of listeners. Few musicians can afford such an ethical decision.[36]

The *Harper's* Letter and Neil Young's case are just two examples of how free speech is a concept that is too big and too vague to do productive work in understanding what is at stake in either case. Had Young's situation been discussed using my clearer distinctions, everyone would not have come to an agreement on the position, but a more articulate and less polarized conversation would have been had. Rather than talking past each other in a yelling match, the participants in this controversy could have realized that, for Young, free speech means an absence of government censorship, whereas for the Rogan defenders, free speech describes a type of discussion where potentially harmful and factually questionable perspectives should be allowed because of an optimism that a positive outcome will ultimately result from a clash of ideas. Or perhaps some Rogan defenders held the views that come from the writings of C. Edwin Baker, discussed below in Chapter One — that the need for human expression outweighs any possible outcome of a competition of ideas.

Domains of Free Speech

Questions of free speech get even more complicated when we address specific realms, such as universities. There is a long, intricate history of how free expression is related to universities well outside the purview of this book. Public, media, and political attention on academia have increased with contemporary controversies, like the one involving Lindsay Shepherd and Wilfrid Laurier University in 2017, or controversies about student protests against Israel's bombing of Gaza after 7 October 2023. Since the 1990s, conservatives and the right wing have become increasingly focused on universities as an object of their criticisms and a site for mobilizing right-wing supporters.[37] Chapter Three focuses specifically on academic freedom, which is conceptually distinct from free speech, though the two are related and often conflated. Moreover, the legal connection between academic freedom and the constitutional protection of free expression is very different in the US than in Canada. Confusing free speech and academic freedom serves to undermine both.

Chapter Three uses academic freedom to highlight some of the problems and confusion that arise when free speech stands as a means to produce knowledge and search for "the truth," as Chapter One describes, and Chapter Two discusses this matter in relation to the metaphor of a free "marketplace of ideas." The legal scholar Brian Leiter challenges the proposition that free speech leads to the truth. He argues that the courtroom and our legal system are clear counter-examples to this connection. In determining perhaps the most important truths in a democratic society — *Has an individual committed a crime for which the state will imprison them?* — the law requires one to pronounce oaths not to lie, rules to determine what evidence can and cannot be presented, and judicial discretion over what the jury may or may not hear. A courtroom may be an example of the opposite of free expression, one of the most highly scripted and regulated arenas of speech. Clearly, to the extent that we take our legal system as legitimate, we accept that there are circumstances in which determining the truth requires such regulation.[38] I pursue Leiter's line of argument, not with the example of the court system, but instead the university. The university has also been viewed as a place for the free marketplace of ideas, but here too the tenets of academic freedom do not support unrestricted speech as the best method by which to pursue truth and knowledge. On the contrary, university knowledge production rests on training and accreditation, disciplinary processes, and professional responsibility that should not be applicable to all those with freedom of expression. Indeed, such a conception of free expression would severely diminish it.

The internet, and more specifically, social media, have clearly transformed the way most communication occurs. As Chapter Four addresses, the fact that it is primarily privately owned is not historically unprecedented, as private companies have dominated the newspaper, book publishing, radio, and television business as well. However, the structure and business models of the dominant social media platforms create a very different terrain where free speech is exercised.

Because my aim is to provide analytic clarity to debates concerning free expression, let me address a few points concerning vocabulary. When I am discussing the legal principle of the freedoms that individuals have or should have in relationship to laws that their governments can legitimately make — that is, issues concerning the Canadian Charter of Rights and Freedoms or the US First Amendment — I will use the phrases "freedom of expression" or "freedom of speech," respectively. When I discuss these concepts generally, I will use the phrase "constitutional protections" with the assumed predicate of freedom of expression. For the most part, this type of freedom is a negative one; it is freedom from restraint. When I consider issues concerning how different speakers do or should interact with one another — that is, the culture of public discussion and democratic debate — I will use the phrase "critical and inclusive discussion." By this, I mean to refer to that ideal of discussion that is open, critical, diverse, lively, and without barriers that would inhibit or exclude anyone's participation. By diverse, I mean that such discussion includes not only different ideas, but also people who bring different life experiences, different ethnic and cultural backgrounds, different class histories, different gender experiences, and have different physical and mental abilities. The more diverse the discussion, the more robust its contribution will be. The value of public discussion is not only a matter of individuals expressing themselves; it also involves how people interact with one another, including listening to and engaging with other perspectives. These ideals can only be realized through a positive sense of freedom, the "freedom *to*," as distinct from the negative definition of freedom as "freedom *from*." This raises a complex and perhaps unresolvable tension between what some may see as expressing critical ideas and others may experience as creating a hostile environment. Discussion in the media often addresses this point by noting freedom of speech does not mean freedom from consequences.[39] This book does not attempt to solve this dilemma. Instead, I acknowledge it as an important tension inherent in the nature of human dialogue, but distinguishable from constitutional questions of the freedom of expression and academic freedom. I also suggest that it plays itself out differently in different realms, whether in public or in private, in a university classroom or on social media. Even on social media, a platform devoted to gardening will have a different culture around these issues than one devoted to politics.

When I am dealing with more general accounts that do not make clear distinctions between the two concepts or include both, I will use "free speech" or "free expression," interchangeably. Some may think this is a matter of American versus Canadian terminology, because the First Amendment contains the phrase "freedom of speech," whereas the Charter uses "expression," but this distinction is far from watertight. The Chicago Principles discuss "free expression," as does John Stuart Mill in his foundational work, *On Liberty*. As Chapter One discusses, C. Edwin Baker uses "expression" as a more encompassing concept than "speech," but this is far from an accepted distinction. For these reasons, I use them synonymously, depending mostly on the context.

Book Outline

This book provides some tools to better understand the key issues at stake concerning free expression. Chapter One investigates the roots of various philosophical ideas and aims of open and unencumbered discussion and this will enable us to separate the idealistic aspirations from laws like the Canadian Charter or the US First Amendment that will be addressed in Chapter Two. Chapter Three illustrates that academic freedom, although having certain similarities, cannot be adequately understood as free speech at universities, especially not in Canada.

Chapter Four grapples directly with the idea that the previous chapters also address — namely, that the historical and social context has always been and will continue to be central to how we understand free expression, perhaps now more than ever. Undoubtedly, the internet and social media have changed everything, or at least created new terrain upon which free expression plays itself out, or is prevented from doing so.

While this book focuses on how free speech is generally understood today, with its dominant ideas rooted in the Western tradition, my position is that these ideas have led us to a place where, ironically, we seem to be endlessly repeating the same old arguments about free speech, despite one of its key tenets being that opening up discussion to new and diverse perspectives will bring about new knowledge. The Conclusion offers some considerations for ways to move forward, including the need to include Indigenous perspectives. This highlights the severe limitations of our current, dominant ideals of free speech which, for thinkers like Kant and Mill, are supposed to ensure social progress, but today seem to be stagnating in the same old debates that often ignore traditions other than the European or so-called "Western tradition."

Clearly, the question of free expression is not one question. It is a series of different questions for which everyone seems to have different answers. When is free speech really a plea for conversational ethics? When is it a prerequisite for pursuing knowledge and truth? When is it an individual right and requires protection from government overreach? When is it a collective process? What place is there for so-called unorthodox views? How has it been weaponized and to what consequence?

CHAPTER ONE

PHILOSOPHICAL JUSTIFICATIONS

THIS CHAPTER EXPLORES KEY FIGURES IN THE WESTERN TRADITION of free speech to illustrate the various justifications for it and parse out the incompatibilities amongst them. Historically, Immanuel Kant, John Stuart Mill, Alexander Meiklejohn, and C. Edwin Baker have all offered influential arguments. In different ways, they are all free speech absolutists, but their arguments contain substantially distinct positions in terms of why free speech should take priority over other values, such as security, equality, or justice. They vary on how free expression relates to democracy, the search for knowledge, and the human need to express oneself. Indeed, their arguments in favour of free expression are often at odds with each other, but they lay out the foundations for how and why free speech has come to be valued and protected in modern democracies. By delineating this tradition, this chapter aims to bring greater clarity to contemporary controversies over free speech that become confused, contradictory, and reductive when they ignore these origins and the principles embedded in them.

Where to Begin?

Many have argued that the ideals of free speech and expression have roots going back to Ancient Greece, Republican Rome, and what has been deemed the "Great Conversation," sometimes qualified as "Western" or "European" history.[1] One might contend, as Timothy Garton Ash has, that "the essence of our modern idea of free speech as a democratic public good is to be found almost fully formed 2500 years ago in Athens and some Greek colonies."[2] But there are important reasons why I focus on the advent of modern democracy in the eighteenth and nineteenth centuries onward. For one, we avoid Garton Ash's circular logic: after a brief discussion of free speech ideas appearing in Confucianism, Japanese Buddhism, and Nelson Mandela's account of his home village in South Africa, that, "There is no ducking this truth … free speech — as we are interpreting the term here — is a specialty of the modern West."[3] It is a disconcerting but common claim that something vaguely labelled "the West" has a special monopoly on dialogue and the "spirit of inquiry," as claimed by the American philosopher of education, Robert M. Hutchins.[4] Not only have such positions fed into racist justifications for slavery and colonialism, but they do not advance the concept or history of free speech, nor do they reflect the diversity of the "global village" in which our personal and professional relationships and communications occur today. In the Conclusion, I point to some examples of Indigenous approaches from Turtle Island that should inform our ideas of free and open discussion moving forward. These issues demand greater attention, but my focus here is on the dominant ideas of free speech because of their pervasiveness and their need to be re-thought.

Our current twenty-first-century terrain of free speech debates builds upon the foundations of free expression, as theorized by Kant, Mill, and Justice Oliver Wendell Holmes, among others, more directly than ancient Greek philosophers or other sources. There is a reason why these figures loom large in the references and reading lists of authors and organizations defending free speech today.[5]

As Mill is perhaps the most frequently referenced theorist in today's free speech debates, I invoke his historical connection between free expression and modern (meaning here, European) democracy. He argues that the age-old struggle between "Liberty and Authority," between subjects and government, changed radically with the advent of modern democracy — the rule of the people via elected representatives. Representative democracy was relatively new and still developing when Mill was writing. As a member of Parliament, he participated in decreasing property qualifications for voters and introduced an amendment that would have given women the right to vote. In this context, Mill wrote:

> The notion, that the people have no need to limit their power over themselves, might [have] seem[ed] axiomatic, when

popular government was a thing only dreamed about . . . . In time, however, a democratic republic came to occupy a large portion of the earth's surface [and] such phrases as "self-government," and "the power of the people over themselves," do not express the true state of the case.[6]

For Mill, the importance of "Liberty of Thought and Discussion" is directly tied to a fear of the "tyranny of the majority" that modern democracy inevitably raises. He worried that democracy based on majority rule dramatically increased the level and type of oppression that minorities might face.[7] Whether it is the printing press, the newspaper, or the digital age that provides our medium of expression, communication technologies and their changes are intimately intertwined with political and institutional developments of modern representative democracy, the public sphere, and public education systems that spread literacy throughout the population. While an important scholarly endeavour, to trace ideas of free speech more widely necessarily abstracts the principle from the context of our current controversies.

If we take our cue from today's free speech advocates, which is my approach in this book, we might start with French philosopher Voltaire (1694–1778), and the famous phrase, "I disapprove of what you say but will defend to the death your right to say it." However, as with many of the catchphrases that arise in current free speech debates, this one is not only pithy, it is apocryphal. Voltaire did not write it.[8] The sentence was penned in 1906, by English writer Evelyn Beatrice Hall (using the pseudonym Stephen G. Tallentyre), to paraphrase Voltaire's position in 1759, regarding the burning of Claude-Adrien Helvétius's *De l'esprit*, published in 1758. As media scholar John Durham Peters argues, it is doubtful that Voltaire, famous for his irony, would have expressed such sincere righteousness. It is unlikely that he would offer his life to defend a position he found superficial. In fact, Voltaire's actual response to the burning of Helvétius's book was, "What a fuss about an omelette!" It was a statement of dismissal rather than indignation.[9] Voltaire's 1764 essay on the "Liberty of the Press" supports Peters's interpretation. His literal attack on censorship is not because books and publications are important to progress and freedom, but because they lack the power to change the world. One could say Voltaire's position is that the sword is mightier than the pen. Books, he argues, are of "little consequence." Perhaps this is all ironic, but those invoking Voltaire never explain this.[10] Considering Spinoza's writings, which Voltaire detested but did not think should have been censored, Voltaire asks: "Have you discovered that this book has changed the face of the world?" His answer is an unequivocal *no*. Instead, he speculates about Spinoza's profits as the sales of the book rose due to the controversy ignited by the censorship.[11] This, of course, foreshadows many discussions today about how bans call attention to that which is banned — a phenomenon known, since 2003, as the "Streisand effect."

As Voltaire and his famous but wrongly attributed quotation do not provide a suitable starting point, it makes more sense to begin with a short essay by Prussian philosopher Immanuel Kant (1724–1804), "An Answer to the Question: What Is Enlightenment?" It was published in 1784, almost three decades after the burning of Helvétius' book and just a few years before the outbreak of the French Revolution, when representative democracy was in its infancy.

Kant's Free Speech Absolutism and Enlightenment

Enlightenment in the eighteenth century was generally understood to mean the spreading of knowledge, with emphasis on educating the public (or at least the male public, as women were prohibited from most schools until the turn of the twentieth century, including at the University of Königsberg where Kant was a student and professor). This spread of knowledge entailed reorienting societal decisions to be based on reason and evidence. Kant famously reformulated this image of the enlightenment, defining it as one's *"emergence from his self-incurred immaturity."*[12] "Maturity," as he defined it, was the ability to "use one's own understanding without the guidance of another," and he emphasized that this required not so much a great intellect or command of facts, but rather "resolution and courage." Kant argued that: "Laziness and cowardice are the reason why such large portions of men, even when nature has long emancipated them from alien guidance …, nevertheless gladly remain immature for life."[13] To this framing of "the public use of reason," as a measure of maturity and moral righteousness, Kant fashions an ethos of individualism pitted against accepting intellectual authority.

It is not necessary here to delve into Kant's influential and complex philosophical system, but these themes of autonomy and individualism are central to his moral philosophy in general. In this particular essay, he emphasizes that the motto of enlightenment was not general knowledge, but specifically, "*Sapere aude!*"— know thyself. This command to think critically for oneself superseded looking to books for guidance or to other experts, like "a doctor to judge my diet for me" or a spiritual adviser (an example that registers Kant's Protestant position against the authority of the Roman Catholic Church). While I have not seen any anti-vaxxers make specific reference to Kant on this point, one can see how his individualistic moralization of free speech would resonate with them.

However, Kant also argues that such thinking is difficult and rare: "Only a few, by cultivating their own minds, have succeeded in freeing themselves from immaturity and in continuing boldly on their way." His advocacy for free speech is limited to the "public use of reason" that pertains to discussions amongst the "reading public" on issues that matter to society at large. He describes a situation where the principles he espouses will be ineffectual for the majority of individuals — not because they lack the cognitive ability, but because they lack the requisite courage and determination.

In other writings, Kant made some untenable and disturbingly racist and sexist claims concerning both women's and non-white people's cognitive abilities and their "motivating forces." As the philosopher Charles W. Mills demonstrates, it is not easy to divorce Kant's racism and sexism from the substance of his philosophy (though many have tried). For instance, Kant states that white people have more "motivating forces and talents" than other races and that Black and Indigenous peoples could never be "genuinely civilized." He held that women and people of colour cannot be truly moral in his sense of the term. Mills is convincing in his conclusion: "Instead of seeing these exclusions [of people of colour and women from Kant's moral philosophy] as merely an embarrassment, we should be taking them as a philosophical challenge."[14] Not surprisingly, other scholars hold very different interpretations of Kant. Political scientist Sankar Muthu, for example, maintains that:

> Kant's understanding of human unity and diversity forms the basis upon which he condemns imperialism and articulates a cosmopolitan conception of global diversity, which defends against the paternalism of European imperial powers, non-European peoples' freedom to organize their societies and to practice their collective lifestyles in the manner that they see fit.[15]

Such debates are clearly beyond the scope of this work, but should not be concealed especially because they relate to the standard trajectory whereby the exclusionary sphere of white men is merely expanded — rather than fundamentally transformed — to include others, such as women, the poor, non-white individuals, religious minorities, and other non-citizens.

Kant argues that free speech for the few who are capable of enlightenment can bring about general enlightenment for all of society. It is worth quoting the passage to see how Kant makes his point:

> For there will always be a few who think for themselves, even among those appointed as guardians of the common mass. Such guardians, once they have themselves thrown off the yoke of immaturity, will disseminate the spirit of rational respect for personal value and for the duty of all men to think for themselves.[16]

Kant's vision is one whereby even most white men will not be able to rise to the excellence required for enlightenment, but a small elite who have courage will lift all of society to a higher level. Of course, such themes of elitism can be found in most Western philosophies going at least back to Plato's emphasis on the difficulty of doing philosophy and thinking critically. Plato famously argued that only the rare, indeed the philosopher king, can truly approach the Truth sufficiently to be a good ruler. Crucial to both Kant and Plato is the notion that no government authority, public opinion, or intellectual elite should be able to determine who these special individuals are. Moreover, both Plato and Kant emphasize the effort required to think critically (and overcome laziness and cowardness) — a position that is in sharp contrast to those, like C. Edwin Baker, as we shall see, who align free speech with the universal human need for self-expression.

For Kant, freedom of public expression is the paramount value, and in this sense, he is a free speech absolutist: "For enlightenment of this kind [one that truly reforms and raises the general way of thinking in society], all that is needed is *freedom*. And the freedom in question is the most innocuous form of all — freedom to make *public use* of one's reason in all matters" (original emphasis).[17] Here, Kant distinguishes this "public use of reason" from expression in the non-public realm, by which he does not only mean the private realm in the sense of one's domestic or personal life, but our roles as employees. In other words, for Kant, the "public realm," or what we might call the "public sphere" following Jürgen Habermas,[18] does not include what we say in either our home or work life. He spends significant space in this short essay discussing how religious ministers and priests must preach the doctrines of their churches and are not free to express their own religious ideas. Similarly, those working in government positions must refrain from expressing their views if they conflict with those of the government. However, Kant insists that even ministers, priests, and government employees must be permitted absolute free expression outside their roles as ministers, government officials, or employees. In other words, as citizens, everyone needs to have the freedom of "the public use of reason." It is important to keep this point in mind as it distinguishes Kant from Mill, and aligns him with Meiklejohn. Chapter Three raises this important distinction between the public and private, as well.

Kant argues that for the "public use of reason" to be available to everyone, the government must maintain stability and security. Kant sums up the necessary political arrangement required for free speech with a dictum he attributes to Frederick II, King of Prussia (1740–86): "*Argue* as much as you like about whatever you like, *but obey!*" (original emphasis).[19] Key here is the absolutely limitless character of those topics about which we should have freedom to speak "about whatever you like." The flip side for Kant is that obedience is necessary. The benevolent ruler must have "at hand a well-disciplined and numerous army to guarantee public security" to protect individuals from dangers posed by the disorder that could erupt from free debate.

Kant describes,

> a strange and unexpected pattern in human affairs . . . A high degree of civil freedom seems advantageous to a people's *intellectual* freedom, yet it sets up insuperable barriers to it. Conversely, a lesser degree of civil freedom gives intellectual freedom enough room to expand to its fullest extent. Thus once the germ on which nature has lavished most care — man's inclination and vocation to *think freely* — has developed within this hard shell, it gradually reacts upon the mentality of the people, who thus gradually become increasingly able to *act freely*. (original emphasis)

In other words, allowing people more freedom of action can disrupt society and make it unruly, ultimately curtailing the free speech of some or all. True civil liberty and individual freedom of action must be delayed, according to Kant, until society as a whole can become enlightened; until then, society needs rules and rulers to enforce them. Kant is vague about how this progress will occur, but he is optimistic that the primacy of free speech will foster reason and one day lead to enlightenment, which will usher in greater freedom in general, including civil freedom and the freedom to act.

We learn two key points from Kant's position regardless of whether we accept it. First, the importance Kant places on free speech in its most absolute form demands severe impingement on all other freedoms. It is precisely the strong army and non-democratic nature of government that enables a benevolent ruler to allow such unbridled free speech. Second, his optimistic faith in "reason" and insistence that the freedom to speak and reason publicly is the paramount requirement for society to progress towards enlightenment. It is crucial to note that Kant's free speech absolutism is not actually absolute. It excludes those he considered incapable of reason and it requires the state with a strong military to maintain order, allowing the few who have the courage to use their reason the security to do so. It does not fit easily with the view common among conservatives that government is a necessary evil that should be kept as limited as possible. For Kant, the limits of government regulation of free public speech are premised on a strong and active government in all other spheres.

Mill, Social Progress, and Truth

In contrast to Kant, Mill's argument for free speech is made in the context of modern representative democracy. Writing seventy-five years later, in England, a constitutional monarchy with political power residing increasingly in a democratically elected House of Commons, Mill saw free speech as, in part, a protection from majority rule (that is, a majority of property-owning adult men). Mill was deeply worried about democracy becoming a "tyranny of the majority." For Mill, free speech and other liberal freedoms are an important check on the power of the democratic government.[20] Mill's articulation of *liberal* democracy, where the power of "the people" or the masses of voters is restrained within the liberal constraints of individualism, has had incredible influence, becoming a part of what one might call "common sense." That his arguments about the importance of free expression have become so dominant is not too surprising.

Before focusing on Mill's specific argument for free expression in *On Liberty*, I need to lay out his book's main argument. Mill states that his purpose is to assert "one very simple principle":

> The sole end for which mankind are warranted, individually or collectively, in interfering with the liberty of action of any of their number, is self-protection. That the only purpose for which power can be rightfully exercised over any member of a civilised community, against his will, is to prevent harm to others.[21]

This idea is often referred to as Mill's "harm principle."

Note here that Mill references a key distinction in his subclause, "individually or collectively." This begins his practice of sometimes referring to government action but most of the time focusing more on the public and the pressures of public opinion. As we shall see, these distinctions are pivotal, and I will discuss them in detail in Chapter Two. While acknowledging this distinction between the government versus public opinion as the agent of restrictions on speaking, Mill combines them in most of this work of his. In his concluding chapter, he raises the question of "government interference," which he states, "do[es] not, in strictness, belong to . . . the principle of liberty," however "closely connected" they are. Thus, it is only as an addendum at the end of the final chapter where he discusses why activities beneficial to society should be left to individuals rather than governments.[22] But in general, Mill presents *On Liberty* as an argument from the perspective of the individual's freedom from external pressures, whether they are other individuals, groups, public opinion, or expectations (or what today we might call "cancel culture" or the tendencies decried in the *Harper's* Letter, discussed in the Introduction), or the democratic government. As I will discuss, this is a key issue that Alexander Meiklejohn and C. Edwin Baker see very differently.

Like Kant, Mill acknowledges that his doctrine of liberty (he uses liberty and freedom synonymously) does not apply universally to all societies or people. He notes that because children are in the care of others and have not developed the ability to reason, the principle of liberty does not apply to them. In a troubling manner, he extends this logic concerning children to whole societies:

> For the same reason, we may leave out of consideration those backward states of society in which the race itself may be considered as in its nonage ... Despotism is a legitimate mode of government in dealing with barbarians, provided the end be their improvement, and the means justified by actually effecting that end.[23]

This idea that, like children, entire societies may be "taken care of by others" is by definition paternalistic and common to racist colonialism.[24] These issues become complex, as Mill was both a radical proponent of women's rights (including introducing a bill in the House of Commons for the women's vote in 1866) and a vehement abolitionist who celebrated John Brown's attempt to foment armed slave rebellion in the US.[25] This is not the place to detail the complex debates concerning Mill and colonialism, or the extent to which Mill's paternalist imperial attitudes undermine or inflect his contributions to political theory concerning freedom, as my aim here is to interrogate critically the tradition of free speech to which Mill is central. These questions of racism and colonialism are vital to our current discussions of whether or not ideals and rationales for free expression can help anti-colonial and anti-racist movements, but that is not my aim here.

We now turn to Mill's specific argument about free expression, which he confines to Chapter Two, marking it off from his wider analysis of freedom in general.[26] Mill opens the chapter with a sentiment that has been embraced by subsequent free speech defenders: "If all of mankind minus one, were of one opinion, and only one person were of the contrary opinion, mankind would be no more justified in silencing that one person, than he, if he had the power, would be justified in silencing mankind."[27] In other words, even a perfectly democratic government — that is, one where "the people," or a majority of them, effectively rule — cannot legitimately infringe upon free expression of any individual. He opposes any majority diminishing individual freedom, especially free speech, whether through government, public opinion, or other social means. For Mill, the danger of such suppression is that it denies everyone progress.

It is important to note that Mill is not making a rights-based argument. He does not argue that individuals have an inherent right to free expression; rather he makes a utilitarian argument that free expression benefits society at large. As Mill puts it, "I forego any advantage which could be derived to my argument from the idea of abstract right, as a thing independent of utility."[28] He followed Jeremy Bentham's utilitarianism which focused on the outcomes of actions, their utility in achieving the desired end of the greatest good for the greatest number. Where for Bentham this good is a matter of maximizing pleasure and minimizing pain, Mill expanded the idea of good to include social progress.[29]

In a pithy summary, Mill encapsulates his rationale: "If the opinion [that is to be silenced] is right, they [all of humanity] are deprived of the opportunity of exchanging error for truth: if wrong, they lose, what is almost as great a benefit, the clearer perception and livelier impression of truth, produced by its collision with error."[30] Here, the purpose or utility is consistently that of striving for truth. Mill then provides a lengthy discussion of each of the elements of this sentence, with examples of how brilliant individuals, such as Marcus Aurelius, and entire societies, such as Ancient Athens that sentenced Socrates to death, have been mistaken. He argues that human knowledge is fallible and thus there is always the possibility that we think an idea is false when it is actually true. The potential veracity of any given speech demands it not be silenced.

However beneficial it is to make sure potential truths are given voice, Mill contends that it is "almost as great a benefit" to society to allow ideas (what he calls opinions) to be aired even if they are undoubtedly false. Once aired they can be challenged and scrutinized, concomitantly preventing the truth from becoming "dead dogma."[31] Here, Mill aligns with Kant on the importance of thinking for oneself, of weighing critical perspectives, and of the clash of ideas in reaching a meaningful truth or valid position. He rails against those who "can once get their creed taught from authority, naturally think that no good, and some harm, comes of its being allowed to be questioned." In order to really understand and hold a position, one needs to hear the contrary position. An individual "must be able to hear them [counter-arguments] from persons who actually believe them, who defend them in earnest, and do their very utmost for them."[32] This description of how a deeper understanding of truth emerges from battling with untrue ideas is what leads people to connect Mill's position with Oliver Wendel Holmes's famous metaphor of the "marketplace of ideas," to be discussed in Chapter Two. Mill's notion is that there should be a free zone or arena for public discussion that neither the government nor dominant opinion infringes on.

This enables both individuals to think for themselves and weigh the arguments of others but also allows new and progressive ideas to take root. The authors of the *Harper's* Letter are making a similar point by supporting even "caustic counter-speech."

As a thorough and analytical author, Mill moves on to cases that are not so clear-cut in terms of being true or false. He gives the example of French philosopher Jean-Jacques Rousseau (1712–78), who Mill admits is very important but with whom he fundamentally disagrees. Mill's description of the impact of Rousseau's writings is worth quoting: "with what a salutary shock did the paradoxes of Rousseau explode like bombshells in the midst, dislocating the compact mass of one-sided opinion, and forcing its elements to recombine in a better form and with additional ingredients."[33] In other words, the consideration of flawed or false ideas, however outlandish or contradictory, can lead towards the truth and a fuller understanding. Mill's robust defence of free speech is geared towards the search for truth in public and premised on our capacity for human fallibility and incomplete knowledge.

When Speech Becomes Action

In the transition to the rest of *On Liberty*'s analysis of freedom more generally, Mill makes a key distinction between action and speech: "No one pretends that actions should be as free as opinions."[34] He continues:

> On the contrary, even opinions lose their immunity, when the circumstances in which they are expressed are such as to constitute their expression a positive instigation to some mischievous *act*. An opinion that corn-dealers are starvers of the poor, or that private property is robbery, ought to be unmolested when simply circulated through the press but may justly incur punishment when delivered orally to an excited mob assembled before the house of a corn-dealer, or when handed about among the same mob in the form of a placard. (emphasis added)

In other words, under some conditions, some speech constitutes the instigation of acts which, if harmful, can be rightly prohibited.

In addition to being relevant to contemporary questions of free expression, including Donald Trump's speech to an excited crowd near the US Capitol on 6 January 2021, this is also Mill's answer to Kant's problem: How can we allow total freedom of speech without society devolving into chaos and violence? Kant's answer was to follow the dictum: *argue as much as you want about whatever you want.* And obedience should be enforced by a strong army. Mill's more democratic solution mobilizes the speech/action distinction: you are free to argue with words but if your actions are deemed harmful the government can force you to obey.

> The liberty of the individual must be thus far limited; he must not make himself a nuisance to other people. But if he refrains from molesting others in what concerns them, and merely acts according to his own inclination and judgement in things which concern himself, the same reasons which show that opinion should be free, prove also that he should be allowed, without molestation, to carry his opinions into practice at his own cost.[35]

Thus, for Mill, when an individual is considered to be "molesting others" or making a "nuisance," both the public and the government should be allowed to curtail their action, including their speech. In such cases, their speech is actually not speech but action.[36] His is a functional definition based on the context and impact of one's speech. Put this way, Mill's principle of free expression applies to one's private and domestic realm in a manner that Kant, and as we shall see Meiklejohn and Baker, do not hold.

Chapter Two will expand this speech/action relationship in legal contexts and Chapter Four will extend it to the realm of the internet, where the only physical action is the movement of electronic data. In the context of Mill's framework, the key point is that the harm principle is how we decide if a certain expression should be permitted, regardless of whether it is false or true. I call this the *"sticks and stones may break my bones, but names [words] will never hurt me"* position. That is, mere words are not harmful in the way that action is. If my words do actual damage to you or are detrimental to your "permanent interests" in the language of some Mill scholars,[37] then they need to be treated not as harmless words but as potentially harmful actions. It also seems to be the presumption, as we saw earlier, of Voltaire, for whom books should not be censured because they cannot do real harm. Mill never addresses any psychological arguments about whether verbal abuse can harm an individual. As Melina Constantine Bell notes, Mill "did not have the benefit of modern scientific knowledge about forms of tangible psychological harm, mechanisms for transmitting cultural norms, implicit bias, structural discrimination, etc."[38] Where she attempts to update and expand Mill's notion of harm so that it includes "bigoted speech" that can be justly prohibited despite Mill's staunch defence of free expression, she agrees that without such updating, Mill holds that insulting speech is unlike physical harm.

Another important point is that like Kant, Mill did not think that most people would avail themselves of the individual freedom he found so precious. In Chapter Three of *On Liberty,* Mill argues that while only a few will even understand the intrinsic worth of individuality and individual freedom, "these few are the salt of the earth; without them, human life would become a stagnant pool. Not only is it they who introduce good things which did not before exist; it is they who keep the life in those which already existed."[39] For Mill, these few are the only source of social progress; without them, society risks slipping back into meaningless nihilism. In these same pages, Mill presents his powerful images that humans in mass society can easily become like "sheep" or "automatons." While the word "sheeple" was first coined in 1945, it has become codified and included in the *Merriam-Webster Dictionary* since 2017 due to its increasingly common usage, especially by the alt-right.[40] Mill's implication is that most people can never live up to their potential unique individualism but will remain like herd animals. It is these people who make up the mass public that Mill feared could tyrannize the few genius individuals.

It is important to remember the historical context in which Mill was presenting this defence of free expression. Compulsory public schooling and thus widespread literacy was a relatively new ideal still to be fully implemented. The realm of the "reading public," to use Kant's phrase, through newspapers, journals, and books, was still developing. We must ask ourselves if Mill's idealized realm of free expression, distinguishable from potentially harmful action, is still, or ever was, persuasive.

To complicate the speech/action distinction further, the twentieth century included important developments in philosophy concerning language. Luminary figures like Ludwig Wittgenstein, J.L. Austin, and others challenged the simplistic distinction between speech and action. This is evident in the very naming of an important, new field, "speech act theory," that analyzes every utterance as a speech act.

As we will see in the next chapter, much of the legal thinking concerning the US First Amendment relies on the type of distinction that

Mill makes between speech and action, whereas Canada has a very different legal tradition, with much more leeway for explicitly regulating or prohibiting speech deemed to be harmful without having to show that it is action, as in the laws against hate speech.

Free Speech and Democracy

As demonstrated above, neither Kant nor Mill considers free speech as part of the process of democratic governance. For Kant, free speech requires a strong, anti-democratic state with a benevolent autocrat, and for Mill, free speech is a bulwark *against* too much democracy or populism.[41] Alexander Meiklejohn's *Free Speech and Its Relation to Self-Government* is important and distinct because it *directly* connects free speech to the workings of democracy and the very mechanisms of the rule of the people.[42] Born in England and raised in the US from the age of eight, Meiklejohn (1872–1964) was a philosopher, university administrator (including the president of Amherst College), and a First Amendment advocate. He frames his version of free speech absolutism in relation to the American Constitution and the requirements of democracy or "self-government" — that is, the citizens' needs in governing themselves.

Meiklejohn argues that the US Constitution provides two different types of freedoms: absolute and relative. Absolute freedoms include the freedom of religion and the other rights included in the First Amendment. He emphasizes the absolute nature of the first clause, allowing no exceptions: "Congress shall make no law . . . abridging the freedom of speech." Relative freedoms, on the other hand, are held in balance with other rights and responsibilities. Such relative rights are protected in subsequent amendments. Private property, for example, is a freedom that is subject to the power of taxation by Congress, and thus is far from absolute, but is still an important constitutional right. Meiklejohn maintains that the relative freedom to say what one wishes, especially in private, is guaranteed not by the First Amendment, but the Fifth and Fourteenth Amendments, which protect one's rights to "life, liberty, and property"; to "due process"; and to equality under the law. These relative protections of an individual's free speech, which must be balanced with other rights and the functions of government, are categorically different from the public or political free speech protected by the First Amendment: the First Amendment right is "*the* freedom *of* speech" and applies only to speech about public concerns. This freedom of speech is absolute, according to Meiklejohn. The First Amendment distinguishes traditional authoritarian control from democratic "self-government" in which citizens operate under laws enacted by representatives that they elect and influence through their capacity for public expression and critique of government.[43] Without such capacity, Meiklejohn argues, elected representatives would not know what the public wanted, and the public could not deliberate concerning decisions that are in its interest. He is adamant that the First Amendment must be interpreted in a "single-minded" way and does not concern the "needs of many men [and women] to express their opinions," which is, he asserts, the terrain of the Fifth Amendment: "The First Amendment has other work to do. It is protecting the common needs of all the members of the body politic. It cares for the public need."[44]

This direct connection between the freedom of speech and democracy is why it must be "unqualified" for Meiklejohn: "It admits no exceptions … That prohibition [of Congress from making laws that abridge the freedom of speech] holds good in war as in peace, in danger as in security."[45] This freedom of speech is truly absolute — except, Meiklejohn argues, in the case of sedition, treason, libel, or slander, which by definition cannot contribute to the public good. Meiklejohn clearly distinguishes the absolute nature of constitutionally protected freedom of speech from free speech more generally: "When self-governing men [and women] demand freedom of speech they are not saying that every individual has an unalienable right to speak whenever, wherever, however he [or she] chooses. . . . The common sense of any reasonable society would deny the existence of that unqualified right."[46] The freedom of speech ensures that:

> no suggestion of policy shall be denied a hearing because it is on one side of the issue rather than another. And this means that though citizens may, on other grounds, be barred from speaking, they may not be barred because their views are thought to be false or dangerous.

For Meiklejohn, the freedom of speech needs to be distinguished sharply from Mill's goal of understanding and attaining the truth and thus social progress, or from Kant's goal of furthering enlightenment. As he explains, "the reason for this equality of status in the field of ideas lies deep in the very foundation of the self-governing process. When men [and women] govern themselves, it is they — and no one else — who must pass judgement upon unwisdom and unfairness and danger."[47] It is the process of collective decisions related to governing that are at issue, not some abstract notion of social progress or pursuit of the truth.

Meiklejohn worries that abridgement of the freedom of speech will deny citizens the "acquaintance with information or opinion or doubt or disbelief or criticism which is relevant to that issue." This mirrors Mill's point about denying listeners the ability to hear counter-arguments in order to strengthen their own. But Meiklejohn's goal is the functioning of democracy as a communal process of decision-making. He mentions nowhere progress and preventing social stagnation, as Mill emphasizes. And unlike Mill, he is not concerned with the "tyranny of the majority," nor of free speech standing as a bulwark against too much democracy. Meiklejohn puts it forcefully: "*It is that mutilation of the thinking process of the community against which the First Amendment to the Constitution is directed*" (original emphasis). The phrase that distinguishes his position from Mill's is "*the thinking process of the community.*" In this way, Meiklejohn is ultimately a communitarian in the tradition of Jean-Jacques Rousseau, focused on the self-governing aspect of democracy.[48] Whereas Mill is an individualist wanting to protect individual geniuses from democracy, Meiklejohn sees freedom of speech as necessary for the formation of the public will.

Much of Meiklejohn's *Free Speech and Its Relation to Self-Government* is a critique of the "clear-and-present-danger" test introduced by US Supreme Court Justice Oliver Wendell Holmes in *Schenck v. United States* (1919), to be discussed in the next chapter. This test presented a way in which the First Amendment could be limited and by which the government could curtail one's freedom of speech. Holmes argued, "The question in every case is whether the words used are used in such circumstances and are of such a nature as to create a clear and present danger that they will bring about the substantive evils that Congress has a right to prevent."[49] While this test is superseded in 1969, by the test of whether the speech in question is likely to incite "imminent and lawless action" (see *Brandenburg v. Ohio*), Meiklejohn opposes any test that constrains the absolute nature of the First Amendment. In this sense, Meiklejohn is a precursor to the arguments of the US Supreme Court that overturned the "clear and present danger" test, expanding the First Amendment, as will also be discussed in the next chapter.

Free Speech and Self-Expression

C. Edwin Baker (1947–2009), a professor of law and communication at the University of Pennsylvania, is the fourth and final theorist of free speech surveyed in this chapter. Unlike Kant and Mill, he does not value free speech as a necessary condition for enlightenment or progress, nor does he see it as an inherent part of the collective democratic decision-making process, as Meiklejohn argues. Baker's position may be closest to many current invocations of free speech as a self-evident right, a freedom that is inherently good in and of itself, rather than a means to a different end, such as enlightenment, progress, or self-government. Put more philosophically, expressing ourselves is so integral to being human that it supersedes other human needs and attributes, including reason, compassion, or the need for self-protection and security (including freedom from verbal abuse). Baker argues, "Speech or other self-expressive conduct [should be] protected not as a means to achieve a collective good but because of its value to the individual."[50] He explicitly rejects Mill's harm principle[51] and arguments for free expression based on the search for truth.[52] It is not that Baker offers a more extreme version of Kant, Mill, or Meiklejohn's rationale for free speech; he values free speech for entirely different reasons. For Baker, expressive activity, including free speech, is central to one's "personhood" and any government infringement undermines the state's legitimacy. Moreover, he allows little grey area, labelling himself "an advocate of almost absolute protection of free speech,"[53] because "respect for a person's autonomy is in general an on/off value" that is denied when one's "right to use her own expression to embody her views" is curtailed.[54]

Baker criticizes Meiklejohn's narrow focus on freedom of expression.[55] He rejects laws against hate speech, not on the usual grounds that it is impossible to define[56] or that such laws may have unintended detrimental consequences in practice,[57] but because "the capacity to engage in expressive activities that can cause harm is essential to the notion of agents capable of uncoerced agreement."[58] Employing the language of individual autonomy, Baker holds that all speech, including racist hatred, should be protected by the US First Amendment, despite the fact that "the mere expression of racist hate speech can cause real injuries and has the potential to stimulate further harm." In other words, Baker is not mobilizing a speech versus action distinction. He is not presenting the "sticks-and-stones" position held by Kant and Mill that words or speech, unlike action, cannot really harm people. Despite the potential for harm, he asserts that "Typically racist hate speech embodies the speaker's at least momentary view of the world, and, to that extent, expresses her values."[59] This human need for self-expression, even of racism and hatred, is primary for him.

Baker also admits that hate speech can undermine the autonomy and legitimacy of others. His position is that "Of course, *her* [hate] *speech* does not respect others' equality or dignity. It is not, however, her but the state's legitimacy that is at stake in evaluating the content of the legal order" (original emphasis).[60] Baker's free speech absolutism applies solely to the government and is akin to what I refer to as constitutional protections of the freedom of expression — that is, restrictions on the government from censuring individuals (also to be discussed in the next chapter). Baker's argument is that it is not the government's role to protect any individual or society at large from the harms of any speech or expressive activity, including hate speech like that prohibited by legislation in Canada. As he explains, "In any minimally decent society that legally permits hate speech, such expression of hate reflexively creates, for those who object to racism, a platform to explain and justify their objections. This expressive activity may provide the greatest safeguard against racist cultures and polities."[61] Thus, unlike Mill, who is as fearful of public opinion silencing expression as he is the government, Baker suggests that the public is the sole and just agent to combat speech that is harmful, violent, or infringes on the safety and well-being of others. Chapter Two examines this idea that "more speech" is preferable to "enforced silence" in detail, and Chapter Four considers whether the expansive social media landscape provides an adequate venue to challenge hateful and harmful speech effectively, as Baker suggests. His position does not support that of the *Harper's* Letter, nor the current critiques of "woke-ism" or "cancel culture," as those critiques focus on public discussion and a culture of tolerance. Baker argues that "People in positions of power or authority do and should lose their influence, and often even their position of authority, for public or exposed private racist expression."[62] Therefore, while he takes an absolute stance that all expression is valid for the full weight of constitutional protection from government infringement, he allows for individual or societally imposed limits on speech in public discourse.

Baker does not, as far as I know, fully investigate the philosophical roots of his position. His emphasis on "expressivist personhood" might suggest he is drawing on the tradition of the Romanticist philosophy of Johann Gottfried Herder, Wilhelm von Humboldt, and up through to the likes of Charles Taylor, perhaps.[63] But this tradition is at odds with Baker's theory of individualism. Indeed, Taylor's critique of "atomic individualism" applies to Baker's arguments.[64] Taylor, who to my knowledge has never engaged with free speech theory per se, sees expressivism dialogically, where we are not atomized individuals expressing ourselves, but we develop our identities within complex, ongoing conversations with others. For Taylor, expressivism is inherently a communitarian approach, whereas for Baker it is individualistic expressivism that is at the heart of his almost absolutist theory of free speech.

While it is outside of the framework of this work, philosophically Baker's position creates an untenable attempt to bridge atomistic individualism with an insistence that being human inherently concerns our ability to do more than communicate, but to express ourselves and our personhood to others.[65] Thus, on one hand, Baker might seem to be in agreement with those like the Canadian legal scholar Richard Moon, who posits, "We become individuals capable of thought and judgement, we flourish as rational and free persons, when we join in conversations with others and participate in the life of the community."[66] But different from Baker, for Moon and myself this position is incompatible with the idea that we must be able to legally express hatred in ways that clearly and intentionally harm others.

Baker distinguishes "civility rules," like those the *Harper's* Letter decries, from issues of free speech. Unlike the *Harper's* Letter, he has little to say about such public discussions and the culture that does or does not allow them to flourish. For Baker, "In a free society, . . . these civility rules must be by people's voluntary allegiance, not through the force of law."[67] Baker's argument is important for us here because it captures the notion that an individual has the right to say whatever they want without the government preventing it, regardless of its effects on others or society at large. Baker is quite explicit: racists need to be able to express their racism because it is central to who they are as people. Since Baker sees the goal of free speech as neither truth nor social progress, but rather unconditional self-expression, he avoids many of the sticky questions that the other thinkers face. However, for those who see expression as a necessary social process, Baker's free speech absolutism may not be convincing.

Summary

This chapter has illustrated that contemporary free speech advocates and even the more subtle but vague calls for open, critical discussion, like the "Open Letter" in *Harper's Magazine*, could be invoking significantly different conceptions of free speech. Yet it is almost always impossible to determine which of these different conceptions they are presenting. Of course, I have only presented four influential options; there are many others, including important non-Western perspectives, as I discuss in the Conclusion. But here I am focused on interrogating the dominant tradition often invoked in current free speech controversies, showing its internal tensions and contradictions. Where both Kant and Mill find free speech essential because it is a method, perhaps the only method, for enlightenment, social progress, and the search for the truth, Meiklejohn and Baker instead root it in democracy, although in very different ways. For Meiklejohn, freedom of expression is central to the people as a collectivity being able to rule, whereas Baker insists a legitimate democracy does not suppress the utterly vital "expressive liberty" of those individuals who must follow its laws. For Kant, free speech requires a strong, authoritarian government that is not likely to be possible in any democracy, at least not in his eighteenth-century context; for Mill. it is a check on democracy as a barrier to individual genius and a discourse in pursuit of truth and progress. For Kant, free speech must be held, even forcefully, above all other civil freedoms but only applies when an individual is speaking in public. For Mill, free speech includes both public and private expression and can be limited only when that speech is deemed to be action and harmful to others. For Meiklejohn, speech that should be given absolute protection is limited to expression on public issues in the context of democratic processes. Baker's concept of self-expression puts the most primacy on the right to free speech, but only from government censure.

Simply invoking the words "free speech" creates confusion: it is vague at best and meaningless at worst. It is mistaken to take this state of confusion to mean, as some suggest, that free speech is an empty vessel that can be filled with any position.⁶⁸ As I raised in the Introduction, Neil Young's decision to withdraw from Spotify over Joe Rogan's spreading of false information about COVID-19 vaccines is fully consistent with his advocacy of the freedom of speech, in the constitutional sense of the absence of government regulating speech — if by free speech he meant an absence of government regulation, which is exactly what he did say. Young, for example, could have supported his position by invoking either Meiklejohn or Baker, and it would have clarified his position. But he would be inconsistent if he tried to justify himself by referencing both, as they have different freedom of speech theories. Either way, critics talked past Young in their diatribes about him going against his 1960s counter-culture roots and Freedom of Speech tour's principles, as the critics seemed to have in mind more so the defences of free speech closer to Mill's theories, including his argument that public opinion can be as detrimental to the search for truth and progress.

CHAPTER TWO

CONSTITUTIONAL PROTECTIONS

THIS CHAPTER EXPLORES WHAT THE DISTINCTIONS ARE BETWEEN *free speech,* as the ideals of open, critical, diverse, and inclusive public discussion (as examined in the Introduction and previous chapter), and the *freedom of expression,* as the specific legal right protected by the Canadian Charter of Rights and Freedoms and the US First Amendment. This constitutional legal principle is fundamentally about limiting government infringement on citizens, residents, and visitors. It is a negative freedom, a freedom from restraint or impediment, like that of Mill's freedom of expression, but concerning specifically governmental infringements rather than the condemnations of public opinion. While related to ideals of critical and inclusive discussion, the constitutional protections from government censorship must be distinguished from them. This is not a novel argument. Canadian legal scholar Richard Moon, for example, writes:

> In much of the writing about the freedom of expression, particularly that from the United States, no distinction is drawn between freedom of expression as a moral or political ideal and as a constitutional right .... Yet, as the book's title [*The Constitutional Protection of Freedom of Expression*] is meant to suggest, it matters whether we are talking about freedom of expression as a political claim or constitutional right.[1]

Canadian political scientist Emmett Macfarlane notes that "free expression extends beyond its status as a constitutionally entrenched right. It is equally fundamental as a societal value."[2] As shown in the previous chapter, Kant does not acknowledge this distinction, whereas Mill recognizes it, but does not use it. It is a central distinction for both Alexander Meiklejohn and C. Edwin Baker. Thus the confusion created when free speech is deployed as a principle with no specification runs deeper than my Introduction's distinction between the *Harper's* Letter and the controversy between Neil Young and Spotify.

This chapter demonstrates that the constitutional right to freedom of expression is primarily about safeguarding society at large and individuals specifically from the overreach of legislative power.[3] As Kant and Mill argued, its premise is that allowing individuals to express their ideas in public will lead to greater knowledge and progress, but the law itself is to ensure this negative freedom. A hopeful result of such constitutional protection may be robust public discussion. It may even be a necessary condition for such dialogue, though not the only one. As Chapter Three will illustrate, many models of truth-seeking are premised on specific forms of regulating speech, whether it be court procedures or academic education and knowledge production. This chapter shows how the idea that protection from government censorship is sufficient to shape productive public discussion relies on an extremely optimistic and unconvincing vision of human reason. The legal principles of freedom of expression are rights in the negative sense in that they remove barriers to speech; there is no positive requirement to foster good, productive content.[4] What faith we may have had that unrestricted speech would unleash critical, diverse, and productive discussions may have been severely undermined by the last decade's experiment with social media, as Chapter Four will examine. When the legal system itself is required to determine truth, such as the guilt or innocence of a person accused of a crime, it makes no pretence to free expression, but creates, as Brian Leiter argues, intense regulations on what and who can express themselves in a court of law.[5] Thus while the Canadian Supreme Court has repeatedly argued that one of the values underlying free expression is that "seeking and attaining the truth is an inherently good activity,"[6] the point is that free expression allows its citizens to pursue the truth and that the court's job in protecting free expression is not to make judgements about the truth of its citizens' ideas.

The key element of this distinction is that the freedom of speech as a constitutional principle should not consider the substance or quality of the speech in question beyond whether or not it harms individuals or presents a danger to society. The determination of harm is different in Canada than in the US, and both have changed over time, but courts have consistently held that the role of government is not to use its coercive power to adjudicate the quality of expression nor whether the speech contributes to truth, legitimate critique, enlightenment, progress, or any other such goal.[7] Government's primary functions require that it uphold the rule of law to maintain a peaceful and orderly society made up of diverse individuals and groups. The principle is that a democratic government should not be in a position to silence or censure the people it represents and rules. Conversely, a government may regulate speech to protect other citizens and society at large, but not to enforce its own determination of what is true, what is valuable, or what is worthy of expression.

While seemingly straightforward, this constitutional principle of freedom of expression does not necessarily apply to all governmental action concerning its citizens' speech. Governments establish public school systems and mandatory attendance to ensure educated citizens can read and write and thus express themselves, ideally as informed people. Governments decide the extent to which they will require that private schools meet certain criteria and curricular objectives to meet such aims. Some governments, such as in France, are very specific about the language that will be used for this education, even the precise rules of grammar and usage (through the Académie Française). Others, like in Canada, have constitutional laws that dictate that education be available in the official languages;[8] still others, like the American government, do not stipulate any official language, at least not at the federal level. Of course, this does not mean that English is not, in practice, the dominant language of the US, but it is not specified in the Constitution, nor have any proposals to enshrine English as the official language passed into federal law.

Democratic governments foster myriad programs for public benefit, such as funding academic and scientific research and supporting business and community groups, for which they must adjudicate the quality and intent of citizen expression to make decisions about what is worthy of support and taxpayer funds. These are positive actions in support of particular content of expression, and governments of different stripes may or may not pursue them, depending on their priorities. In some ways, then, governments can and do adjudicate the quality and content of speech, but only within the limitations of their own constitutional protections of their citizens' individual rights, especially the right to the freedom of expression. And we must distinguish these two types of actions that governments make. The first includes what I have labelled "critical and inclusive discussion," which we can think of as positive expressive freedom, and the latter, the "constitutional protection of the freedom of speech."

This chapter does not aim to provide a comprehensive account of the complex legal issues involved in right to free expression. There is extensive legal scholarship on the First Amendment in the US, and a respectively large literature concerning the Charter right to free expression in Canada.[9] Richard Moon and Emmett Macfarlane, for example, offer thorough analyses of why the Canadian courts should maintain a wider approach, taking into account social context when adjudicating the Charter right to free expression.[10] Similarly, there is a rich literature on Canada's laws against hate speech and hate propaganda, including in contrast to the absence of such laws in the US.[11]

It is no accident that the distinction I am making here has recently been increasingly confused and misused. Donald Trump's class-action lawsuit against Facebook, Twitter, and Google, for suspending his account after he violated their codes of conduct, is a clear example of a conflation of these two distinct principles, and likely deliberately so. While there may be a sound argument that the suspension of Trump's accounts by these private companies curtails some ideals of critical and inclusive discussion or free speech culture in the amorphous sphere of social media, there is no sense in which it is a breach of the US First Amendment, which only constrains Congress.[12] The legal consensus is that this lawsuit will go nowhere in the courts.[13] Facebook, Twitter, and Google are private companies, not Congress or government entities in any way.[14] Indeed, it would be a violation of the First Amendment for the government to force private social media companies to host any particular content or individual.[15]

Commentators and legal experts have suggested that Trump's lawsuit is merely a media stunt to gain attention and generate campaign donations,[16] but it also appears to be part of a pattern that may be a conscious strategy to confuse Americans about the meaning of the First Amendment. Staunch Trump supporter Senator Josh Hawley responded with a similar misuse of the First Amendment when his publisher

Simon & Schuster cancelled his book contract after the insurrection attempt on Capitol Hill on 6 January 2021. As a graduate of Yale Law School, Hawley must have understood that his threat to sue a publisher for First Amendment infringement was legally nonsensical, and yet he still tweeted that the cancellation of his book contract was a "direct assault on the First Amendment … We'll see you in court."[17] As with Trump's lawsuit, most commentators consider Hawley's threat to take his publisher to court as merely a ploy to get attention. Nonetheless, such tactics exacerbate confusion about what the First Amendment entails.

This chapter also considers several of the slogans and ideas that have originated from US court cases on the First Amendment that have migrated into general discussions of critical and inclusive discussion. These include the example of the false cry of "fire" in a crowded theatre, the analogy of the "marketplace of ideas," and the notion that more speech or counter-speech is preferable to imposed silence. These concepts have been imported into public discussions of free speech and yet they do not specifically refer to the constitutional concept of the freedom of speech of the First Amendment, as seen, for example, in the *Harper's* Letter that I discussed in the Introduction. Instead, they are most often used as ideals that should structure public discussion. I argue that this situation further confuses the current debates around free speech and its goals.

Constitutional Foundations in Canada and the US

This is not the place for a full discussion of the complexities of constitutions, including important differences between written constitutions in the republican tradition of the US or France, as distinct from Britain and Canada's inclusion of unwritten components of constitutions, but it will help to understand that constitutions delimit the various functions of a government and what powers they may or may not exercise. Constitutions legitimize democratic governments by explicating the purposes of their various components, such as the House of Commons, the Senate, and the courts. In this context, the important points of similarity between the US and Canada are that both constitutions are the highest law of the land, and any legislation that is deemed to contravene them is null and void. In both countries, the federal Supreme Court interprets the Constitution and rules on these matters (this is called judicial review).

In Canada, Section 2 of the Charter of Rights and Freedoms states, "Everyone has the following fundamental freedoms: (a) freedom of conscience and religion; (b) freedom of thought, belief, opinion and expression, including freedom of the press and other media of communication; (c) freedom of peaceful assembly; and (d) freedom of association." This delineation of freedoms is, however, preceded by an important qualification in Section 1: "The *Canadian Charter of Rights and Freedoms* guarantees the rights and freedoms set out in it subject only to such reasonable limits prescribed by law as can be demonstrably justified in a free and democratic society." Thus, in Canada, the right to free expression has been repeatedly limited when the courts have determined that the limitations are "reasonable" in a "free and democratic society."

In the US Constitution, the First Amendment is more categorical with no sense of balancing the freedom of speech by reasonable limits. It could not be more explicit: "Congress shall make no law respecting an establishment of religion, or prohibiting the free exercise thereof; or abridging the freedom of speech, or of the press; or the right of the people peaceably to assemble, and to petition the government for a redress of grievances." It limits government action, specifically by Congress (and, since the passage of the Fourteenth Amendment, by state legislatures as well). This right to the freedom of speech is more specific than a general goal of fostering critical and inclusive discussion, and it is more limited in scope than Mill's principle against anyone, individually or collectively, silencing the expression of another.

While the Charter right to freedom of expression parallels the First Amendment, there are significant differences. In Canada, freedom of expression was entrenched in the Charter in the Constitution Act of 1982, replacing a Bill of Rights (1960) that was not part of the Constitution and thus did not have precedent over other legislation (nor did it apply to the provincial legislatures). Whereas the US has over 200 years of history with the First Amendment freedom of speech, the Canadian Charter right to freedom of expression is much more recent. The significance of this difference, however, can be overstated, as there were few Supreme Court cases that dealt with First Amendment speech issues before Justices Holmes and Brandeis inaugurated the freedom of speech as a defining feature of American law after World War I. Nevertheless, there have been far fewer free expression cases before the Canadian courts and they, of course, date back only to 1982 with the passage of the Charter, compared to the US where such cases have been developing in their reasonings since 1919.

The Charter's stipulation of "reasonable limits" to freedom of expression is perhaps more important to distinguish the Canadian situation from the US. Whether it concerns upholding prohibitions against tobacco companies sponsoring sporting and cultural events or overturning a ban on political advertising on public buses, the Supreme Court of Canada's decisions on expression protected under the Charter have most often hinged on Section 1, "the reasonableness of the limitation." For example, while the court decided that Canada's laws against hate speech contravene in Section 2(b)'s guarantee of freedom of expression, it ruled that such restrictions were a reasonable limit that "can be demonstratively justified in a free and democratic society."[18] Whereas the Canadian right to freedom of expression is balanced against the needs of a democratic society, the American framework is more absolute and categorical. Among other important consequences, this is why the US, unlike most other liberal democracies, does not have legislation against hate speech.

Yelling "Fire!" — When Speech Becomes Action

However absolute the First Amendment may read, the US Supreme Court has always interpreted it to exclude some speech from its protection. In broad terms, the rationale for such exclusion is that when the speech in question causes, incites, or constitutes harmful action, it is not actually *speech* (that the First Amendment must protect), but *action* (that can be "abridged"). As Justice Oliver Wendell Holmes famously argued in 1919, "falsely yelling 'fire' in a theatre" is not speech that the First Amendment must protect. Rather, such an utterance is an action that government can and should regulate to prevent harm to others. Holmes invoked the comparison of falsely yelling fire to the distribution of pamphlets, encouraging eligible men to resist the military draft, in *Schenck v. United States*. Indeed, in this very case, Holmes articulated what became known as the "clear and present danger test": "The question in every case is whether the words used are used in such circumstances and are of such a nature as to create a clear and present danger that they will bring about the substantive evils that Congress has a right to prevent."[19] Thus, while the First Amendment reads as if all speech is protected from congressional legislation, if the speech is deemed *action*, it can be constitutionally prohibited. While the legal reasoning differs in important ways, the end result is often quite similar to the Canadian process whereby the courts balance free expression rights against other interests.

This "clear and present danger" test was a more robust protection of the First Amendment right to free speech than the previous precedents during the First World War, where speech that would produce a "bad tendency" could be prohibited by the government despite the First Amendment.[20] Nevertheless, the decision ruled against the Socialist Party Executive Members, Charles Schenck (Secretary General) and Elizabeth Baer. Later the same year, however, Justice Holmes insisted that the "clear and present danger" test must be refined to include the provision that the danger of the speech in question must not only be "clear and present," but also "imminent." In *Abrams v. United States* (1919), both Holmes and Brandeis dissented from the majority decision, which upheld the Espionage Act (1917), and ruled that the First Amendment did not protect Abrams' right to distribute flyers critical of sending American troops to fight in Russia against the new Bolshevik government. This dissenting opinion also gives rise to the metaphor of free speech being a "marketplace of ideas," to be discussed at length below.

Concurring with Justice Brandeis's decision in *Whitney v. California* (1927), Holmes and the court further refined and constrained the "clear and present danger test," and in 1942, *Chaplinsky v. New Hampshire*, the Supreme Court developed the doctrine that "fighting words" were not protected speech under the First Amendment. In this case, a Jehovah's Witness called a police officer a "God-damned racketeer" and a "damned Fascist." These phrases were deemed not free speech but rather "fighting words" — that is, speech that is actually action. These refinements would continue until the test was finally supplanted altogether in *Brandenburg v. Ohio* (1969). This case involved a Ku Klux Klan member, Clarence Brandenburg, who had been convicted for an antisemitic, white supremacist speech he gave at a Klan meeting. The Supreme Court overturned Brandenburg's conviction, finding that the law used to convict him abridged his First Amendment freedom of speech rights. That decision set forth a new test for the courts: Is the speech under consideration "directed to inciting or producing imminent lawless action and is [it] likely to incite or produce such action"?[21] This complex history illustrates the changing nature of the line between permissible and impermissible speech in terms of the law.[22]

The key point is that while the First Amendment is often held up as an absolute prohibition against government legislation criminalizing any speech, the Court has never interpreted it to mean that *all* speech is allowed. Arguably the Supreme Court has been expanding the First Amendment protections, but there is still a line — despite it historically changing — beyond which the US government has constitutionally restricted people's speech. Indeed, no country in the world has lived up to the absolute principle.[23]

It is worth noting that the US Supreme Court's struggle to draw the line between speech and action — a line I highlighted in relation to Mill's defence of free speech — was taking place at the same time as the so-called linguistic turn in philosophy involving the relationship between speech and action. In *Philosophical Investigations*, the influential Austrian philosopher Ludwig Wittgenstein audaciously declared "the meaning of a word is its use in the language,"[24] thereby repudiating the idea that words are just containers for ideas and speech is fundamentally a method of transporting ideas from one individual to another. Instead, for Wittgenstein, meaning is something we produce, and this production of meaning is akin to an action. His emphasis on how language is used troubles any stark distinction between speech and action. The English philosopher J.L. Austin's *How to Do Things with Words* provides a long attempt to distinguish words that themselves are actions (for example, "fighting words"). He offers examples, like saying, "I do," in a wedding ceremony (what he called "performatives") from speech that is solely expression. Austin, unable to succeed in making any watertight distinctions, concludes that most speech acts include a performative element and must be analyzed in the context in which the words are uttered. Austin asserted that to understand speech, we must include both the intention of the speaker and the effect it has on the listener.[25] In short, to varying degrees, all — or most — speech is, to some degree, action.

Before turning to the Canadian legal principle of freedom of expression, there are two other concepts that have emerged from First Amendment jurisprudence that have become central to free speech debates regarding "critical and inclusive discussion" (as I have called it so as to distinguish it from the constitutional protection of the freedom of speech): the first is the concept of the "marketplace of ideas"; the second, what is sometimes called the "counter-speech doctrine" — the idea that the best response to harmful speech is "more speech, not enforced silence."

The Marketplace of Ideas

The analogy that free speech acts as a "marketplace of ideas" originated with Justice Holmes's comparison to speech being valued like a consumer buys products, functioning as commodities for sale on the open market, as was expressed in his dissenting opinion in *Abrams v. United States* in 1919:

> But when men have realized that time has upset many fighting faiths, they may come to believe even more than they believe the very foundations of their own conduct that the ultimate good desired is better reached by free trade in ideas — that the best test of truth is the power of the thought to get itself accepted in the competition of the market, and that truth is the only ground upon which their wishes safely can be carried out.[26]

This "marketplace of ideas" analogy[27] presents the First Amendment to be that which enables and allows for a space where the best ideas are able to emerge and thus fulfills the goals of enlightenment or social progress as argued for by Kant and Mill. However, despite its widespread influence, the analogy is rather counter-intuitive, as commodities traded in markets are usually material objects with unique physical existence. Ideas expressed in speech do not have such exclusivity: if you sell me an apple or a bottle of bourbon, you can no longer consume it; when you convince me of an idea, you do not relinquish it. The competition of ideas in a debate or discussion is not at all like the competition among commodities for the available dollars in a market. Copyright, patent, and intellectual property law is an exception whereby, in a very limited manner, the exclusive ownership of specific ideas is granted to individuals. But this is not what Holmes was getting at, nor what is meant when the marketplace of ideas is invoked. Most of the ideas that circulate in public discussion are not inventions nor anything trademarked or copyrightable.

Moreover, history and experience have shown that the free market does not produce equality, justice, or particularly high-quality products. Markets place high value on some products, especially scarce ones in high demand, and do not on their own facilitate equitable distribution of wealth. Moreover, the marketplace of goods enables consumers to choose inferior products at lower prices instead of quality goods that cost more. Mill accepts this as a positive feature of real markets but does not think the competition of ideas should lead to lower-quality ideas.[28]

Many have interrogated and challenged the analogy of a marketplace of ideas. English political philosophers Robert Sparrow and Robert Goodin expose its many weaknesses in detail. They argue that we should replace the market of ideas metaphor with a more accurate and productive "garden of ideas," which better captures the active process of diversity and vibrancy of ideal public discussion.[29] American legal scholar Vincent Blasi analyzes additional problems with the market metaphor: "One reason to doubt the efficacy of the market mechanism as a means of ordering beliefs derives from the concept, well recognized by economists, of market failure. Except in models, markets are imperfect. Differential access to information distorts markets. Collective behavior can distort markets."[30] Public discussion understood as a marketplace would be rife with such market failures, according to Blasi.

More profoundly, English post-colonial studies professor Anshuman Mondal argues that the "marketplace of ideas," along with Mill's depiction of an arena or zone of free speech, assumes a "planar" space that ignores the differences of power, circumstance, and experience that speakers and listeners bring to any dialogue. "Rather than visualizing freedom in terms of its scope and extent, across a flat and uniform social space that is emptied of context, I suggest we conceptualize liberty in terms of forces and flows channelled by and through an irregular and uneven terrain."[31] Media studies professor Gavan Titley draws on Mondal's analysis of "the shape of free speech" to illustrate how the illusory homogenous marketplace of free speech "has been drawn into validating, amplifying and reanimating racist ideas and racializing claims."[32]

Similarly, in an article concerning free speech debates at American universities, "The Marketplace of Racist Ideas," legal scholars Nancy Leong and Kevin Whitfield argue that the "anti-regulatory approach" (their term for the free marketplace of ideas) obscures structural inequality among students, faculty, and others at universities and that it also defies logic.[33] First Amendment scholar Jared Schroeder offers a less critical reimagining in order to update the metaphor for the digital era, dubbing our social media environment as a "discursive marketplace of ideas."³⁴ Professor of public policy Philip Napoli presents a more critical analysis of what he calls the "algorithmic marketplace of ideas" of social media, showing how prone it is to "market failure" and other "red flags," illustrating that "it seems increasingly dangerous and misguided to maintain confidence in the notion that the marketplace [of social media] is inherently oriented towards assuring that truth will effectively overcome falsity."³⁵ These examples are just a sample of the host of diverse arguments, from various angles, questioning and rejecting the very influential marketplace analogy, especially in the current context of the twenty-first century. This analogy has been central for illustrating the negative freedom that merely prohibits regulation as a sufficient condition in securing the positive, productive requirements needed for critical and inclusive discussion. By falsely analogizing the interaction and diffusion of ideas with those of goods in a market, the idea of the marketplace obscures the different principles of government overreach restrictions and the search for truth and knowledge and eclipses any consideration of free speech as an effective and essential expression for individuals in a democracy.

In addition to questioning the analogy of free speech to that of a marketplace of ideas — especially for its evasion of inherent power dynamics amongst speakers and its potentiality for becoming an excuse for, or even fuel for, racism and other hurtful speech — I want to call attention to how the marketplace concept functions to confuse the differing goals of constitutional protection of the freedom of expression and the fostering of productive spheres for critical and inclusive discussion. Holmes mobilized the metaphor in 1919 to assert that anti-war propaganda ought to be protected expression. While he clearly disagreed with the defendants' position, he argued that competition with better ideas would quash the propaganda's impact. However, had these ideas *succeeded* in the marketplace, Holmes's test of a "clear and imminent danger" would kick in and allow Congress to stop their spread. In other words, Holmes's famous invocation of a marketplace of ideas was an argument against government suppression of the competition of ideas, but with a backstop of the "clear and imminent danger" test to protect society from what might be called "market failure." Behind Holmes's seeming faith in reason and his confidence that dangerous ideas would be defeated by rational discussion was a safety check that could prohibit speech that was likely to cause "substantive evils," as he noted in *Schenck*. And Holmes saw Congress's job as preventing such evils.

Counter-Speech: Quantity Produces Quality?

US Supreme Court Justice Louis Brandeis contributed another key element to the pantheon of free speech slogans. In *Whitney v. California* (1927), he elaborated that, "If there be time to expose through discussion, the falsehoods and fallacies, to avert the evil by the processes of education, the remedy to be applied is more speech, not enforced silence." This summation has become known as the counter-speech doctrine. As historian and legal scholar James Belpedio contends, the *Whitney* opinion written by Brandeis, with which Holmes concurred, sided with the majority decision of the Court but presented a more eloquent and substantial reasoning concerning the freedom of speech.[36] The case centred on a speech given by Charlotte Whitney while organizing to form the Communist Labor Party of California. Brandeis and Holmes concurred with the majority opinion of the Court that her speech was not protected by the First or Fourteenth Amendments. Thus, the idea of "more speech" was not, in this case, deemed an adequate remedy to evil speech. Moreover, Brandeis went out of his way to note that there was no imminent danger and there was sufficient time for discussion to expose Whitney's supposed fallacies. Perhaps Belpedio is correct that overriding Brandeis's eloquent defence of free speech was his belief that Whitney had participated in the conspiracy that was the organization of the Communist Labor Party and her speech should be prohibited.[37] Once again, like the marketplace of ideas analogy, the counter-speech doctrine becomes a mere platitude that obscures the legal regulation of speech. Brandeis is lauding the positive effect of the freedom of speech while simultaneously arguing that, in the case at hand, it must be abridged.

Invocations of the doctrine of counter-speech imply that ideas that could be harmful are best combatted by allowing private individuals to speak against them. Not even Mill went this far, given his consistent application of the harm principle. Brandeis clearly had some faith that "more speech" would produce better, more convincing speech. Justice Anthony Kennedy took the onus off mere quantity and shifted it to the quality of speech in his opinion in *United States v. Alvarez* (2012): "The remedy for speech that is false is speech that is true." But this formulation introduces exactly what Holmes and Brandeis avoided: how is the government to trust that speech that is true would be produced? Moreover, in 1927, Brandeis's faith in "more speech" was not strong enough for him to reject the Court's majority decision to convict Charlotte Whitney. Even for its founder, the more speech doctrine was substantially limited.

As Napoli illustrates, Facebook and X have both adopted the doctrine that counter-speech is better than censorship or regulation. But Napoli suggests (and this will be addressed in Chapter Four), that the social media environment casts even more doubt on the counter-speech position.[38] Richard Moon argues that the counter-speech doctrine is "inadequate in a communication environment that is increasingly fragmented and which a significant element of the population is not only receptive to 'false news,' . . . but is also (relatively) hostile to competing opinions and evidence that contradicts their views."[39]

In her exquisite history of the development of the ACLU's position on free speech and the First Amendment, Laura Weinrib shows how, in the 1930s, "Seizing on the conservative rhetoric of time-honored individual rights [as contrasted to collective rights to picket, strike, and boycott of earlier ACLU commitments], the ACLU attracted supporters within and outside the courts." In this way, "More than any other entity, it was the ACLU that crafted the constitutional compromise of the post-New Deal era" between conservative individualism and ideals of free speech.[40] This historical context should cast further doubt on the applicability of the US constitutional understandings of the freedom of speech to current Canadian situations. This brief discussion of the origins of free speech ideals in American jurisprudence culminates in the irony of the case, *Citizens United v. Federal Election Committee* (2010). In this decision, the court equated political campaign donations by corporations, non-profits, and unions with protected "speech" that could not be curtailed by election laws. Here, the "more speech" principle of the counter-speech doctrine is transformed into a "more money" doctrine. Inequalities in wealth are directly translated into inequality in power and influence. The qualities of the arguments presented are overshadowed by the quantities of money used to propagate them.[41]

The Canadian Charter Right to Free Expression

The Canadian Charter is much less overt textually about who it restricts than the American First Amendment which clearly limits the power of Congress — not of individuals or the public — to curtail people's freedom of speech. Section 2(b) of the Charter grants the freedom of expression but is silent about who or what must allow such freedom. It is not until Section 32(1a) that it stipulates, "This Charter applies to the Parliament and government of Canada in respect of all matters within the authority of Parliament including all matters relating to the Yukon Territory and Northwest Territories." The Supreme Court addressed this issue in *RWDSU v. Dolphin Delivery* (1986), shortly after the Charter became law. This case was about the freedom of association related to picketing, articulated in Section 2(d), but the precedent applies to the freedom of expression of Section 2(b). In its decision, the Court ruled that the Charter as a whole applies only to the government. *McKinney v. University of Guelph* (1990) clarified:

> The exclusion of private activity from Charter protection was deliberate. To open all private and public action to judicial review could strangle the operation of society and impose an impossible burden on the courts. Only government need be constitutionally shackled to preserve the rights of the individual. Private activity, while it might offend individual rights, can either be regulated by government or made subject to human rights commissions and other bodies created to protect these rights.[42]

This decision concerned mandatory retirement at the University of Guelph, however, it is important concerning the application of the Charter to universities.

The *McKinney v. Guelph* decision addressed whether organizations funded by the government — like universities — are considered within the "authority" of the government and thus subject to Charter restrictions. While the Court decided in this case that universities were not a part of the government, and thus the Charter did not apply, it did stipulate that neither the federal nor provincial governments could delegate their activities to private organizations which would then be free from Charter considerations. In *Eldridge v. British Columbia* (1997), the Court made it clear that the Charter applies to hospitals because they operate through the delegated authority of the provincial governments. Chapter Three's discussion of academic freedom will look more closely at the relationship between universities and the Canadian Charter of Rights and Freedoms, but even where there are grey areas, the principle is that the Charter applies to governments and not organizations that are non-governmental.

The history of the Charter right to freedom of expression in Canada includes many cases where the Court ruled that expression had been infringed but determined that such infringement was "reasonable" and "demonstratively justified in a free and democratic society," as set out in Section 1. Thus, unlike the US framework, the idea of balancing free expression with other values is built into the very wording of the Charter. For example, one of the early freedom of expression cases, *Irwin Toy Ltd. v. Quebec* (1989), decided that the Quebec statute against advertising to children under thirteen years of age did restrict the toy manufacturer's freedom of expression. The decision did not overturn the law, however, because the court determined the limit was reasonable and justified to protect children's well-being. Similarly, in *Little Sisters Books and Art Emporium v. Canada* (2000), the Court ruled that the government could confiscate "obscene" materials imported from the US, despite the infringement on the bookstore's freedom of expression, because it deemed obscenity a social harm that could reasonably be restricted by government. On appeal, however, the Court ultimately sided with Little Sisters because the confiscation contravened the Charter's equality rights of the LGBTQ+ customers of Little Sisters.

The classic case in Canadian free expression jurisprudence is *R. v. Keegstra* (1990), which ruled that laws against hate speech are constitutional. Part VIII of Canada's Criminal Code, entitled, "Offences Against the Person and Reputation," includes Sections 318–20 that focus on "Hate Propaganda." Section 319 makes it an indictable offence to incite or promote "hatred against any identifiable group," defined as "any section of the public distinguished by colour, race, religion, national or ethnic origin, age, sex, sexual orientation, gender identity or expression, or mental or physical disability."[43] *R. v. Keegstra* tested whether this part of the Criminal Code contravened the Charter right to free expression.

James Keegstra was a high-school teacher in Alberta, convicted of using antisemitic speech, including Holocaust denial, in his classes. The court ruled that the law that prohibits any communication that "Wilfully promotes hatred" against identifiable groups is constitutional as a reasonable limitation on freedom of expression. As Richard Moon has argued, the *Keegstra* decision, written by Chief Justice Brian Dickson, significantly questioned the capacity for free expression to determine the truth. It is worth quoting Dickson's reasoning at length because it demonstrates a very different perspective than the American thought on freedom of speech:

> Since truth and the ideal form of political and social organization can rarely, if at all, be identified with absolute certainty, it is difficult to prohibit expression without impeding the free exchange of potentially valuable information. Nevertheless, the argument from truth does not provide convincing support for the protection of hate propaganda. Taken to its extreme, this argument would require us to permit the communication of all expression, it being impossible to know with *absolute* certainty which factual statements are true, or which ideas obtain the greatest good. The problem with this extreme position, however, is that the greater the degree of certainty that a statement is erroneous or mendacious, the less its value in the quest for truth. Indeed, expression can be used to the detriment of our search for truth; the state should not be the sole arbiter of truth, but neither should we overplay the view that rationality will overcome all falsehoods in the unregulated marketplace of ideas. There is very little chance that statements intended to promote hatred against an identifiable group are true, or that their vision of society will lead to a better world. To portray such statements as crucial to truth and the betterment of the political and social milieu is therefore misguided.[44]

Thus, the Canadian Court sees the invocation of the marketplace of ideas as a potentially extreme position that rationality will overcome falsehood and thus justifies any harm caused by them. As addressed in Chapter Four, the advent of social media reinforces this doubt in such an optimistic faith in unregulated free expression.

Keegstra was far from a unanimous decision; the court split 4–3, with a strong dissenting opinion written by Beverley McLachlin (who would become Chief Justice in 2000), joined by Justices La Forest and

Sopinka. Justice McLachlin specifically argued that "the claims of gains to be achieved at the cost of the infringement of free speech represented by s. 319(2) are tenuous. Indeed, it is difficult to see how s. 319(2) fosters the goals of social harmony and individual dignity." While critics of Canada's hate speech legislation often raise questions about its efficacy, the *Keegstra* decision has held. Both *R. v. Butler* (1992) and *R. v. Krymowski* (2005) cited the *Keegstra* precedent to define hate speech and uphold legislation against it. *Saskatchewan (Human Rights Commission) v. Whatcott* (2013) also upheld *Keegstra* but added that "hatred" must be applied as an objective not subjective definition.[45]

The Criminal Code provisions concerning hate speech are not the only venue through which Canada restricts hate speech. Section 13 of the 1977 Canadian Human Rights Act (CHRA) declares:

> It [to be] a discriminatory practice for a person or a group of persons . . . to communicate telephonically . . . , repeatedly, any matter that is likely to expose a person or persons to hatred or contempt by reason of the fact that that person or those persons are identifiable on the basis of a prohibited ground of discrimination.[46]

The Supreme Court ruled in *Canada (Human Rights Commission) v. Taylor* (1990) that this section of the CHRA did not contravene the Charter right to freedom of expression — though once again Justice McLachlin dissented, along with two other justices.[47] Controversy persisted over such hate speech regulation being adjudicated by human rights commissions, including provincial bodies in BC, Alberta, Saskatchewan, and the Northwest Territories.[48] Section 13 of the CHRA was repealed in 2013, following the recommendations of a commissioned report written by Richard Moon in 2008. Justin Trudeau's Liberal government presented Bill C-36 in 2021, and re-introduced it as Bill C-63, the Online Harms Act, to address the gap left in terms of dealing with hate speech on the internet, as will be discussed in Chapter Four.

Summary

The main point of this chapter has been to explore the legal and constitutional principles of freedom of expression, explaining how they are distinct from the ideals of critical and inclusive discussion. This distinction can be broadly understood as that of the negative freedom focused on preventing governments from infringing on an individual or group's opportunities to express themselves, as different from the type of positive freedom that enables people not only to express themselves, but effectively be heard and have an impact on public discussion.

Another key theme has been to highlight the differences between the legal terrain of the US and that of Canada. Despite the absolute wording of the First Amendment, the courts have consistently drawn some line beyond which some speech cannot be allowed if it will likely cause harm to individuals or society at large. Similarly, however powerful the metaphor of the marketplace of ideas and the doctrine of counter-speech as the best response to false and harmful speech, ultimately there is always a line where such ideals give way to the need to regulate speech, in some cases, if that speech is deemed to be, or may incite, dangerous action. The Canadian legal system has approached the question differently, explicitly balancing free expression against other rights and values. By defining certain speech as harmful to specific marginalized groups in society, the Charter legitimizes government regulation. Canada's Supreme Court considers how best to prevent government legislation from creating a "chill" on Canadians' expressions of their ideas, but does not hold this as an absolute goal above all other values. While these complex issues are related to attempts to foster critical and inclusive discussion in order to achieve public debate and democracy, they are constrained by the constitutional principle of free expression so as to prevent government from overextending its power and jurisdiction.

In both the legal arena of the freedom of expression and the realm of ideals of public discussion, there is great emphasis from John Stuart Mill's thought, on through the twentieth-century court decisions and the pervasiveness of the "marketplace of ideas," on how ideas and perspectives make gains from conflicting with alternatives that assume an adversarial relationship. The exclusivity of free speech to this Western tradition, as well as its presumed antagonistic nature, has been challenged by Indigenous thinkers. For example, John Mohawk describes how Haudenosaunee and other Indigenous peoples in North America "carried with them a tradition of meeting and democracy, of free speech, of free thinking, of tolerance for each other's differences of religion, of all those things which got attached to the [American] Bill of Rights."[49] The Western tradition needs to reconsider how important this influence is as it could direct society in a new way forward, as I suggest in the Conclusion. Similarly, Indigenous scholars, such as Anishinaabe legal scholar John Borrows, explore how reintegrating Indigenous law and tradition into the Constitution of Canada reconfigures how dissent and critique can be integrated and better harmonized with traditional values of respect for the community and living a good life.[50]

Before further consideration of the obvious technological and social developments that have altered the terrain of free expression, I will address the specific context of academia as a place where confusion over what freedom of expression entails has become increasingly evident.

CHAPTER THREE

ACADEMIC FREEDOM IS NOT FREE SPEECH

IN THE FALL OF 2017, MOST MAJOR NEWSPAPERS, RADIO STATIONS, television news programs, dozens of pundits, and social media platforms were abuzz in Canada with the story of a teaching assistant at Wilfrid Laurier University in Waterloo, Ontario. Lindsay Shepherd was a graduate student enrolled in a one-year, interdisciplinary master's degree in Cultural Analysis and Social Theory. As a teacher's assistant (TA), she was assigned a first year Communications course, taught by Dr. Nathan Rambukkana. For the tutorial on essay writing, Shepherd decided to show a short video clip from the Ontario public television show, *The Agenda with Steve Paikin*.[1] In the video, controversial psychology professor and public commentator Jordan Peterson argued that his freedom of expression guaranteed by the Canadian Charter should allow him to use his choice of pronoun when referring to others, including his students at the University of Toronto. He was upset about the then-proposed federal Bill C-16 that would force him, so he argued, to use "made-up" words that he rejected on "ideological grounds." In fact, the bill — now law — amended the Canadian Human Rights Act and Criminal Code, adding "gender identity or expression" to the list of characteristics protected from discrimination and hate speech. It made no reference to pronouns (nor to any other grammar issues).[2] Shepherd decided that this video clip "would be very instructive for my students: it was fascinating how a grammar and language-related debate was a hot topic on a TV panel show," she explained.[3]

Some days after the class, Shepherd was called into a meeting with Professor Rambukkana. That meeting included the coordinator of her graduate program, Dr. H. Pimlott, and a representative from the Office of Gendered Violence and Sexual Assault Prevention, Adria Joel. Shepherd was told that how she handled showing the video had created "a toxic environment for some of the students."[4] A tense and emotional conversation ensued in which Rambukkana tried to explain why, in his judgement, the tutorial she led was inappropriate. He later issued a written apology for some of those comments and for not supporting and mentoring her sufficiently.[5] The meeting culminated in Shepherd being told to provide Rambukkana with her lesson plans prior to each class; she was also informed that he might sit in on some of her future tutorials.[6]

National Post columnist Christie Blatchford jumped on the story to decry that the "thought police strike again," after Shepherd contacted her with a secretly made recording of the meeting.[7] Many others leapt on the bandwagon to castigate Rambukkana, the meeting, and the remedy. They presented these events as indicative of a crisis of free speech at Canadian universities, where leftist ideology allegedly suppresses dissenting ideas and perspectives. From CBC's satirist Rick Mercer to editorialists in *Maclean's* and the *Globe and Mail*, most mainstream and progressive commentary lauded Shepherd as a champion of free expression, as did the far right, including white supremacist group Proud Boys and white nationalist Faith Goldy. It seemed that much of Canadian society interpreted the event as an outrage against free speech, sometimes even dragging in the Charter right to free expression. The basis of outrage — whether Shepherd's freedom to show the video, the students' freedom to watch it in class, or Peterson's free expression — was usually unclear. As is typical of free speech controversies, the nuances of free expression and academic freedom were blurred under the banner of "free speech." On the rare occasion that academic freedom was mentioned, it was usually conflated with free speech. Moreover, the media and public fury insisted that this incident epitomized the supposed infringement of free speech at universities in general. As will be demonstrated in this chapter, no TA nor professor has a Charter right to free expression while performing their duties as a university employee. This case illustrates how journalists, commentators, university administrators, and most of the Canadian public have no understanding that academic freedom and free speech are not synonymous. This significant and prolonged outrage and public discussion about what universities are supposed to be like and do shows how most Canadians think academic freedom is simply free expression at universities. Regardless of whether or not a TA should have been allowed to show a Jordan Peterson video, discussing it as an issue of free speech is counter-productive and misses the important issues at stake.

Many commentators emphasized that they disagreed with Peterson, but that his ideas should not be silenced in university classrooms, often invoking a paraphrase of one of the free speech slogans, "I disapprove of what you say, but will defend with my life your right to say it," wrongly attributed to Voltaire as discussed in Chapter One.[8] The coverage that ensued made it clear that the Canadian public, and the media leaders who inform it, have a frighteningly weak grasp of the important principles and distinctions between the freedom of expression and academic freedom, not to mention how universities can best fulfil their roles in society, most especially in the age of social media. There was no acknowledgement that Canadian Charter rights do not apply to university classrooms, unlike the case of the First Amendment in the US. The confusion between academic freedom and freedom of expression, as well as between the distinct situation in Canada versus the US, was further exacerbated when the premiers of Ontario and Alberta, Doug Ford and Jason Kenney, threatened to withhold funding from universities that do not comply with the recent provincial free speech policies. To make matters worse, the Quebec government passed Bill 32 in 2022, which defines "academic freedom" as a right that everyone has with no regard to their status as academics.[9] The confusion evident in the case of Lindsay Shepherd has thus been further entrenched in Canadian society.

Remarkably, only a few media accounts pointed out that the situation at Wilfrid Laurier University concerned academic freedom and not freedom of expression or speech.[10] Despite the clarity these contributions offered on the conceptual difference between the two, they had little impact on the public discussion. Most of the coverage used the terms interchangeably, some invoking a standard trope, especially common in the US, that academic freedom is just free speech on campus.[11] This chapter will show how these points of confusion are partially caused and further entrenched by the inappropriate adoption in Canada of American perspectives, namely, the "Chicago Principles"[12] and Sigal Ben-Porath's concept of "inclusive freedom."[13] However commendable the ideals of critical and inclusive discussion may be, confusing and conflating them with the constitutional protections of the freedom of expression or academic freedom creates conditions for the weaponization of free speech in institutions dedicated to the pursuit of truth and knowledge. These latter goals, as I explored in the Introduction, involve positive freedoms that successfully enable and foster environments of critical, inclusive, and diverse communication, whereas the legal conceptions of free speech, as analyzed in Chapter Two, are negative freedoms, restricting government and authority from being able to restrict individuals from speaking.

What Is Academic Freedom?

Academic freedom is the freedom to pursue teaching and research activities in accordance with professional, disciplinary, and scholarly standards and obligations. Its purpose is the furthering of knowledge and understanding for the public good, not the individual gain of the professor. As historian Joan Wallach Scott argues in the American context, "Academic freedom is highly specific to institutions of scholarly research and teaching; it is not, like liberty or equality, a universal human right. It is not a general right to free speech, although the two are often confused."[14] Canadian philosopher Shannon Dea goes further, illustrating the recent trend whereby "campus free speech legislation wrongly treats free speech rather than academic freedom as the freedom that is proper to post-secondary institutions."[15] Stanley Fish, a literary theorist and prominent American intellectual, explains that competence, accuracy, and relevancy are the core academic values that need to guide academic freedom.[16]

These principles of academic freedom are clearly in conflict with Lindsay Shepherd's view that "in a university all perspectives are valid," especially when referring specifically to a classroom, as distinct from the general spaces on campus.[17] For any university to abandon the ideals of competence, accuracy, and relevancy (inside or outside the classroom) is a "colossal failure," notes Fish. As Michael Bérubé and Jennifer Ruth insist:

> Some ideas don't deserve a hearing, and one of the primary roles of the university is to distinguish between those that do — and should continue to be explored and built upon — and those that should not be seriously entertained by any legitimate institution

of higher education. Conflating free speech with academic freedom obscures this basic truth.[18]

This does not mean there is agreement about what constitutes competence, accuracy, and relevancy. It is often challenging, time-consuming work to determine those ideas that are worth pursuing and those that are not, but it is what academics do, using the methods appropriate to their disciplines and subjecting their work to collegial scrutiny and peer review.

In addition to freedom in the realms of teaching and research, academic freedom normally includes "freedom of intramural expression" — the right to criticize the workings of the university itself — and "freedom of extramural expression" — the right to engage in public expression without negative repercussions on one's position as professor. This capacity for extramural expression is the one aspect of academic freedom that may be unrelated to a professor's professional expertise or experience. These last two freedoms have significant overlap with (but are still distinguishable from) free speech, though neither applies to the Shepherd situation. The idea of intramural and extramural academic freedom does not just reproduce the Charter right to freedom of expression that all Canadians enjoy. Rather, the point of intramural speech is that collegial governance is an aspect of what it is to be a professor. Unlike other workplaces that can legally demand loyalty from their employees and insist that they represent their company well, university faculty have a distinct and far more independent relationship from their employer, the university. This is part of the university's role as an institution that produces new knowledge and critical-thinking students. Extramural academic freedom is also different from freedom of expression because it restricts the university — not the government — from taking punitive actions against an employee for speech outside the workplace. Academic freedom is a freedom necessary for academics to perform their duties of producing knowledge and educating students.[19] Without academic freedom, the knowledge and education made available by universities for society would be greatly diminished.

To insist that everyone has academic freedom undermines its specific meaning as the freedom to pursue teaching and research, and ignores its function in the production of knowledge, making the qualifier "academic" superfluous. This is, however, exactly what the right-wing

Coalition Avenir Québec (CAQ) government did with Bill 32. In response to a controversy outside of Quebec, at the University of Ottawa, when a lecturer was suspended for using the "N-word" in a class, the CAQ government passed this legislation, defining academic freedom as "the right of every person to engage freely and without doctrinal, ideological or moral constraint, such as institutional censorship, in an activity through which the person contributes to carrying out the mission of an educational institution."[20] Below, I will show how the Quebec definition also runs counter to the academic freedom clauses that result from collective bargaining between faculty associations and university administrations. Indeed, the only other Canadian province that has legislation that mentions academic freedom, to my knowledge, is Manitoba. Manitoba's Advanced Education Act stipulates the exact opposite of Quebec's law. It connects academic freedom to the autonomy of universities and exempts it from government definition and regulation.[21] The ramifications of Quebec's law have yet to be seen, but its broad definition of academic freedom opens the possibility that a student uses it to object to receiving a low grade, arguing that the grade infringes on their academic freedom because grading is based on "doctrinal" constraint that the law prohibits. Of course, the Latin root for "doctrinal" is *doctrina*, the same root for "doctor" and "doctorate," and it means "to teach." The irony is that the Quebec government has passed a law that grants students the freedom from being taught by their professors at university.

American legal scholars Matthew Finkin and Robert Post provide a sharp example to drive home the distinction between academic freedom and constitutional free speech: for a physics professor to confuse astronomy and astrology must certainly hold consequences and prevent her from being permitted to teach astronomy at a university. Yet, for the US government to censor the *New York Times* for the same mistake would be an authoritarian breach of the First Amendment.[22] Of course, customers of the *New York Times* may complain or cancel their subscriptions over such ignorance, but this has nothing to do with constitutional rights to freedom of speech. To confuse the legal principle of freedom of expression that should not involve veracity, competency, or knowledge production with academic freedom narrows the expression protected by our Charter and at the same time increases the grounds on which the courts or legislators could justify limits on expression. As Canadian political scientist Dax D'Orazio explains, "while the principle of freedom of speech emphasizes content neutrality (on the part of the state, institution, etc.), the university is typically *not* neutral regarding the content of speech."[23]

Simultaneously, the conflation debases the specialized knowledge upon which the university is founded and undermines the reason why students pay tuition for higher education. University education is not just about imparting information. Joan Wallach Scott's position complements Canadian scholar Ian Angus's insistence that the "idea of the university can be defined as loving the questions" and that the ability to "ask and confront genuine questions" is paramount.[24] However, it takes experience and substantial investigation of the subject matter to develop an appreciation for what questions are profound, what questions have been asked before, which questions have been answered or abandoned, and which questions are irrelevant to the material. These processes are also central to research production as seen in peer review and tenure decisions.

Academic freedom is a complex concept with various components that developed historically and are far from uncontested. For example, Eve Haque has raised important questions about why the Canadian Association of University Teachers (CAUT) has defended cases as if "academic freedom is a superordinate freedom which must be defended from any form of attack no matter why and no matter what actual 'academic' content is being defended in the name of academic freedom."[25] In this sense, academic freedom has definite limitations as a principle based in the status quo of academic procedures. It is based on standards that have been accepted in the past and is slow to change to accept new perspectives.

It is beyond the scope of this book to provide a thorough analysis of the concept of academic freedom and I focus on how academic freedom is distinct from free expression.[26] My point is that the Charter right to freedom of expression does not judge the quality of the expression but rather its effect, whether it harms others or society at large. Academic freedom is premised not only on the merits of the person granted this freedom — an academic at a certain stage of their career and development of expertise — but whether or not the expression fits within their professional and scholarly obligations. All of this is related to judgements about the quality of the expression. For example, the Charter gives me the freedom to lie (provided that it does not have the effect of slander or libel), but as an academic, I do not have this freedom: I cannot present information to my students or colleagues that I know to be false. As an individual, I should be able to tell people what my gut feelings are, or a wacky hunch I have. But it is unprofessional of me to give a lecture to my students about some idiosyncratic notion that I have not investigated the scholarly merits of or tested. Academic freedom is rooted in accepted methods for continually testing important values and truths.

Joan Wallach Scott describes this ambiguous aspect of academic freedom: "The critic of orthodoxy thus, ironically, must find legitimation in the very discipline whose orthodoxy he or she challenges."[27] There is a reason fields of study are called "disciplines," and the etymology is pertinent. To be a member of an academic discipline, one must act with discipline according to its accepted rules. One may use those rules to challenge, improve, and expand them, but academic freedom is not the negative freedom to say whatever you want, ignoring the criteria on which granting academic freedom is based. The expertise upon which this very particular type of freedom is allotted is carefully monitored and assessed by members of the profession. For new research and knowledge to be accepted as part of the discipline of mathematics, for example, evidence will be required that is different than that required in literature or sociology. Formal proof is necessary for mathematics, whereas detailed textual analysis is necessary in literature and a methodologically sound investigation for sociology.

Scott is a historian who devoted significant portions of her career to arguing that "Women's history was not just another topic, a minor theme in the exalted stories of nations and their [mostly male] leaders; it was for many of us an inquiry into the founding assumptions of so-called mainstream history (African American history, postcolonial history, and queer history offered similar interrogations)."[28] She had to struggle, with the help of many other historians, to change those founding, disciplinary assumptions of what and whose stories constituted history. It took time and much collective effort, but she did it by following the rules of history as an academic discipline, presenting evidence, and gaining influence and support among other scholars in the field. There may be historians who still view women's history as a minor subfield and bemoan why there are so many journals, prize-winning books, and prestigious lectures devoted to gender history, but history as an academic discipline has been changed. Developments in academic disciplines and what may be considered their core principles proceed with scholarly rigour, including processes such as peer review.

Freedom of Expression and the Workplace

As discussed in Chapter One, the idea of free speech articulated by Kant concerned only the "*public* use of reason," and excluded the speech of people in private life, by which he meant official roles and occupations. Kant's examples focus on religious ministers, noting that they should have free speech as individuals but not as representatives of their church, such as when they are preaching. At the time Kant was writing in Prussia, most educational institutions were operated by religious authorities, and thus his distinction would apply also to many teachers. His position is that restricting expression in these private realms will not adversely affect society's ability to move toward "enlightenment." This is implicitly the case for every thinker discussed in Chapter One. Stanley Fish puts it bluntly: "Do you and I have free speech in the workplace? No. Can an employer discipline or dismiss us because he doesn't like what we say or what our T-shirt says? Absolutely."[29] This is as true in the Canadian context as it is for Fish's discussion of the First Amendment.

If you are a worker at Starbucks or Toronto-Dominion Bank and while at work you tell your customers that Tim Horton's coffee is better or that the Bank of Montreal is a more reliable bank, you will not have much luck arguing that you cannot be disciplined because you have "freedom of expression" guaranteed by the Charter. Don Cherry was fired by SportsNet from *Hockey Night in Canada*'s "Coach's Corner" for expressing what were understood to be racist ideas.[30] Wendy Mesley left the CBC after her suspension for having used the N-word in more than one staff meeting.[31] Neither proposed taking their employer to court on a Charter violation of free expression. Freedom of expression does not extend to the workplace in the US, Canada, or anywhere else in the world. One of the key skills that many people in such positions are being hired for is their ability to communicate, including the content of that communication. It would be draconian and nonsensical for the government to prevent employers from judging their employees for the quality and content of their communications, including firing, hiring, or promoting them.

Of course, one might argue that these corporate decisions were wrong or misguided — whether in Cherry's or Mesley's case — and criticize them for not upholding the ideals of critical and inclusive discussion. This is an important argument that should not be obscured by the conflation of it with constitutional free expression protections. I might use those same ideals to defend the SportsNet and CBC's decisions, arguing that those expressions of racism stifled the participation of racialized individuals in hockey or CBC editorial discussions. This would be an actual debate. However, to think the argument in defence of Cherry or Mesley would be strengthened by invoking the Charter is simply a misunderstanding. Any legal questions would depend on the grounds of wrongful dismissal, not the Charter right to free expression. To extend free speech — whether as a legal principle or an ideal — to *all* workplaces would be a truly radical position. It would also be inconsistent with not only supposed free speech advocates, like Jordan Peterson and Lindsay Shepherd, but also with media figures like Rick Mercer or the editorial board of *The National Post*. None of them has, to my knowledge, argued that employers are treading on the free expression rights of their employees by adjudicating their expressions at work.

Obviously, a teaching assistant, like Lindsay Shepherd, is different in important ways from an employee at a café or a bank. Universities are different from such businesses. But the key to that difference is found precisely in academic freedom, not free expression.[32] The core purpose of a university is to contribute to the common good of society by producing and disseminating knowledge and critical thinking. This is done primarily by educating students and conducting research. Academic freedom is essential to these goals. As Joan Wallach Scott summarizes, academic freedom entails the "autonomy of the university from state intervention; freedom of individual faculty to pursue research and to teach in their areas of expertise as well as the teacher's right — that of any citizen — to express political views outside the classroom; an accused faculty member's right to due process and to the judgement of his or her peers."[33]

As Scott notes, there is an overlap between academic freedom and freedom of speech. An academic may use their free expression to criticize their own universities (intramural academic freedom) and make other political arguments in public (extramural academic freedom). However, where the freedom of expression protects an academic as a citizen from the government censoring their speech, academic freedom protects them from administrative interference in their production of knowledge and public expression. Bérubé and Ruth explain in the American context: "The idea is that no professor gives up their First Amendment rights as a citizen when they take an academic position."[34]

This overlap should not lead to the general conflation of the two different concepts. As Shannon Dea points out, "Deans (and other senior administrators) don't have full academic freedom because it is important that they serve their institution first and foremost. Professors have academic freedom because — in principle at least — they should serve truth, not any particular organization."[35] Unlike my dean, who may have to put the interests of the University of Winnipeg above her own search for knowledge, the faculty are obliged to put the search for knowledge first. It is not incidental that deans and higher university administrators are not covered by the collective agreements that secure academic freedom.

The Charter Right to Free Expression and the Academy

In addition to academic freedom being a different principle from those of free expression, in Canada, there is an important legal distinction between them. The Supreme Court of Canada decided in 1990 that the Charter does not generally apply to universities, as noted in Chapter Two, when it ruled in *McKinney v. University of Guelph* that universities, while substantially funded by government, are not part of it.[36]

James Turk explains that the Alberta courts have decided that the Charter applies to some university activities in specific cases, but these do not involve classroom teaching.[37] *R v. Whatcott* (2012) and *Wilson v. University of Calgary* (2014) both address protests on university campuses and how the universities dealt with them. In these cases, the Alberta court ruled that the Charter applies to universities as custodians of public spaces, or at least quasi-public spaces. *Wilson v. University of Calgary* notes that the university is a place of scholarly inquiry and that "the nature and purpose of a university as a forum for the expression of differing views" needed to be considered. However, the Court's application of the Charter was to individuals expressing their political ideas in a public area of the university campus, not to activities of students and professors as such. Neither case pertained to course-related activity.[38]

Another case, *Pridgen v. University of Calgary* (2010), involved students who had been disciplined under the university's Non-academic Misconduct Policy for posting negative comments about their professor on a Facebook page. The Alberta court likened the administration's non-academic misconduct policy to delegated governmental authority and specific governmental purposes and ruled that the university had violated the students' Charter right to freedom of expression.[39] Had this case involved the Academic Misconduct Policy, the outcome may have been different. This is a complicated case, but part of the determination was that the students' expression occurred on Facebook, not at the university itself. The Supreme Court, the ultimate arbiter of the Charter, has yet to make any decision that affirms or rejects the Alberta rulings.

In 2017, at Dalhousie University, the administration's attempt to discipline Masuma Khan provides more evidence of confusion concerning the distinction between academic freedom and freedom of expression among university administrators. This event happened the same year as the Lindsay Shepherd controversy, seven years after the *Pridgen* case. Responding to backlash against the student union's decision not to participate in the Canada 150 events, Khan, vice-president of the student union, posted on Facebook: "White fragility can kiss my ass. Your white tears aren't sacred, this land is." The university administration tried to discipline her, suggesting that she receive counselling and write a reflective essay. She refused. Two years later, Dalhousie University administration apologized over Twitter.[40] That the *Pridgen* case involved white students criticizing their untenured, non-white professor, and that Khan, a Muslim woman of colour, was responding to criticisms received regarding the student union's critique of colonialism, is not insignificant.[41] These two cases would seem to support Moskowitz's assessment in the American context that discussions of free speech on campus are "really about much more than free speech, but about everything that free speech can mask: namely, our unsettled history of racism."[42] If we want to better protect and defend principles of free speech on campus, such hypocrisy needs to be kept at the forefront of our analysis. These are issues not of academic freedom but free expression of students outside the classroom.

Most recently, in *UAlberta Pro-Life v. Governors of the University of Alberta* (2020), the Alberta court again furthered the extent to which student protestors have Charter-protected expression on campus. While the court did not decide fully in favour of UAlberta Pro-Life, it did find that the university's requirement that the group pay for prohibitively expensive security costs to hold their protests on campus infringed on their freedom of expression.[43] But this ruling again did not extend Charter protections into classrooms or to course-related activity. In BC and Ontario, the courts have not shown such willingness to apply the

Charter to universities, and no case has reached the Supreme Court of Canada to set a precedent.[44]

It may be the case, as James Turk has argued, that these recent provincial cases could herald a future trend to apply the Charter to universities, but the decisions are careful to delineate their application of the Charter to non-academic expression *outside* the classroom.[45] In these cases, the courts were considering individuals protesting abortion in a public space on campus and individuals expressing their views about a professor on Facebook, not any student expression made in a classroom or made by professors or teaching assistants performing their duties. Nonetheless, these cases still support my specific point that the main pedagogical work of the university is not, and cannot reasonably be, subject to the legal protection of the Charter right to freedom of expression.

Academic Freedom and the First Amendment

As Shannon Dea points out, "It is important to remember that both the constitutional supports for freedom of expression (as we call it in Canada) and the institutional culture supporting academic freedom are very different in Canada and the US for a number of reasons."[46] Unlike in Canada, the US Supreme Court has ruled that the First Amendment applies to public (but not private) universities as an extension of the government and has legally connected First Amendment freedom of speech protections to academic freedom.[47] Adding to this difference is that the vast majority of universities in Canada are public, whereas in the US a much higher portion of universities are private. Moreover, unlike in the US, most Canadian universities are unionized, and the teeth of academic freedom today can be found in faculty collective agreements. These differences are critical to how academic freedom works in both countries.[48]

The connection between the freedom of speech and academic freedom in the US goes at least as far back as *State of Tennessee v. John Scopes* (1925), famously described by H.L. Mencken as the "Scopes Monkey Trial." This case concerned a law that prohibited anyone in a publicly funded institution from teaching material inconsistent with the Biblical account of the origins of humanity. The American Civil Liberties Union (ACLU) took on the case to defend the substitute biology teacher, John Thomas Scopes, for teaching evolutionary theory. The ACLU argued that the law infringed on his First Amendment rights but described the specific freedom of speech of a teacher as academic freedom.⁴⁹ This connection between academic freedom and the First Amendment was strengthened in the 1950s context of McCarthyism and the Red Scare when teachers and professors faced attempts to root out "subversive teaching" connected to communism.⁵⁰ The first explicit Supreme Court discussion as to why academic freedom is included in the First Amendment came in Justice William Douglas's dissenting opinion in *Adler v. Board of Education* (1952), with Justice Hugo Black concurring. Like the *Scopes* case, this case involved a public school teacher (in the state of New York), and not a university professor. Justice Douglas reasoned that no one needed the First Amendment protections of free speech more than teachers, arguing that public schools are increasingly the "cradle of democracy" and laws infringing on teachers' ability to express themselves freely would turn the school system into a "spying project."⁵¹

This initial foray into connecting university professors' academic freedom with the free speech protections of the First Amendment was cemented in *Sweezy v. New Hampshire* (1957). That majority decision overturned the conviction of University of New Hampshire professor Paul Sweezy for "subversive behavior" in refusing to answer the Attorney General's questions about the Marxist content of his university lectures. Justice Felix Frankfurter wrote a concurring opinion, joined by Justice Harlan, that went further in describing the specific nature of freedom for university professors, although the decision did not actually use the term "academic freedom." Moreover, Frankfurter relies mostly on the Fourteenth Amendment's right to due process, not First Amendment freedom of speech.⁵² Nevertheless, this case is commonly understood as central to the US court's interpretation and defence of academic freedom.⁵³ Many other cases followed that presented academic freedom in public universities as a sort of special application of the First Amendment freedom of speech. This legal terrain has created different frameworks for understanding the distinction between academic freedom and free speech in the US and in Canada, and confusion reigns when it is ignored or misunderstood.

Where Academic Freedom Finds Its Teeth

As examined with freedom of expression, we can distinguish between the legal right that has the force of the law from more subjective and harder-to-enforce ideals of free speech. Similarly, while academic freedom is also often used in a vague sense of ideals we aspire to, its formal application also has substantive force backed up by the law. That legal provision is specifically located in collective agreements between faculty and universities across Canada. As Jeffrey Sachs argues, by "locating academic freedom within administrative law, Canadian faculty generally enjoy greater free speech protection than non-unionized faculty elsewhere, particularly in the United States."[54]

Neither "academic freedom" nor "freedom of expression" are mentioned in the Wilfrid Laurier University (WLU) mission statement,[55] whereas they are invoked at many other universities, including my own place of employment, the University of Winnipeg.[56] The Wilfrid Laurier University Act (1973) — provincial legislation that established the university — states, "The objects of the University are the pursuit of learning through scholarship, teaching and research within a spirit of free enquiry and expression," with no further explanation or stipulations.[57] These are not unimportant statements; they are aspirational, and when it comes to their substantive enforcement, they are not very effective.[58]

Where the principle of academic freedom has real enforcement potential and legal standing is in collective agreements between the faculty associations or unions and the university administration. At WLU, like most unionized Canadian universities, the collective agreement for full-time professors and professional librarians has specific clauses devoted to academic freedom. At WLU, academic freedom is limited in that "Members have a duty to exercise that [academic] freedom in a manner consistent with the academic obligations of teachers and scholars, and librarians."[59] This language is common in most Canadian universities' collective agreements. It is how, as a professor of political science, I have significant freedom to decide how I teach and conduct my research, but it does not give me carte blanche — I cannot teach biology or engage in non-academic activities in my classroom.

If I decided to devote my "Introduction to Political Science" course entirely to my fascination with beer brewing techniques in ancient Egypt, for example, my university could legitimately discipline me for not fulfilling my obligations as a professor assigned to teach an introductory course in political science. Such discipline would not be an infringement on my academic freedom; it would be an insistence that I do the job I was hired to perform. If I had a blanket negative freedom akin to a Charter right, I could teach anything I wish as long as my students were not harmed by what I said in class. For universities to function, professors must abide by the decisions of their department chairs and deans concerning their teaching assignments and the senate-approved descriptions of the courses they teach. They must follow the rules of collegial governance set out by their departments.

In case of a dispute, most universities would begin the resolution process in the political science department, with my colleagues who also have expert knowledge about (and academic freedom to determine) what constitutes "political science." These judgements take place on more substantive and qualitative grounds than any legal principle of free expression that needs to be adjudicated according to whether it harms others. In this case, the academic community would need to decide whether beer brewing in ancient Egypt is a topic central to the discipline of political science, whether I am adequately serving my students' needs in understanding the topic of the course, and whether the course adequately prepares students for subsequent courses they may choose or be required to take.[60] Were I to discuss policies about beer brewing and interprovincial laws on selling beer in Canada, this might or might not be an acceptable topic, even in an introductory course, and depending on how much of the course I devoted to it. However, if I were told I could not discuss topics involving alcohol consumption because of a teetotalling university administrator or committee, I would take the issue to my faculty association on the grounds of a violation of my academic freedom. Either way, a judgement would have to be made as to the suitability of such material for the course. This is why universities have departmental committees that review course outlines yearly, departmental curriculum committees that work to determine what is appropriate to teach for the discipline, as well as senate committees that approve new courses after a rationale is given as to why they should be offered. This oversight is part and parcel of collegial governance, whereby the faculty as a collective body makes decisions concerning academic matters. That many, if not most, professors in Canada have not been submitted to such disciplining does not change the fact that it is the structure in which academic freedom takes place and has teeth. Indeed, as indicated at the opening of this chapter, many university administrators and professors are not well-informed about the differences between free speech and academic freedom nor how they are adjudicated, as was amply demonstrated in the public debates around the Lindsay Shepherd situation.

Ideally, academic freedom supports professors to create environments of critical and inclusive discussion in their classrooms and at other university events, but it cannot be conflated with that ideal of free speech. It is not constructive to see academic freedom as an individual, negative right. Shannon Dea has argued that we should understand academic freedom as a "group-differentiated right" — meaning that while individual professors enjoy this right, "they do so in virtue of their membership in a group," and the purpose is not individual self-realization, self-fulfillment, or advantage, but a social good.[61] Moreover, academic freedom comes with substantial responsibility and is fundamental to the function of academia and the pursuit of knowledge and education.

It is true, however, as Canadian legal scholar Michael Lynk has demonstrated, that the adjudication of academic freedom through collective agreements ultimately boils down to labour law and arbitration. Lynk argues that these processes often do not acknowledge the specific nature of academic freedom but see it through general employee-employer frameworks.[62] I agree, but the solution to this is not to further diminish the specificity of academic freedom by conflating it with free expression but rather to insist on its unique nature in labour law and arbitration.

Another key issue here, especially considering the Shepherd case, is that these collective agreements and their provisions for academic freedom apply only to professors and librarians and do not extend to teaching assistants or other university staff. At many universities across Canada, TAs and markers are unionized, but not at WLU. While these collective agreements often do not provide TAs with the same level of academic freedom as faculty collective agreements, those who truly believed that Shepherd was unfairly restrained from teaching how she wished should have advocated unionizing TAs as a struggle for academic freedom. However, none of the outrage about the Shepherd case acknowledged that academic freedom at Canadian universities is a bargaining issue, and not one recommended that TAs should be unionized at WLU.

There are pertinent reasons why academic freedom is awarded to professors based on qualifications. Obviously, graduate students who have been chosen for teaching assistantships have many qualifications. But the undergraduate students in their courses, often only a few years behind them in education, may rightfully question if important pedagogical decisions about course content and methods should be the responsibility of professors (with many more years of experience and education, not to mention higher pay) and not relegated to TAs who have often just finished their undergraduate degrees. In this case, Shepherd described how she decided to include the video clip of Peterson by looking around on YouTube for videos that would make the classes on grammar livelier and more relevant.[63] While I have no objections to such methods, they are hardly the hallmark of quality university pedagogy. Indeed, to the extent that they are *celebrated* as examples of free speech at the core of the university's mission, they undermine the actual purpose of universities in providing more rigorous and grounded knowledge than one can find on YouTube.

Had the national controversy sparked by Shepherd's showing of the Peterson video included a debate about the extent to which TAs should have academic freedom, I would have welcomed it. Indeed, the CAUT's 2018 policy statement on academic freedom notes that it should apply to "all academic staff."[64] It nowhere mentions students but presumably includes TAs, markers/graders, and other such academic staff positions. Dea suggests that both TAs and students should have some type of academic freedom, but she notes that it would not make sense for them to have the same level of academic freedom as professors.[65] The idea that students have some sort of academic freedom is implied in many Canadian universities' mission statements. For example, the University of Winnipeg's mission statement includes two vague references to academic freedom being a core value and essential part of the tradition of the university.[66] These are important issues that I think deserve more attention and consideration, but they have been lost in the public misunderstandings and outrage over some poorly formulated commitment to free speech.

Following the public and media outcry about Shepherd's censure, WLU President Deborah MacLatchy issued an apology. As the regional newspaper reported, "MacLatchy confirmed Shepherd did nothing wrong in showing the clip from TVO, and added there's no reason to believe she didn't handle the class discussion appropriately."[67] Thus a university president made pronouncements about what was and what was not appropriate in a professor's course. MacLatchy, trained as a zoologist, decided the suitable pedagogy and content for a course in communications, overriding the professional judgement of a professor trained in that field and the entire department. WLU's apology is a disconcerting example of administrative overreach into a professor's academic freedom over content and methods taught in the classroom. It pre-empted the faculty's ability to determine in consultation with their colleagues what is appropriate course content. MacLatchy's concern — perhaps appropriate — with protecting the interests and reputation of WLU amid the public backlash ironically led to what I see as a serious degradation of academic freedom in the name of freedom of expression. It is disappointing that the WLU Faculty Association was not more active in countering what I saw as an infringement on Professor Rambukkana's academic freedom.

Joan Wallach Scott argues that "by collapsing the distinction between free speech and academic freedom, they [those on the right like David Horowitz] deny the authority of knowledge and of the teacher who purveys it."[68] Blatchford expressed surprise and outrage that in the initial meeting with Shepherd, "Pimlott [the chair of Shepherd's graduate program] seemed obsessed with scholarly qualifications."[69] Of course, this "obsession" — *scholarly qualifications* — is at the core of the university and is the heart of academic freedom that enables knowledge production and dissemination.

Conflating Free Speech and Better Speech

Among her several unsuccessful attempts to quell the storm raised by the Shepherd controversy, WLU President MacLatchy published an op-ed in the *Globe and Mail*, in which she wrote: "Universities have a greater responsibility than merely protecting free speech. We must also promote better speech in an increasingly polarized and complex world."[70] She discussed how universities must "set the bar for how people with very diverse perspectives can engage in difficult discussions;" and concluded that: "Students must learn how to examine ideas, identify faulty logic and counter opposing opinions with better, evidence-based arguments. This embodies the higher standard for expression that is truly better speech." Of course, I agree with her lofty description of the purpose of universities. It would be hard not to, but I contend that these are the very goals academic freedom was designed to protect, above and beyond the general fray of free speech and constitutional protections of expression.

To move, as MacLatchy does, from "protecting free speech" — which sounds like constitutional language — to facilitating "better speech" by teaching students to identify "faulty logic," develop "evidence-based arguments," and thereby communicate from a "higher standard," contributes to this conflation of the Charter right to freedom of expression with academic freedom. When we set a bar, by definition we curtail the expression of those who fail to clear that bar. The pole vaulter does not move on to the next round if they do not get over the bar. As discussed in Chapter Two, the Charter protection of free expression is adjudicated on whether it harms others. To confuse such clarity by adding "better speech" to the principle of "free speech" opens the door at least to mild suppression of speech that is not deemed "better." As I have been arguing, professors and academics need to encourage "better speech" all the time in our activities of grading assignments, responding to students' comments and questions in class, leading discussions, and so on. In effect, much of what university teaching is about is encouraging quality expression — better speech. This is why the Charter right to free expression has no place in the classroom (except as a very important document to be studied thoroughly enough to realize it is not like academic freedom). It could potentially encroach on students as public individuals with rights to free expression outside the classroom if the type of reasonableness described in Section 1 of the Charter is conflated with the reasonableness that professors use to promote "better speech." To meet their professional obligations, professors need to explain why, for example, a student's question is irrelevant, in a reasonable manner. But this is very different from the reasonable manner in which the Supreme Court judges whether hate speech can be prohibited by legislation despite it contravening Section 2(b) of the Charter.

Both MacLatchy's op-ed and the "Statement on Freedom of Expression" passed by the WLU Senate and approved by it in the wake of the Shepherd case refer to Sigal Ben-Porath's concept of "inclusive freedom" in an attempt to describe academic freedom as freedom of expression with the addition of inclusivity, respect for others, and critical evaluation.[71] Ben-Porath is a professor at University of Pennsylvania's Graduate School of Education whose 2017 book, *Free Speech on Campus*, develops this concept of "inclusive freedom" solely in the context of the US (Canada is not mentioned in the book). Her analysis of free speech and framework of "inclusive freedom" are intricately connected to the US First Amendment. She makes the important distinction between public universities, where the First Amendment applies, and private ones, where it does not but is often adopted on principle. As discussed above and in Chapter Two, the context in Canada is very different, raising serious questions about whether Ben-Porath's "inclusive freedom" can be transported unchanged into the Canadian context. This is, however, just what the WLU Statement does and, as we shall see below, it is also the case with the Chicago Principles recently invoked by the provincial governments of Ontario and Alberta.

Ben-Porath coined and developed the concept of "inclusive freedom" to address some of the problems that I have raised in terms of the limitations of the legal principle of freedom of speech as a narrowly defined negative right. However, where I emphasize the importance of the distinction between academic freedom and free expression, Ben-Porath attempts an additive approach, layering ideals of critical and inclusive discussion onto these legal protections against government censorship. She writes:

> An inclusive freedom framework for speech on campus takes seriously the importance of a free and open exchange as a necessary condition for the pursuit of knowledge and as a contributing condition to the development of civic and democratic capacities. It lends similar weight to the related demand that all members of the campus community be able to participate in this free and open exchange if it is to accomplish the goals of free inquiry, open-minded research, and equal access to learning and to civic development.[72]

With the metaphor of weight, Ben-Porath acknowledges there is a balancing act, and thus tension, between inclusiveness — including the participation of people whose identities have experienced and continue to experience oppression and discrimination — and the permission for anyone to say anything they wish regardless of whether they contribute to the continuation of another's oppression and discrimination. She describes this goal (of what I regard as "squaring the circle") in many eloquent ways, but they all consistently confuse or try to combine two distinct principles: "Inclusive freedom demands that speech on campus be protected as broadly as possible while aiming to ensure that all members of the campus community are recognized — and know that they are recognized — as members in good standing."[73] In other words, unlike the First Amendment that would strike down as unconstitutional any law against using the "N-word," or other utterances that attack or undermine others' identities, as long as the speech is not, as stated in *Brandenburg v. Ohio*, "directed to inciting or producing imminent lawless action and is likely to incite or produce such action,"[74] "inclusive freedom" has to balance the need to allow expression but limit verbal abuse or derogatory language that might negatively impact the inclusiveness of the discussion. The debate here is about what constitutes "as broadly as possible," a point on which free speech absolutists will have a much different assessment than others who hold free speech in balance with other values, such as security and equality. Disagreements will also inevitably arise over what constitutes being a member "in good standing" and how it is ensured.[75]

In terms of trying to balance these distinct principles, Ben-Porath's work has merit, especially her detailed discussion of many specific cases, including those she was involved in as the chair of her university's Committee on Open Expression. While slightly more sophisticated, Ben-Porath's framework of "inclusive freedom" serves to re-employ the linear metaphors discussed in the Introduction. And though it gives more contours to the question of where to draw the line between one person's free expression and the respect and inclusivity required for critical and inclusive discussion, it still leads to a simplistic framework. By focusing on free speech and subsuming academic freedom into it, Ben-Porath's analysis minimizes the importance and distinct nature of academic freedom.

In my Conclusion, I suggest that a better way to achieve Ben-Porath's goals of "inclusive freedom" is to turn to Indigenous approaches, such as that of Indigenous studies professor David Newhouse (Onondaga from the Six Nations of the Grand River), who focuses on "extending the rafters" and insists that including those previously excluded is fundamental to academic freedom rather than being considered only after the requirements of a negative freedom of free expression have been met.[76]

The Chicago Principles in Canada

President MacLatchy and Wilfrid Laurier University are not alone in looking to the US for resources (and perhaps, prestige?) to deal with the supposed free speech crisis at Canadian universities.[77] The premiers of Ontario and Alberta, Doug Ford and Jason Kenney, respectively, both insisted that universities in their jurisdictions adopt free speech policies based on the Chicago Principles.[78] These Principles are contained in a three-page statement issued in 2014 by the University of Chicago Committee on Freedom of Expression. As I will detail below, it extols the virtues of unrestrained free expression, arguing free expression should take precedence over considerations of civility and mutual respect.

The committee was appointed by the university's president Robert Zimmer and the provost Eric Isaacs, but was never approved by the university senate or any faculty body.[79] In that sense, while written by faculty, it was a project of the university administration which should be a red flag for those who understand academic freedom to include faculty autonomy and intramural academic freedom. Many American universities have adopted the Chicago Principles, but they are not without critics in the US, including Sigal Ben-Porath. On 11 December 2018, *Inside Higher Ed* published an article by Ben-Porath, entitled "Against Endorsing the Chicago Principles," and it was accompanied by a rebuttal and several other responses. Ben-Porath argued that while the Principles "represent an admirable effort to restate and reinforce colleges and universities' long-standing commitment to free speech," the problem is "the false assurance they offer the colleges and universities who endorse them." She continued: "They rely on a legalistic and formal framework that purports to offer a response to a set of problems that has little use for such blunt tools."[80] In other words, they rely solely on the legal premises of freedom of speech and fail to grapple with the tensions that her concept of "inclusive freedom" articulates. This may be a rather generous reading of the Chicago Principles, but her core criticism is solid. Shama Rangwala develops a more substantive assessment, concluding that "the Chicago Principles are symptoms of a looming crisis of academic freedom: they threaten to defang the university as an institution of critique."[81]

The president and provost state that they created this committee "in light of recent events nationwide that have tested institutional commitments to free speech and open discourse." The Chicago Statement, as some call it, nowhere mentions "academic freedom" and seems to be primarily focused on the question of invited speakers and public talks given at universities. It does not distinguish between events organized by the university itself, whether by departments or faculties, or events that are held on campus but organized by students or non-affiliated individuals or organizations.

The Statement begins by quoting a 1902 speech by the University of Chicago President William Rainey Harper that "the principle of complete freedom of speech on all subjects has from the beginning been regarded as fundamental in the University of Chicago" and that "this principle can neither now nor at any future time be called in question." Harper's absolutist position holds the freedom of speech above all other values. While perhaps a mere rhetorical flourish, the pronouncement that freedom of speech cannot be called into question is clearly hypocritical. Indeed, this book that you are reading is premised on the insistence that we call into question such truisms. That the authors of the Chicago Principles chose to begin with this quotation sets the tone for addressing free expression not as a complex and important principle that should be thoroughly investigated but rather as a three-page rallying cry for the already converted.

After three more quotations from previous University of Chicago presidents, the Statement reads, "Because the University is committed to free and open inquiry in all matters, it guarantees all members of the University community the broadest possible latitude to speak, write, listen, challenge, and learn." The Statement raises some of the issues that Ben-Porath is concerned with, noting that the university greatly values "civility" and "mutual respect." But it separates its position from Ben-Porath's balancing of such concerns with clear postulations that "these [other considerations that may limit free expression] are narrow exceptions to the general principle of freedom of expression, and it is vitally important that these exceptions *never* be used in a manner that is inconsistent with the University's commitment to a completely free and open discussion of ideas" (emphasis added). Thus, where Ben-Porath begins with the First Amendment and asks universities to augment its protections with a higher standard of "inclusive" and "better speech," the Chicago Principles aims at limiting any exceptions to absolute free speech.

As shown in Chapters One and Two, even the most absolute theorizations of free speech and applications of the First Amendment invoke some limits at some point, whether interpreted by where speech becomes action that incites or inflicts harm, as with Mill and Holmes, or where it is confined to topics of public concern, as with Meiklejohn. Sure enough, the Chicago Statement also invokes something like a harm principle:

> The freedom to debate . . . does not, of course, mean that individuals may say whatever they wish. The University may restrict expression that violates the law, that falsely defames a specific

individual, that constitutes a genuine threat or harassment, that unjustifiably invades substantial privacy or confidentiality interests, or that is otherwise directly incompatible with the functioning of the University.

To this complex list, it then adds a blanket but standard practical caveat that the university can "reasonably regulate the time, place, and manner of expression."

In articulating these limits, this section of the Statement provides the crucial definition of what its authors mean by free expression and where the Principles become more than lofty platitudes. But it is exactly here where both grammar and logic become muddy. Its initial point is clear: a university is taking it upon itself and its policies to *actively* prohibit illegal speech. While unlikely, presumably a university could decide that such legal questions will be left to the police and law enforcement, but the Principles are noting this should not be the case. The Statement then goes on to specifically forbid expression that "falsely defames a specific individual" and that which constitutes a "genuine threat or harassment." These are already crimes in Illinois, so these restrictions are redundant but not unclear, per se. One might wonder how neither the English professor nor the law professor on the committee pointed out the redundancy of "falsely defames" — by definition, there is no such thing as true defamation.

However, as the list continues, things become much less clear. It moves into territory of speech that may not be illegal, such as breach of privacy and confidentiality. While Illinois does have specific legal requirements under certain circumstances of confidentiality, the Statement is not clear on whether only such legal restrictions are included or if other instances may be prohibited by the university. In any event, the final phrase is entirely vague: it suggests the university itself, rather than the law and the courts, may determine what is "directly incompatible with the functioning of the University" and can be restricted without contravening the Principles. In other words, the key part of the Statement that should provide its real meaning and substance is unclear. As Rangwala argues persuasively, "Ultimately, the [the Chicago Principles Statement] acknowledges limits — the university, after all, would not function without a mandate and parameters — but the vagueness allows these limits to be manipulated or shifted to suit the interpreter." As she notes, the Statement effectively gives university administrators the power of interpretation with no space for the faculty or a faculty union to be involved in such determinations.[82]

The absence of any reference to academic freedom that should protect faculty from administrators is most troubling. By eclipsing academic freedom adjudicated by faculty with unclear sentiments of free expression to be interpreted by university administrators, the Chicago Principles undermine the very mission of the university and its reliance on academic freedom. Shannon Dea demonstrates brilliantly how the Chicago Principles' silence concerning academic freedom is an example of freedom of expression being substituted for academic freedom which raises important problems.[83]

As Shama Rangwala, James Turk, and Richard Moon have all noted, Ford and Kenney's adoption of the Chicago Principles for universities in Ontario and Alberta has much more to do with appealing to their right-wing supporters than with safeguarding the quality of higher education.[84] Their analyses show how these provincial requirements are dangerous infringements on the autonomy of universities to determine how best to conduct teaching and research. Turk's major criticism is that it "overrides the institutional autonomy that historically has provided some protection for free speech and academic freedom on campus."[85] He makes a strong case that this move is based on the false premise that there is a free expression crisis at Canadian universities.[86] Canadian political scientist Dax D'Orazio offers an excellent account of the historical dynamics leading to the Chicago Principles and what he calls a "feedback loop" to explain why they came to be adopted in Canada for political reasons.[87]

Despite my agreement with Turk's key point here, we diverge where Turk holds that there should be a closer relationship between academic freedom and free expression. Indeed, he concludes that, despite all the problems with Premier Ford's policy on free expression at Ontario universities, it may have the unintended positive consequence of causing "Ontario courts to reconsider their position on the Charter applicability to universities."[88] Only time will tell, but from my analysis in this book and the arguments of Shannon Dea noted above, applying the Charter to universities would not necessarily lead to more critical and inclusive discussion and could hamper the practices of academic freedom. But Turk's position that academic freedom should be more closely aligned in Canada with free expression has some support from other Canadian academics.

For example, historian Mark Gabbert argues that to adequately secure the principle of academic freedom, "it is best understood as a special case of the right of freedom of expression." For Gabbert, "Academic freedom can therefore be understood as an offspring of freedom of expression."[89] He mounts an important critique of my insistence that academic freedom is based on accepted methods and rules of a discipline. Yet, historically, his analysis is grounded in the American context and does not address the Canadian legal differences. He does not show how academic freedom would be strengthened in the Canadian context where most professors are covered by collective agreements by using this parent-child metaphor to relate it to free expression.

The broader point here is that the complex issues of the freedom of expression and those of academic freedom are further muddied when we overgeneralize from one freedom to the other. As I have shown, freedom of expression must be universal and not based on qualitative judgements about the speech involved beyond its potential harm to others. In contrast, academic freedom is necessarily bestowed on professors based on their qualifications and is premised on adjudicating the quality of expression. Confusing the two weakens both.

Summary

We should resist the former University of Chicago president William Harper's sentiment, quoted in the Chicago Principles, that free expression is a tenet that we must not critically question or interrogate; as Mill insisted, that is a sure way for free expression to become a dead dogma that is not well understood. Indeed, *Rethinking Free Speech* insists that we must seriously analyze the general concepts of free speech. This chapter has argued that the concept of "free speech on campus" debases a more sophisticated conception of academic freedom tailored to the Canadian context. We must be wary of conflating academic freedom with the Charter right to freedom of expression or more general ideals of critical and inclusive discussion. None of these three important and overlapping principles is easy to practice or enforce on its own, but more is lost than gained by ignoring or conflating the nuances that distinguish them. Eve Haque has made a persuasive argument that, in Canada, "academic freedom is an important principle that continues to need defending on many fronts. However, our current conception of academic freedom also remains fossilized because only 'expert' voices are given the platform to guide the discussion."[90] As Haque also argues, we need to grapple with how academic freedom is unproductively pitted against and often used to shield explicit and systemic racism. In a similar vein, Dea presents a "restorative" rather than "juridical" approach to academic freedom that goes beyond being merely a "negotiated job prerequisite" but changes with the developing role of universities so that it can work in the interests not of individual professors, but society.[91] These are vital points that raise critical concerns with our common understanding of academic freedom. However, to better develop academic freedom we need to be clear that we should not equate it to the Charter right to the freedom of expression nor a general principle of critical and inclusive discussion. To use the metaphor from my Introduction, you may not like Robertson's screwdrivers, but if that is the screw you need to remove, there is no point insisting on using a Phillips.

Many of these discussions about free expression at universities repeat the comedian Rick Mercer's outrage that the supposed suppression of Lindsay Shepherd's free expression undermines a major purpose of university — to expose young people to a wide variety of ideas including unpopular ones.[92] Ben-Porath describes universities as places where students are exposed to tensions and disagreements outside of their "bubble."[93] Prior to the internet, especially during the post-war expansion of universities to much broader cross-sections of the population, perhaps this type of exposure to unpopular and perhaps unthinkable ideas was an important role for universities. But since the advent of social media, the idea that universities are places where students are exposed to such unorthodox, radical, and diverse ideas is antiquated. An hour spent on social media can bring students into contact with more controversial, radical, and unthinkable ideas than one could ever introduce in a meaningful way in a university course. As Chapter Four explores, the dominance of social media needs to be thought through in much more profound ways.

Edward Said suggested that "Our model for academic freedom should be the migrant or traveller," voyaging beyond familiar places and confronting the unknown.[94] Recent events and the general state of public discussion in Canada, including the adoption of American approaches, seem only to offer us a twisted version of Said's model — the stereotype of the ugly American tourist, both ignorant and confident enough to travel the world, being entertained by the unknown without really engaging it, protected by their coat of "free speech."

CHAPTER FOUR

SOCIAL MEDIA

IN 1960, A.J. LIEBLING LAMENTED, "FREEDOM OF THE PRESS IS limited to those who own one."[1] Free speech is similarly restricted by people's ability to disseminate their expressions and be heard. However, these limitations seem to be vanishing as digital technology allows anyone with a smartphone or access to a computer the amazing potential to communicate with billions of people across the world.[2] This capacity for any group or individual to distribute information and opinions has blurred our ability to distinguish what is and is not professional journalism, leading to the current crisis in traditional media. Initially spurred on by the availability of cheaper and smaller video cameras in the 1990s, the ability to communicate increased exponentially with the widespread adoption of smartphones and the platforms offered by social media. Free speech advocates from the eighteenth to the twentieth centuries, including Kant, Mill, Meiklejohn, and Holmes, would be astonished by our easy access to such an expansive public sphere. As American judge Stewart Dalzell stated in 1996: "It is no exaggeration to conclude that the internet has achieved, and continues to achieve, the most participatory marketplace of mass speech that this country — and indeed the world — has yet seen."[3] He made this remark in a US federal district court decision that struck down much of the Communications Decency Act (1996), which attempted to regulate the internet.[4] The portion of the Act left intact included the much-discussed Section 230 that will be analyzed in detail below.

While technology has broken down innumerable barriers to free expression, we also need to pay attention to the qualities of the spaces for discussion and communication it has created. The internet is not simply one massive forum in which its billions of users participate. Rather, it is a medium used by platforms such as Facebook, X, TikTok, and myriad other social media that now structure so much of our social discussion. As Anshuman Mondal highlights (and as noted in Chapter Two), the space of free expression is never flat, nor is it a homogenous arena in which all speakers and listeners participate equally.[5] Social media offers different formats for expression, from X's 280-character limit (originally 140 when it was launched as Twitter), to the videos on TikTok and YouTube, to the multimedia options available on Facebook, Instagram, and Snapchat. On 4chan, 8chan, and Reddit, users remain anonymous, but most platforms allow them to choose their own usernames with differing levels of transparency and other requirements to create accounts. Substack, Spotify, Discord, and Twitch all offer unique formats for communication. Multiplayer video games create yet more venues for global communication, as do networking sites like LinkedIn or dating apps. At one level, users have a wide variety of platforms and means to express themselves, but as we shall see, such an abundance of options does not guarantee free speech as a negative freedom that eliminates all obstacles or regulations. Nor does the plethora of platform options necessarily advance open, critical, diverse, and inclusive discussion — that is, positive expressive freedom. In terms of the commitment and ability to enforce user codes of conduct and maintain an environment free of harassment, hate, and polarization, this new public sphere of social media leaves much to be desired.

Whether the creation of an alphabet, the invention of the printing press, or the development of digital cyberspace, technology itself does not safeguard public discussion that is at the heart of the various rationales for free speech. The structures that determine how we use these technologies, from standardized lexicons to internet protocols that enable communication, are shaped by the laws and social conventions that govern public discussion. This chapter focuses specifically on the legal structures that have made it possible for social media platforms and apps — that provide today's global public sphere of expression — to be fiscally viable, or more accurately, wildly profitable.[6]

Both users and social media companies have developed a new vocabulary to describe the vast number of innovative means by which we organize our discourse today, including words such as "hashtag," created initially by Twitter but now used more generally on social media platforms and even in spoken conversation (otherwise known as "IRL"

— in real life). Facebook developed the notion of "friends" (regardless of whether you have ever met IRL), "likes" were added in 2009, and then came more reactions — love, laughter, sadness, anger — and "care," during the pandemic. Facebook and other social media have developed different account settings for sharing and viewing content, including public or private pages, and various ways to access "threads" and "channels." When Elon Musk bought Twitter and changed its name to "X," he contemplated an "edit" option that is standard on most social media. Platforms like Reddit and Wikipedia created entirely new infrastructures to support different types of communities, often at the global level. These are all ways in which the digital public sphere structures our possibilities for critical and inclusive discussion.

If Justice Oliver Wendell Holmes once described free speech as an experiment, so Judge Dalzell in turn described the internet and social media as an experiment in free speech, the public use of reason, and critical popular debate.[7] It is increasingly clear that this new experiment is far from an unambiguous success. Almost no one is satisfied with the current outcomes.[8] Even those free speech absolutists who argue against any regulation of the internet do not do so in celebration of the quality of discussion and progress produced by social media, as was common a decade ago. Rather they reject regulation out of fear of potential unintended consequences or the futility of enforcement. Jacob Mchangama cautions that restrictive rules for social media "may be a curse worse than the disease," but there is no question that issues of hate speech, fake news, and polarization constitute some type of disease that threatens public discussion on the internet. Mchangama ultimately suggests we must live with the downsides and the only way forward is to champion free speech, despite his lack of any clear definition of what it entails.[9] Social psychologist Jonathan Haidt connects these social media ailments directly to the state of public discourse and governance: "Social media's empowerment of the far left, the far right, domestic trolls, and foreign agents is creating a system that looks less like democracy and more like rule by the most aggressive."[10] But like Mchangama, Haidt's proposed solutions steer clear of anything that could suggest "regulation." Many others mount various arguments that boil down to the idea that any attempt to suppress or regulate any expression — including the polarizing spew of hatred and "fake news" that occupies so much of social media — will necessarily undermine free expression.[11]

Others argue that the concentration of power in a handful of major social media companies could lead to the suppression of free expression unless we have government regulation.[12] As Michael Bérubé and Jennifer Ruth contend, "The context-collapsing and democracy-destabilizing nature of social media makes it extremely difficult to cling to the traditional liberal belief that the best remedy for hate speech is more speech."[13] Without more awareness of the differing objectives of free expression — ideals of critical and inclusive discussion, legal principles that restrict government censorship, and academic freedom's search for knowledge — any attempt to advocate free expression is likely to fail. How we cope with technological innovation must be guided by a better understanding of the disparate goals of free expression.

The backlash — or "techlash" — against social media in general, and Facebook, X, and Google in particular, has become increasingly prominent. In addition to concerns that social media is addictive and potentially harmful to physical and mental health,[14] there are growing anxieties about the lack of transparency in the collection, sale, and use of data by the private companies that provide the platforms. This came to a crisis with the Cambridge Analytica scandal in 2013.[15]

Even more troubling, in 2018, Facebook admitted it had not sufficiently responded to the use of its platform to foment hate and violence against the Rohingya population in Myanmar. Algorithms designed to maximize Facebook profits amplified hate speech and inflammatory posts, contributing to the campaign of genocide against the Muslim minority. The company's lack of local support for its platform or timely removal of inciting posts is at the centre of a £150-billion lawsuit.[16]

In Canada, filmmaker and law professor Joel Bakan is suing Twitter, alleging it breached his freedom of expression by refusing to run a paid ad for his film that is critical of big tech.[17] However, unlike other lawsuits, such as Trump's and Hawley's (discussed in the Introduction and Chapter Two), Bakan's allegations do not directly rely on the constitutional protection of free expression but rather on contract law. At the time of writing, it is unclear how successful this strategy will be legally.[18] Regardless, all this attention has brought revelation after revelation about how these platforms operate, and this new information has added to the general disillusionment with social media, particularly as a forum for productive and democratic free expression.[19]

Ro Khanna, Representative to the US House of Representatives for California's Seventeenth District, which includes Silicon Valley where the major social media platforms are headquartered, points out that "It may seem hard to remember, but at the time [in 2011] tech companies were seen by many as beacons of freedom, and their leaders as respected global statesmen."[20] Today, almost everyone, including Congressperson Khanna and most free speech absolutists, admits that the space for discussion on the internet is deeply flawed and that earlier democratic dreams have yielded a nightmare rife with misinformation and polarization. As Canadian political scientist Ronald Deibert summarizes,

> Once, it was conventional wisdom to assume that digital technologies would enable greater access to information, facilitate collective organizing, and empower civil society.... Indeed, for much of the 2000s, technology enthusiasts applauded each new innovation as a way to bring people closer together and revitalize democracy. Now, social media are increasingly perceived as contributing to a kind of social sickness.[21]

If we view social media as a massive experiment in unfettered free expression, the results currently seem far from positive.

Canada, the US, and many other governments and intergovernmental organizations around the world are working on legislation and other means to curb hate speech on the internet, as well as the "fake news" and increased polarization.[22] Underlying these legislative impulses is the admission that traditional measures to protect public discussion and individuals' capacity to speak are not sufficient for the digital medium. The question is: What can governments or society at large do when the space for discussion and communication is provided by private, for-profit companies with no or little obligation to consider the public interest? How have private companies come to dominate and structure the public sphere so profoundly?

The public sphere has been historically constituted by newspapers and other print media that were also primarily private and for-profit. Governments later became more active in regulating radio and television, including public broadcasting systems like the CBC in Canada or the BBC in Britain (both funded by the government but at arm's length), and PBS in the US (funded by donors). For much of the twentieth century, the public sphere, while importantly constituted by for-profit commercial media, also had considerable non-profit components and significant government regulation.

Just as the principles of free speech took their modern form with the advent of representative democracy, so too has the advent of the digital age fundamentally altered the contours of free expression.[23] Social media has had an impact on all the related principles of free speech. Jennifer Petersen traces how the US Supreme Court has changed its conception of "speech" due to technological developments to a point where now "there is less distinction between speaking and the work of computation and less need for speakers at all in legal reasoning" concerning the First Amendment.[24]

The case of *Pridgen v. University of Calgary* (2010), discussed in Chapter Three, concerning university students criticizing their professor on Facebook, illustrates new questions raised by the ubiquity of social media as a forum for expression. As a platform for expression, Facebook is neither on-campus, nor off-campus, but rather it is both. In *Pridgen*, the court blurred the traditionally distinct university jurisdiction and determined that students' Charter protection of the freedom of expression trumped university policy on non-academic misconduct. In *Mahanoy Area School District v. B.L.* (2021), the US Supreme Court was tasked with deciding whether a high school cheerleader's profane expression of frustration on Snapchat could be punished by the team's code of conduct. School administrators worried that if students' speech on social media was considered to be outside of school grounds, much of their ability to regulate student behaviour while at school would be diminished. Similarly, as argued in Chapter Three, the internet has also eclipsed the university as a vehicle through which many young students are exposed to provocative and sometimes outrageous ideas. Now the internet is the venue where young people first encounter ideas that challenge social standards.

This chapter cannot possibly delve into all the tricky lines that digital technology blurs. Earlier boundaries between different places of speech — at school or outside of school, at home or in a public meeting — disappear in the ever-present hyperspace of social media. Moreover, this new space is provided by private companies that are based on a new business model. A closer look at social media helps to situate the changing nature — and recent growth — of free speech controversies, reveal the inadequacy of many common ways of thinking about free speech, and suggest ways to re-think free expression in the digital age. Specifically, social media makes even clearer how inadequate it is to think of public discussion as a marketplace of ideas. I argue the social media landscape requires that we clearly distinguish the legal or constitutional rights from the other — more idealistic — goals of critical and inclusive discussion.

Absolute Free Speech Cannot Exist on a Social Media Platform

While free speech advocates straightforwardly reject all impingements on free speech, this objective is impossible, or at least no one has managed it yet on a social media platform. This is because social media platforms are subject not so much to laws, but the needs of businesses that require user attention. Jason Miller, one of Trump's former communications advisers, admits as much in regard to his supposedly pro-free speech social media upstart, GETTR. Buried in GETTR's Terms of Use, after much legalese, is Section 2.iv that stipulates:

> GETTR holds freedom of speech as its core value and does not wish to censor your opinions. Nonetheless, GETTR may, but will not have any obligation to, review, monitor, display, post, store, maintain, accept, or otherwise make use of, any of your UGC [User Generated Content] and GETTR may, in its sole discretion, reject, delete, move, re-format, remove ... UGC without notice or any liability.

Furthermore, despite Miller accusing Twitter and Facebook of "censoring" Trump,[25] GETTR's Terms of Use include the following:

> Without limitation, we may, but do not commit to, do so [as above] to address content that comes to our attention that we believe is offensive, obscene, lewd, lascivious, filthy, pornographic, violent, harassing, threatening, abusive, illegal, or otherwise objectionable or inappropriate .... For example, this may include content identified as personal bullying, sexual abuse of a child, attacking any religion or race, or content containing video or depictions of beheadings.[26]

This list of restrictions is much more expansive than what is illegal under US laws, including the First Amendment. GETTR retains precisely the type of regulation criteria, such as offensiveness, that free speech advocates, including Miller, condemn. "Filthy," "lascivious," or "lewd" expression alone would not meet the bar for Mill's harm principle, nor does it encroach into action that might warrant suspension of First Amendment protections in Holmes's reasoning. Regardless of whether one thinks any of Trump's posts were "offensive," he was banned by Facebook, Twitter, and YouTube for encouraging violence when his supporters stormed the Capitol Building on 6 January 2021.[27]

The restrictive terms of use on even the most absolutist free speech platforms are not (only) due to hypocrisy or lack of will; they are structural components of these platforms. As discussed in the Introduction, content moderation (and thus, "censorship") is an inescapable aspect of social media. Even Donald Trump's Truth Social platform goes beyond prohibiting just what is illegal: it prohibits nudity, content it deems to be pornography, and material it determines to be spam. It also provides "guidelines" meant to "promote productive, civil discussion."[28] In 2012, Twitter claimed that it was "the free speech wing of the free speech party,"[29] but unless one is operating elsewhere — namely, on the dark web where users are *totally* anonymous — there is no social networking site that allows one to post whatever one likes: *all* have user agreements that give the platforms much wider latitude to restrict expression than does the law.[30] The business model of social media could not sustain the potential legal liability for anything users might say, as I explain below. A social media platform that allowed all speech that is legal is unlikely to produce an environment with widespread appeal and profitability. Without mechanisms to protect and determine the quality of content, it is also unlikely to contribute to democratic goals or achieve Mill's or Kant's goals of advancing truth or "enlightenment."

Legal Protections of Free Expression Increasingly Miss the Point

In 2009, Jack Balkin, the Knight Professor of Constitutional Law and the First Amendment at Yale Law School, wrote: "Gradually, I have come to the conclusion that we face a transition of enormous irony. At the very moment that our economic and social lives are increasingly dominated by information technology and information flows, the First Amendment seems increasingly irrelevant to the key free speech battles of the future." As a law professor who has devoted much of his career to the First Amendment, Balkin argues that while the principles underlying twentieth-century debates about free speech are still significant, "the most important decisions affecting the future of freedom of speech will not occur in constitutional law; they will be decisions about technological design, legislative and administrative regulations, the formation of new business models, and the collective activities of end-users." [31] Even in 2009, Balkin was focusing on issues that he argued could not be adequately addressed by the First Amendment, such as net neutrality (the idea that internet service providers treat all customers and content the same), and Section 230 of the Communications Decency Act (1996), discussed below.

Richard Moon comes to a similar conclusion, reflecting on the impact of social media in the Canadian context. He writes, "Public discourse is in crisis, but the remedy is no longer simply 'free speech' — the breaking down of state censorship. Indeed, a robust protection of free expression may actually contribute to the crisis."[32] Timothy Wu, technology adviser to President Biden and Law Professor at Columbia Law School, agrees with Balkin and Moon, arguing that due to social media, censorship is no longer primarily an issue of direct government action. Wu argues that new mechanisms now restrict speech, including techniques such as "flooding tactics," "filter bubbles," or the unleashing of "troll armies" — whether they be real people or bots, orchestrated by governments (often foreign governments) or private organizations. First Amendment conceptions of free speech assumed information scarcity, but now, as Wu describes it, we face information overload. When we received our news from print, radio, and network TV, the question was how to get our issues, concerns, or perspectives into one of the limited number of prominent media venues. Now the question is how to make our issues, concerns, or perspectives stand out from the massive amount of content anyone can post on the web. Wu adds that this shift from information scarcity to abundance has been accompanied by an opposite shift from attention abundance to attention scarcity as social media platforms compete not for our dollars or even loyalty to their products, but primarily for our time and attention. As Philip Napoli notes, the "attention economy" is "grounded in the notion that audience attention represented an increasingly — and thus increasingly valuable — resource to the growing number of competitors."[33]

Wu concludes that either the First Amendment will remain "confined to the harms that fall within the original 1920s paradigm," or the First Amendment protection must be adapted and "broaden its own reach to encompass the new techniques of speech control" inherent in social media.[34] Not surprisingly, there are a plethora of arguments that the First Amendment needs to be expanded so that it not only restricts the government but may be used to restrict private social media platforms from infringing on the free speech of users.[35] Such approaches eventually come up against the conundrum that such government regulation of private companies would infringe on those companies' freedom of speech.

A "Virtual Space for Others to Speak"?

We must pay attention to the profound ways in which the legal framework always structures expression on social media. In the 1990s, as the internet was developing, the question for governments was whether the new digital networked technologies and entities that used them, such as bulletin boards and listservs (the precursors to social media) were like newspapers, radio, and television. The question was: Were they producers and curators of news, or were they "neutral" carriers that transported information, like telephone companies, postal services, and couriers? Monika Bickert, head of policy management at Facebook, maintains that social media companies are different from traditional publishers because "they generally do not create or choose the content shared on their platforms; instead, they provide the virtual space for others to speak."[36] Despite the fact that prominent figures such as Nadine Strossen (president of the ACLU, 1991–2008) and congressperson Ro Khanna agree with Bickert's distinction,[37] the view does not withstand scrutiny.

In the US, prior to the passing of the Communications Decency Act (Chapter V of the Telecommunications Act of 1996), internet service providers, bulletin boards, list-serves, and what would become social media were in a legal limbo between two different conceptions of information providers. Conceived in one way, they would be regulated like publishers of newspapers, magazines, or books, who have a degree of legal liability for the material they publish. The other option would be to consider them merely as carriers of information, like telephone companies or courier services that transport materials with no liability for their content. For example, if one is defamed in a newspaper article, one can sue both the author who wrote it and the newspaper that published it. But if one is defamed over the telephone, one can sue the person who defamed them, but not the telephone company. A telephone company only provides the means of communication; it does nothing to curate or sanction it. Two decades later, Bickert maintains this position is still true for Facebook— that it is simply a carrier of the information content made by others.

The history of Section 230 of the Communications Decency Act is important to our ability to understand our current situation. In 1995, the New York Supreme Court in *Oakmont, Inc. v. Prodigy Services Co.* ruled that because Prodigy, an internet service provider (ISP), moderated some of the content on one of its internet bulletin boards, it was acting like a publisher and thus was liable for all the content posted on its site, including a post by an anonymous user that defamed Stratton Oakmont, an investment firm.[38] Members of Congress were concerned that this ruling would discourage internet platforms from making any effort to prevent harmful, defamatory, and pornographic material on their websites because such curation would make them liable for all the content posted on their platforms. Congress thus passed a piece of legislation entitled, "Protection for 'Good Samaritan' Blocking and Screening Offensive Material," as part of the 1996 Telecommunications Act, included as Section 230.

Section 230(1) states: "No provider or user of an interactive computer service shall be treated as the publisher or speaker of any information provided by another information content provider."[39] As long as a social media company does not create the content, it is merely a provider, not a publisher. This legislation prevents these platforms from being sued for content posted on their sites.[40] Without it, social media platforms like Facebook, X, Google, YouTube, and TikTok would not be able to disseminate the massive number of posts that they do and make profits as they currently do. When both President Trump and then President Biden discussed repealing Section 230(1), the strong reaction from social media companies illustrates its importance.[41]

In 1996, Facebook did not yet exist, but this piece of legislation is essential to the business model of most social media platforms. Since the prominent social media companies do not sell access to their platform but offer it to users for free, they need to attract as many users as possible to glean the data they then sell to advertisers. The larger their pool of users becomes, however, the more difficult it is to control the content posted on their sites.

As Facebook, X, and most other social media increasingly use complex and secret algorithms to determine what users see on their feeds, the distinction between them and traditional media becomes untenable. According to Pew Research surveys, nearly half of social media users say that they use those platforms to get their news "often" or "sometimes."[42] In other words, consumers substantially treat many social media platforms as they have traditional media news sources, and, like traditional media, those platforms curate and manage what their users have available to consume. Emily Bell describes social media platforms as "the unintentional press," explaining that while the companies themselves resist this description, "their decisions and behavior are increasingly indistinguishable from those of editorial organizations." They are gatekeepers of expression and make decisions about what and how content is displayed.[43] This need to manipulate user content creates an insurmountable tension between the private interests of social media companies and the public good of critical and inclusive discussion. Section 230 is what creates this possibility.

Of course, Section 230 is an American law and not on its own applicable outside the US, yet it has helped to structure the global digital public sphere. The United States–Mexico–Canada Agreement, which replaced NAFTA in 2018, contains Article 19.17, which obliges Canada and Mexico to comply with Section 230; other global trade agreements have similar clauses. There is some debate on the extent and meaning of this Article, as well as what may happen if the US alters or abolishes it.[44] While I have been careful to attend to differences between Canada and the US, they are negligible in the case of free expression on social media. Thus, the rest of this chapter will focus mostly on the US, despite the importance of both the Canadian context and the global nature of the digital public sphere.

"Senator, We Run Ads"[45]

Social psychologist Shoshana Zuboff describes in detail how Google initiated the business model that Facebook, X, and most other social media adopted — a model in part made profitable by Section 230. Initially, Larry Page and Sergey Brin, the founders of Google, scorned other search engines that sold advertising to create revenue. They were convinced that being beholden to ad sales would adversely affect their search engine's effectiveness and reputation. Instead, their revenue came from other sources, including various licensing agreements (for example, to portals like Yahoo! for the use of the search engine); standard sponsored ads on the website observable to all users; and venture capitalist investment.[46] But when the tech bubble burst in 2002, the need for profit became dire. Their previously neglected AdWords branch developed a new way of connecting individuals' data collected from their Google searches to third-party advertisers, enabling them to target specific niche markets with ad content tailored to individual users based on their Google search history. In other words, unlike traditional newspapers, TV, or earlier ad sales that sold "space," AdWords developed the key new product, selling data collected from users to advertisers. Later, Google and other platforms extended this collection of user information beyond searches to many user activities with the use of internet "cookies," code that embeds itself in a user's computer and then allows the website to track the user's actions. This new economic model came to be the core of many social media companies, especially YouTube (owned by Google since 2006), Meta (Facebook's parent company since its 2021 rebranding), and X.[47] Zuboff calls this collection and analysis of massive amounts of data from non-paying users, "surveillance capitalism," in which companies profit from their users' attention and engagement, rather than their money or labour, as happens in conventional business models. Zuboff's reflection on Google's initial critique of this model shows that our current social media situation is not determined by the technology itself. There is nothing inherent in the technology that requires these current structures; they exist because of decisions made by lawmakers, corporate leaders, and users. Alternatives exist, as I will address near the end of this chapter.

Among many of the effects of this new model is that social media platforms are incentivized to increase the number of their users as much as possible, even though most users do not pay anything. Another is that the platforms need to keep users on the sites for as long as possible and to provide as much data as possible, whether by "liking," "retweeting," or just lingering on a post or video. Their goal is to maximize engagement so as to enable their algorithms to collect and analyze as much data as possible in order to maximize its value to advertisers. Many have called this the "attention economy," but Zuboff's analysis provides a richer framework that includes behaviour and engagement. Zuboff and others document the many profound impacts that social media's business model has on society at large; however, for questions regarding free expression, the key point is that these companies have no economic incentive to create a healthy public sphere. Quite the contrary. Facebook quickly learned that polarization and echo chambers work very well to keep people scrolling, clicking, and responding.

Social media platforms increase their profit by using algorithms to cater to each individual user's experience to maximize the time and intensity of their engagement with the site. Not only do they claim that their algorithms are proprietorial and refuse to share any details about them, they argue that if they let users keep their news feeds chronological without algorithms dictating what their users see, their users would miss what Facebook deems to be "important content" that users, they argue, find more "meaningful."[48] They have conducted research finding that users are "better off" with the algorithm news feed, and without them users would "spend less time in their news feeds, post less often and interact less."[49] In other words, the algorithms are important to social media companies' need to attract and keep our attention because this is what generates its profits. Thus, social media is not like the telephone system or postal service that simply transmits the content provided by the users. For one, telephone companies and postal services have paying customers. More importantly and relatedly, they do not create or curate the communications conveyed via the infrastructure they provide. The algorithms social media companies have developed to generate profitable data are not merely neutral conduits of user-created information. As Zuboff and Nick Srnicek, a philosopher and scholar of digital economy, show, social media companies must do more than just create a platform for users to interact in order to monetize their technology, they must also be proactive to harness the attention of their non-paying users.

Mark Zuckerberg, head of Meta, has suggested that Section 230 is outdated and needs to be revised. He has advocated for provisions that protect social media from allegations of third-party libel and defamation, but "only," as reporters summarized his testimony, "if they follow best practices for removing damaging material from their platforms."[50] Predictably, social media lobbyists want a regulatory environment in which they can maintain their ability to generate massive profits and not be penalized for disseminating illicit content. Hence, Facebook is willing to create its Oversight Board and a massive structure of artificial intelligence content moderation supplemented by a large human staff. Their profits can sustain such resource costs as long as they are not accountable if the process fails at times. Some argue that such new legislation could give the old social media giants like Facebook, Google, and X a competitive advantage against smaller upstart platforms with fewer resources to cope with the massive work of such content moderation, including Parler, GETTR, and Truth Social that pitch themselves as "free speech" platforms.[51]

Section 230 is supplemented by another legal classification that exempts social media from normal copyright law in the US: the Digital Millennium Copyright Act (1998, revised in 2018). If social media platforms were liable for copyright infringements, they would not have become such major sources for the sharing of news and information. If a newspaper republishes an article from another newspaper without permission, it can be sued. On social media, it is primarily users who share links to news stories from other sources (and now many media outlets purchase posts on Facebook and X). The platforms themselves are not subject to copyright prohibitions, despite the benefit they incur from the reposting of copyrighted material. As internet activist, technology expert, and science fiction writer Cory Doctorow writes, explaining the details of how the Digital Millennium Copyright Act works:

> It doesn't exactly treat an online service like a bookstore or movie theater (which would face copyright liability if one of the works it offered to the public was found to infringe copyright).
>
> Nor does it treat online services like a technology . . . .
>
> It also doesn't treat online services like a private speech forum—like a bar or a restaurant, which has no obligation to monitor its customers' conversations for copyright infringement or act to prevent them.
>
> Instead, it "borrows a little from all of these," allowing these platforms to monitor its users' speech and apply content moderation but that it is not liable for either taking down content it objects to, or failing to take down content that is harmful.[52]

In 2021, Australia attempted to address this issue, hoping to steer some of the massive profits garnered by social media companies to the embattled media outlets with legislation that would create a mechanism for social media companies to pay for journalism. After a brief period when Meta blocked news links, negotiations led to an amendment, and Meta and Google have negotiated deals with Australian media.[53] In April 2022, Canada passed similar legislation, the Online News Act (Bill C–18), which, after several important amendments, received royal assent in June 2023, and took effect in December 2023.[54] The Act applies only to social media companies with more than 20 million unique monthly users and annual revenues of over a billion dollars. Thus, it only affects Meta and Google. Meta responded by blocking users from posting any links to media outlets months before the Act went into effect. Negotiations with Meta have been suspended with no indication of them being resumed. Google, however, came to an agreement with the Government of Canada whereby they will negotiate with a single group that will represent Canadian media to distribute something in the range of $100 million a year to media outlets.[55] In a narrow sense, such legislative developments are more related to questions of social media's effects on media outlets than free expression per se.[56] However, from a broader perspective, it is very relevant. In Canada, individuals debating on Facebook, for example, can no longer support their points with media links. Perhaps more importantly, Facebook and Instagram that had been major vehicles through which people accessed news produced by media outlets, do not play that role anymore. If news consumers adjust their practices and go straight to the news outlets (perhaps involving paying subscriptions or viewing ads), such effects will be tempered. Otherwise, it could lead to a diminishing of informed people. Moreover, if similar legislation spreads, for example, to the European Union or other countries, this extension could affect the business model of these social media giants and the structure of the public sphere. These developments relate to the broad questions of how, and in what venues, public discussions take place.

In addition to Section 230 and the Digital Millennium Copyright Act, another element that enables social media to monetize user data is the ability to track them across the internet. The technological development of the cookie allowing platforms to track users' movements as they use other websites was initially seen as a significant privacy concern but is now commonplace and difficult to avoid or deactivate. As Shoshana Zuboff discusses, after Netscape invented the cookie in 1994, the Federal Trade Commission (FTC) attempted to regulate it and the Clinton administration banned their use on all federal websites. Advertisers arguing against government regulation ultimately won the day by creating an association for "self-regulation," the Network Advertising Initiative.[57] The result is that users are often asked about their cookie preferences, but also warned that if they do not allow cookies, the functionality of the site may be compromised. Cookies on their own may do little to foster or impede critical and inclusive discussion, but without them, or with tighter regulation of them, social media companies would have much greater difficulty monetizing the space that they provide for expression. Eliminating or severely restricting the use of cookies by social media companies could alleviate many of the privacy issues and problems with data leaks that are part of the tech backlash, but it could also fundamentally alter the dominance and operation of social media.

Section 230, the Digital Millennium Copyright Act, and the decision to allow the free flow of cookies are legal frameworks that have shaped the social media landscape as we know it. They are also all subject to change and some are facing increasing pressure in different jurisdictions around the world. Of course, the law has previously structured how radio and television operate, from issuing broadcast licences and channel frequencies of the Fairness Doctrine (1949–87) of the Federal Communications Commission (FCC) in the US to Canadian content requirements in Canada. Legislation is also the most practical avenue through which governments can alter and shape social media as a sphere of so much public debate and discussion. In the US, from 1949 until the deregulation era that began in the 1980s, the FCC's Fairness Doctrine required public broadcasters to devote some airtime to matters of public importance and that they include contrasting viewpoints, with specific time stipulations, for controversial issues. *Red Lion Broadcasting v. FCC* (1969) upheld the constitutionality of the equal time provision, noting that there is only a finite bandwidth of radio frequencies, and the government must control this finite resource. The repeal of the Fairness Doctrine in 1987 paved the way for one-sided media outlets like Fox News. In Canada, the government regulates mass media with Canadian content requirements and has recently augmented programs that fund media outlets threatened by social media.[58]

The advent of social media has radically changed the public sphere, with new avenues for expression extending around the world, in spaces designed and controlled by a handful of corporations driven more by profit than the public good. These broad strokes demonstrate how the law and changes in business models substantially impact how and where we express ourselves and listen to the ideas of others. The distinctions between legal principles of freedom of expression and ideals of critical and inclusive discussion have become more pressing. Important too is being able to distinguish the principles of thorough inquiry in search for the truth (as found in academic freedom), as well as the processes of our judicial systems from free expression.

The Historical Structuring of the Public Sphere

In his influential work *The Structural Transformation of the Public Sphere*, Jürgen Habermas defined "the public sphere" as a space historically arising from European royal courts, but then really coming into being in the seventeenth and eighteenth centuries via the salons in France, the *Tischgesellshaften* (table societies) in Germany, the coffee houses in England, and elsewhere throughout Europe. These sites transformed the space in which private individuals engaged publicly in ongoing conversations about issues of common concern. In this new modern public sphere, the common practices of both the state and the market were ideally suspended so that the ideas presented could be evaluated in terms of reason untarnished by political or financial interests.[59] This is the background for our current conception of the public sphere as the major realm for free expression and an inherent part of the development of a democratic society.

Habermas notes the significance of the French salons as places where women had great influence, in contrast to the male-dominated spaces of coffee houses elsewhere. He argues that these transformations of public spaces created new conditions for how ideas and values could circulate and their merits debated. These public spaces, however different from one another, influenced the development of journals and newspapers, the "society of letters" (including publications that still exist today, such as *The Guardian, The Spectator,* and *Tatler*),[60] creating what Immanuel Kant refers to as "the reading public," and facilitating the "public use of reason."

Many scholars have questioned Habermas's idealized views of reason being able to overcome political and economic motives as well as many other issues of power relations,[61] but even such critics accept his broader conclusion that the public sphere is structured in particular ways that change historically. Feminist political theorists like Nancy Fraser have criticized Habermas for downplaying the exclusions of the public sphere and casting it (even in ideal theory) as equal and open to all. Fraser is also critical of the way Habermas divided the public from the private in ways that entrench the former as masculine and confine women predominantly to the latter.[62] Habermas argued that it is the power of reason and free speech that allows for such criticisms; indeed, he subsequently accepted the feminist criticism. More importantly from his perspective, it would be the open and critical nature of the public sphere that allowed feminists to argue for its expansion and enabled them to successfully demand that women have as much right as men to participate and frame the nature of that participation. For Habermas, it is critical reason that made possible the type of public sphere that arose in the seventeenth and eighteenth centuries, a space that could transcend its exclusions and inherent inequalities to progressively become more inclusive and diverse.[63]

One of Habermas's main contributions to this book's consideration of free speech is his demonstration of the extent to which the public sphere is always structured, and that structures change over time and with social and technological developments. This insight is crucial today as our public sphere is reshaped by a new medium of communication technology and monopolized by private social media companies.[64]

Similar insights may be best known in Canada through the work of Marshall McLuhan, the Canadian author of the phrase, "the medium is the message," and the influential scholar who showed how media shapes our communication. Harold Innis, another prominent Canadian communications scholar and economist who influenced McLuhan, also demonstrated how culture, politics, and communications were intimately connected to economic and technological developments.[65] The research emanating from media theorist and cultural critic Neil Postman, and his major work, *Amusing Ourselves to Death,* also explores this basic point — that the public sphere is structured, especially with the then "new" medium of television in its network form, but with a special focus on the increasingly prevalent blurring of previously distinct spheres of entertainment and news as the material for public discussion. Of course, Postman was not a technological determinist; rather, he demonstrated how the new media of network television encapsulated and altered the dominant ideological public commitments, making us less able to recognize contradictions and the incoherency of much news and information that was presented to us as entertainment.[66] The Canadian scholar of rhetoric Jason Hannan has taken up Postman's critique, expanding and updating it to the vastly different terrain of social media. Hannan argues persuasively that in the new terrain of social media, "one of the primary moves is the speech act of trolling," an activity that he analyzes as driven by fear, resentment, and distrust.[67]

Back in the middle of the twentieth century, Alexander Meiklejohn mounted some similar criticisms about the advent of radio technology.[68] Just as people in the early 2000s initially had high hopes for the internet to produce an active, open, critical, and democratic public sphere, Meiklejohn saw such potential with the radio. He hoped that it would enable the expression of differences, the sharing of joys, sorrows, and fears, and most importantly. increase mutual understanding. Yet, without mincing words, Meiklejohn writes: "But never was a human hope more bitterly disappointed. . . . It [radio] is not engaged in enlarging and enriching human communication. It is engaged in making money."[69] He argues that despite the hard work of many intelligent men, the educational value of commercial radio is "terrible destruction." In rather melodramatic fashion, he describes commercial radio as a "catastrophe" that corrupts our morals and intelligence. Today's reader cannot help but think of social media when reading Meiklejohn's scathing criticism of radio, that "it reveals how hollow may be the victories of the freedom of speech when our acceptance of the principle is merely formalistic." Ultimately, Meiklejohn worries that we "are giving the name 'freedoms' to the most flagrant enslavement of our minds and wills."[70]

Just as Meiklejohn's critique of *commercial* radio was a statement not about the technology itself, but about the structures that dominated its usage (especially the for-profit motive), so today we must concern ourselves with the way specific structures and business models of social media dominate the internet. This pattern goes even further back in history. While celebrating and using the new technology of the printing press that vastly increased his ability to reach readers, the Renaissance humanist Erasmus bemoaned its propensity to "fill the world with pamphlets and books that are foolish, ignorant, malignant, libellous, mad, impious and subversive; and such is the flood that even things that might have done some good lose all their goodness."[71]

Platform-Free Expression?

Contemporary scholars and activists have deepened Meiklejohn and Erasmus's insights into how profit mobilizes technology. Scholars have drawn on Karl Marx's notions of commodification and the extraction of surplus value to analyze how capitalism's profit motive plays out in understanding the contemporary world of social media. The details of such analyses are beyond this book, but they demonstrate a long-standing tension between the ideals of critical and inclusive discussion and the practices of the companies that provide the forums for it. Digital economy scholar Nick Srnicek develops an analysis of "platform capitalism," paying greater attention than Zuboff to an array of different types of tech companies beyond social media.[72]

Non- and anti-Marxist scholars also consider the role of private companies' need for profit versus the public good of free expression. Timothy Garton Ash uses the concept of "private owned public spaces" (POPS) to describe the nexus and tensions between the public good of free speech and the influence of private companies over the public good.[73] It is telling that the acronym "POPS" came from urban planning around the turn of the millennium to articulate the resurgence — and address the problems— of the old phenomenon of private development encroaching on public space. Originally, POPS were conceived to enable governments to negotiate with developers to include plazas, parks, atriums, and other public spaces. Although privately owned, these spaces were to be harnessed for the public good: freely accessible and contributing to the livability of urban spaces. For the twenty-first century, Garton Ash updates the concept for the technological domination of the public sphere to understand the ways in which "free" expression plays out on the terrain of social media. But just as governments that negotiate with private developers need to know what the developers' goals are concerning the "public space" for the public good, one too must understand whether the private owners of social media and the discussants around it are aiming for a check on government power, a search for knowledge production and the truth, an increase in democratic participation, or an enlargement of space for individual expression. In the planning realm,

POPS have been criticized for prioritizing the interests of developers and ceding them too much control over such pseudo-public spaces.[74] These critiques also present important parallels to social media, as private companies are granted the wherewithal to generate massive profit on the condition that they devote a proportion — a very small proportion — of their resources for the public good.

The developers of big technology companies defend and attribute their profits and dominance to their high-tech innovations that enable people to access a truly massive amount of information in microseconds and make possible an amazingly connected world. Nevertheless, their success depends on a very specific model of regulation developed thirty years ago, based on older, different technologies of communication and the politics of deregulation of the Reagan era. The founders of Facebook, Google, and Apple did not invent the internet. It was developed initially with public funds by the Advanced Research Projects Agency Network (ARPANET) to connect the US Department of Defense with military contractors and university researchers. The development of standard protocols for transferring data has been essential to its massive expansion and in large part to its privatization. This standardization is a form of regulation. As with many industries, government legislation continues to provide the necessary framework that structures how the internet and social media platforms operate and without which they could not function.

Social Media and the Goals of Free Expression

Scholars, such as Philip Napoli, have focused less on the economic imperatives of social media and more on the problems of the digital public sphere's capability to evaluate anything considered to be in the public interest.[75] Jennifer Petersen argues that "networks and big data restructure speech so that individual users unwittingly produce traces that are made legible by machinic interpretation . . . [and thus] many normative principles central to free speech law are subverted."[76] The Canadian new media and communications scholar Wendy Chun demonstrates just how far big data is from allowing us to tolerate differences or move past earlier discourses (such as eugenics and racist pseudo-science that dehumanized many); in fact, big data serves to re-introduce and exacerbate social conflict and hate.[77]

There are a host of different proposals for reforming these many problems of social media. Of course, there are overlaps with other problems, such as our general dependence on networked technology that can and does fail, as it did with the global outage that disrupted Facebook, Instagram, and WhatsApp operations for nearly six hours in early October 2021, and the Roger's system failure across Canada in July 2022.[78] There is concern that the monopolization of social media by a handful of companies stifles competition from new, innovative companies and technologies. The security of our personal data and the risk of it being used by hackers or businesses, such as insurance companies, is another growing source of anxiety. Many of the proposals I will discuss also attempt to address these problems, but my focus here is on questions of free expression and the requirements for social media to operate effectively as a public, democratic space of critical and inclusive discussion. If we take C. Edwin Baker's position, as discussed in Chapter One, whereby the goal of free expression is not democratic participation nor the creation of new ideas nor the search for knowledge and truth, but is instead solely personal expression, then perhaps today's social media landscape is sufficient. But if we accept any of the other three positions that I considered, today's social media landscape is failing. There is little evidence that social media has increased public discussion in the manner Meiklejohn argues is required for democratic self-governance. As noted above, Mill's and Kant's goals of critical discussion to foster new knowledge, social progress, and "enlightenment" are also threatened in the current social media environment. Viewing the internet as an experiment in free expression as merely the absence of regulation, we can see that what Meiklejohn called "unlimited talkativeness" does not lead to critical and inclusive discussion.

Some proposed reforms for social media are more piecemeal and others more comprehensive. For example, Francis Haugen, the former Facebook developer turned whistle-blower, made public documents that she argued demonstrated Facebook was putting profit before the well-being of the users, empirically confirming the analysis of Zuboff and others discussed above. One of her main suggestions was to force Facebook to revert to its previous practice of not using algorithms and data derived from other users to determine what a user sees on their Facebook feed. Instead, she proposed that the news feeds be displayed in chronological order of items posted by the users' Facebook friends, as

Facebook did before October 2009.[79] Facebook's response was that their research clearly showed that user engagement decreases when news feeds are purely chronological. Nevertheless, government regulation could force social media companies to abandon such manipulation of data; they could make the algorithms public and transparent, or they could at least give users the ability to opt out of their applications.

Others suggest allowing users more choice and input into which algorithms dictate the content they see.[80] Law professors K. Sabeel Rahman and Zephyr Teachout, for instance, argue for a prohibition of targeted ads. Like Zuboff, they contend that the current model that allows social media companies to provide incredibly specific ads on users' feeds based on personal information is a key reason that traditional media cannot compete. More importantly, the model, they assert, drives the incessant push for social media to collect ever more data. Like many harmful products, targeted ads could be restricted.[81] Another proposal would levy a data tax on social media companies that collect personal data.[82]

Critiques of social media often point to user anonymity as a key to the decline in civility and heightened divisions in public discourse. Anonymity allows individuals to evade accountability for what they say. With speakers and audiences often separated by geography, anonymity exacerbates and entrenches the distance between speech and its consequences. The ability to create anonymous user accounts is also central to how artificial bots work to flood social media with divisive, often false, information and opinions.[83] Again, government regulation could compel social media companies to require users to verify their identities.

Such reforms can be thought of as part of a broader campaign to treat social media companies as "information fiduciaries," a concept proposed by Jack Balkin and his co-author, Jonathan Zittrain, a Harvard law professor. They suggest that, like accountants, doctors, and lawyers, social media platforms could be required by law to temper their own interests and act "in trust" of their users: "To deal with the new problems that digital businesses create, we need to adapt old legal ideas to create a new kind of law — one that clearly states the kinds of duties that online firms owe their end users and customers."[84]

From a more technical perspective, Tim Berners-Lee, one of the developers of the standard protocols that made the World Wide Web possible in the 1990s, has similar worries about the dysfunctional nature of current social media "silos." His solution is to change the technical protocols so that individuals control their own data, and accordingly, companies like Facebook or X would have to negotiate fairer ways to access it.[85] Cory Doctorow offers a version of this approach, grounded in an argument that internet technology is already, by default, "interoperable" (meaning, it is designed to be connectable with other technology, either voluntarily or with the capability of being open to adversarial upstarts who build new technology that can interact with established systems, despite the desires of the companies that own the established technologies). Doctorow argues that big tech has used copyright law and Section 230 to fight this inherent interoperability and changing these laws would allow immediate remedies to problems of big tech that could go along with longer-term initiatives to break apart their monopolies.[86]

Such shifts to interoperability would make social media posts more like an email, whereby a post to one social media platform could appear on other platforms, just like one can send and receive emails with other people regardless of one's service provider or email program (for instance, Google Gmail or Microsoft Outlook). Facebook and Instagram, both owned by Meta, already offer such cross-posting options, but more widespread sharing across platforms would decrease the unique attributes of each. Snapchat's defining feature that posts disappear after a given period and X's character limits, for example, would be decreased. Such technological regulations may have noticeable consequences in limiting the power of private social media companies, but it is not too clear whether they would have much impact on the digital public sphere's ability to meet the diverse goals of inclusive and critical discussion.

Organizations like OpenMedia offer a host of proposals to improve social media, including a strong emphasis on education, yet see almost no role for government regulation on the internet.[87] Instead, they encourage an array of non-profit organizations to either compete with or provide alternative platforms that would challenge the dominance of the oligopoly of Meta (Facebook, Instagram), Google (YouTube), and X. These alternatives could be modelled after state-funded public broadcasters or other non-governmental organizations.

Such reforms could contribute to the goals of free expression in fostering more critical and inclusive discussion by decreasing the extent to which the social media companies intervene in and structure online discussions to benefit their bottom line. But, as the next section discusses, many scholars, activists, policy-makers, and politicians doubt that such measures would be sufficient. They call for more systemic changes, including breaking up the big tech companies, or even demanding social media to be a public utility — thereby obliging social media to be, as some describe it, the truly "common carriers" (like phone companies or couriers) that Section 230 regulates them as.

Reforming the Social Media Public Sphere

The most cautious or conservative (both in the literal sense and in the more political sense) proposals for comprehensive social media reform come from those like Peter Menzies — former vice chair of telecommunications with the Canadian Radio-television and Telecommunications Commission (CRTC) and senior fellow at the right-leaning think tank, the Macdonald-Laurier Institute — and Konrad von Finckenstein, former chair of the CRTC. They call their proposal a "social media responsibility act." The proposed legislation would apply to large social media companies and impose on them a "duty of care," clarifying their responsibilities to include the "preservation and promotion of Charter freedoms" and curtailment of the most "heinous adorations" on the internet. They argue that because the Canadian Criminal Code already applies to the internet, the act would supplement existing regulatory structures and would be implemented and enforced through a government council.[88] Their approach would extend the way that the Canadian government regulates banks, older forms of mass media, and other privately owned companies that offer essential services, to encompass social media.[89]

The seemingly more radical proposal to break up big tech also relies on historical precedent to deal with current problems, looking at how antitrust law was used to disassemble monopolies like Bell–AT&T in the 1980s or Standard Oil in the 1910s and 1920s. The co-founder of Facebook, Chris Hughes, argues explicitly that mere government regulation, much of which Facebook is willing to accept, is not sufficient to curtail the harms Facebook creates. Hughes left Facebook in 2007 and has now called for the FCC to break it up. He argues that while Mark Zuckerberg has done nothing wrong and Facebook's success is not due to ill-will, Zuckerberg nonetheless "has created a leviathan that crowds out entrepreneurship and restricts consumer choice." Hughes continues: "It's on our government to ensure that we never lose the magic of the invisible hand."[90] As with many advocates for breaking up big tech,

Hughes's main concern is that their dominance stifles competition and innovation; issues of free expression are secondary.[91] In proposing a government agency to regulate the pieces left after a breakup of the tech giants, Hughes simply shifts questions of free speech from private entities back to the government:

> The agency should create guidelines for acceptable speech on social media. This idea may seem un-American — we would never stand for a government agency censoring speech. But we already have limits on yelling "fire" in a crowded theater, child pornography, speech intended to provoke violence and false statements to manipulate stock prices. We will have to create similar standards that tech companies can use.

In Hughes's dream scenario,

> the biggest winners would be the American people. Imagine a competitive market in which they could choose among one network that offered higher privacy standards, another that cost a fee to join but had little advertising, and another that would allow users to customize and tweak their feeds as they saw fit.

Thus, even though Hughes favours regulation, his vision is still limited to free speech as achieving a check on power; he does not address how a space for critical and inclusive discussion could be fostered in a for-profit environment.

Left-wing politicians like Bernie Sanders and Elizabeth Warren also support dismantling tech monopolies. Elizabeth Warren made breaking up big tech a central plank of her 2020 bid for the presidential nomination. She has long been focused on addressing the monopolies and oligopolies in the banking sector, which has developed to include a broad antitrust position to address economic inequality, fairness, and lack of competition.[92] Sanders focuses on the importance of protecting quality, independent journalism. He proposes antitrust legislation that rejects mergers and prevents the type of dominance that Facebook and Google maintain. His plan also includes strategies noted above, such as taxing targeted advertising and strengthening unions for journalists.[93]

Neil Chilson and Casey Mattox, both senior fellows at the right-wing Charles Koch Institute, offer a critique of such proposals, specifically in response to free speech issues on social media. As they argue, "Many have proposed using antitrust law to address these speech-related concerns. But while antitrust is a powerful tool, it is not the right tool for this job." They doubt whether a larger number of smaller social media companies would lead to a diversity of content moderation practices or any other correctives to free expression issues that plague the internet.[94] The tensions between profit-driven private corporations, especially those that sell targeted ads and utilize other algorithm-driven business models, and the public good of critical and inclusive dialogue will persist even with an increase in the number of smaller social media platforms.

Many scholars, activists, and policy-makers have argued that a solely economic approach to social media reform is not sufficient — they need to be democratized in some way. While these types of proposals, like those discussed above, are often offered as a means of solving problems other than free expression, they still may also help resolve the inherent tensions in protecting and facilitating the public good through critical and inclusive discussion. As legal scholars Sabeel Rahman and Zephyr Teachout argue, any effective proposal "must alter the fundamental business model and dynamics of the firms themselves." They explain why the changes need to be structural: "Measures that fail to do so will leave in place the incentives that drive the problematic practices of surveillance and data mining and negative forms of misinformation and amplification."[95] Rahman and Teachout distinguish structural responses to the problems with social media, like their own public utilities approach, from managerial reforms, like the ones Hughes, Sanders, Warren, von Finckenstein and Menzies offer. Drawing a line between managerial and structural proposals (reform or revolution) is, however, always contentious and perhaps not terribly constructive, yet it reinforces that issues of free speech are always intricately connected to broader social, political, and economic questions as to how democracy works, how resources are distributed, and how society's needs are produced and fulfilled.

Rahman and Teachout place targeted ads at the centre of their public utilities approach. They note that selling ads has been a common method for news media to generate revenue since 1833, when *The New York Sun* introduced it to reduce dramatically the cost of a newspaper — the "penny press," as it was called. But the social media model, they argue, has three profound differences from previous advertising-dependent models: the legal sheltering of social media by Section 230; the harvesting of personal information and attention; and the extraordinary range of activities that increasingly rely on social media, including family gatherings, like birthdays, job searches, public events, and general communication.⁹⁶ Rahman and Teachout argue that banning targeted ads needs to be combined with other structural policies that recognize and address the profit incentives behind social media communication. While critical of any forms of "self-regulation," like Facebook's Oversight Board, they stop short of insisting that we need a social media option outside the for-profit market.

Nick Srnicek also draws on the public utility model but offers a more radical version of "platforms owned and controlled by the people," adding that they be "independent of the surveillance state apparatus." Srnicek calls for "investing the state's vast resources into technology necessary to support these platforms and offering them as public utilities."⁹⁷ Scholars like political scientists Derek Hrynyshyn and James Muldoon have separately developed similar proposals under the concept of "platform socialism,"⁹⁸ while others have offered a like-minded concept of "platform cooperativism."⁹⁹ Although there are important differences among their approaches, they all agree, as Hrynyshyn puts it, that:

> For platforms to serve the public, they must be removed from private operators, and an alternative source of financial support must be found. It may be very difficult to envision the exercise of legal or state power putting an end to the private operation of networking platforms, but if we are to believe in the possibility of a more democratic form of communication, then we need to imagine how platforms could be socialized so as to serve the needs of the public rather than the needs of private capital.¹⁰⁰

As Srnicek indicated, there is concern with governments having too much control, and all of these authors call for decentralization and differing levels of platforms, including local ones. Chapter One demonstrated that understanding free speech as merely the limitation on government power does not capture the goals of critical and inclusive discussion. In a similar manner, limiting the power of both private companies and governments, as many of these proposals rest on, will also not necessarily enable the type of public sphere required for such goals.

Rahman and Teachout insist that the public utility model must enforce both interoperability requirements (so users can move easily between different platforms and carry their own data with them) and equality measures to be used against those companies charging different rates for data transfer to different customers ("price regulations," for example, so as to ensure "fair pricing").[101] Hrynyshyn contends:

> An open source social media platform could serve users as well as the monopolistic platforms do now, without needing to serve the interests of advertisers or corporate owners. It would allow users to customize their own access to information, so that users could control the conditions in which they communicate, rather than having those conditions chosen for them.[102]

Hrynyshyn is aware that while his proposals have consequences for free speech, they do not fully address the issues we confront today:

> Defining exactly what constitutes "fake news" or "hate speech," or whether to prevent the distribution of misinformation about public health crises, for instance, might always be controversial. But there are many forms of communication, such as online harassment, threats of violence, child pornography, and other forms of expression that are universally seen as undesirable and for which freedom of expression is not considered adequate justification, and these forms of content could be stopped by protocols built into platforms at the highest level.[103]

Regardless of their particular focus, these proposals that recognize and confront the inherent tension between private profit and the public good of free expression contribute to our understanding that, as Jack Belkin notes, our constitutional protections against government censorship or overreach are not sufficient for free expression in the digital twenty-first century.

It is most telling that even the more cautious and reformist positions share with "platform socialism" and "platform cooperativism" a vision for a much greater role for non-profit social media platforms. As congressional representative Ro Khanna writes, "Any diversified market of digital platforms should also include social media options, funded by tax dollars and free of data collection, where people can debate ideas without fear of manipulation."[104] Khanna then discusses a host of potential public social media models, including that of PBS, which is funded by corporate and individual donations and is fully independent of the government. Khanna cites current examples, such as the for-profit

Nextdoor app, where people post information about community events and issues in their neighbourhood.[105] More significant perhaps is the "fediverse," a network of consciously smaller online sites and communities that use free open-source software, such as Mastodon and Pixelfed, to create an alternative, community-regulated social media forum.[106] In Robert Gehl's words: "Fediverse sites eschew surveillance capitalism, largely in favour of more mutualist ways of supporting each other," and "can defederate with those who act unethically."[107]

However, as Khanna points out, it is "hard to imagine that any public sites would replace Facebook, Twitter, or other emerging apps as places that drive the national conversation."[108] Rather, he contends that their existence would increase competition, facilitate consumer choice, and enable more public scrutiny. Few readers may have heard of the fediverse, but its presence and impact could grow if the "techlash" against the social media behemoths increases. While this entire discussion opens many cans of worms, it drives home my key argument: that a host of differing appraisals of social media today point beyond a simplistic free marketplace of ideas model to a need for a new model with new measures to protect the quality of social discourse. As Habermas and others have shown, the public sphere of communication is always structured by law, history, and technology. In democratic societies, "we the people" must determine what those structures are and how they support our needs. If we recognize and accept that social media inevitably structures dialogue, we can concentrate on solutions to manage that space to better foster the democratic goals of free speech.

Of course, one could imagine a decentralized, democratic social media environment where users own their own data, have many options for platforms, and can control how they wish to engage, yet they still end up with public discussions dominated by racist, misogynist, and transphobic content and colonialist assumptions that create barriers for many people to participate. Such changes may have many positive effects but still not meet the goals of critical and inclusive discussion. In other words, we should be suspicious of technological fixes for ensuring that public discussion is truly inclusive and critical as opposed to merely abusive and hateful. While the need for engagement and the manipulation of data through algorithms may exacerbate such divisive conflict, its elimination will not necessarily alleviate it. In other words, none of the analyses I have raised makes a persuasive argument that the problem is fundamentally capitalism — be it surveillance, platform, or any other variety — and that none of the other obstacles to free expression can be dealt with until capitalism is vanquished. Such a position would be a form of reductionism that I certainly do not hold. But all the various positions raised in this chapter accept the idea that unfettered individual freedom is similarly reductionist and unrealistic, despite its popularity among free speech advocates. This book does not aim at making proposals for social media reform per se, but rather insists that to address problems with free speech on the internet, we need to have a more nuanced understanding of what free speech is, what are its rationales, and what are its goals.

Summary

Digital technology and social media have changed the way we express ourselves, so it is no surprise that they raise complex issues related to free speech. My goal has been to illuminate how the key qualities of free expression are thrown into relief by examining the structural framework of social media. In the face of general agreement that there are significant downsides and harms of social media, many have clung to the responses of Mchangama, Haidt, and others in doubling down on the principle of free speech and "more speech" as the only possible way forward.

As I have demonstrated, recent free speech controversies rarely address the heart of the problem. Rather, due to their simplistic understanding of free expression that refuses to address the different and sometimes contradictory reasons why we value it, the public discussion of these issues is at best useless, and at worst exacerbates the polarization of society. The internet in general and social media in particular are still venues for knowledge production and dissemination but given the rise of mis- and dis-information, and the frustrations and harms that have ensued, institutions of learning, especially universities that uphold academic freedom, are more suitable and successful. My analysis in this chapter shows how merely negative freedoms that eliminate all regulation, whether governmental or that provided by the platforms themselves, will not likely produce the goals of critical, inclusive, and diverse discussion. Merely restraining government regulation of social media does not necessarily give individuals freedom of speech if the platforms manipulate such expression for their own profit and ends. Instead, the ideals of critical and inclusive discussion must be fostered by positive freedoms. Moreover, whether the goals of free speech are the search and dissemination of truth, a check on the centralization of power over individuals, democratic participation, or solely individuals' ability to express themselves, they will likely clash with, or at least not be a priority for, social media companies aiming at maximizing their profits. This does not mean that the negative freedoms of constitutional protections of free expression are less important. While often lagging behind private organizations in sophistication, governments have learned new ways of suppressing criticism and enforcing their control. Thus, the legal principles curtailing government encroachment on public discussion remain crucial. Perhaps the major tasks facing us are how to address our needs for truly productive discussions that are critical, inclusive, and diverse.

CONCLUSION

THIS BOOK ARGUES THAT FREE SPEECH IS VITAL FOR A DEMOCRATIC, vibrant, diverse, and inclusive society but to understand it as a single idea or principle is to invite confusion, misunderstanding, manipulation, and polarization. Simplistic approaches to free speech as one principle reduce complex questions into a single dimension of whether the speech in question has crossed a line by going too far, or whether it should be allowed. This reduction tends to obscure what are often the crucial questions: Who is making such determinations and by what mechanisms are they discouraging expression, or are they, in fact, suppressing speech? Is it the government, the social media companies, the public, or other individuals or groups who are said to be failing the principles of free speech? What resources are involved in curbing speech, and do they involve government forces, the denial of resources, or the design of the media through which we communicate? Or is the restraint on free speech coming from moral, public persuasion?

More importantly, this book insists that we interrogate *why* free speech is valuable, not only what free speech *entails*. I have shown that there are several different reasons to hold free speech as beneficial, and they have different ramifications. If the objective of free speech is to enable a quest for truth and knowledge, then the implications for it are different than if free expression were primarily needed as a check on the tyranny of the majority inherent in democracy. Academic freedom as instituted at universities is more appropriate for certain types of knowledge production, and tightly controlled rules of speech are, in fact, needed for the types of truth a court of law tries to determine. To check government power, freedom of expression needs to allow falsehoods, lies, and absurdities, including about issues that are not related to public concerns. These goals are different from the case when free speech is deemed a necessary condition for a democracy viewed as self-government because then participation in public discussion about public issues by everyone is key. If the main reason for free speech is that humans require the ability to express themselves — that it is an inherent aspect of being human — then free speech takes on a different meaning altogether.

When other scholars and free speech advocates raise such issues, they most often hold one of these positions and ignore the others, or they assume these importantly different rationales for free speech are complementary, fitting seamlessly together. I have shown this not to be the case, at least for important figures in the so-called Western tradition that is said to have fostered free expression. And I have yet to come across any account that explains how all of these different goals fit together harmoniously. Specifically, Chapter One focused on Kant, Mill, Meiklejohn, and Baker to illustrate how they each answer the above questions differently, leading to distinct conceptions of free speech and why it matters.

We need a set of conceptual tools to address issues that are raised under the moniker of free speech that go far beyond merely taking differing contexts into account. Rather, entirely different distinctions are required when asking how much a government can regulate the expressions of those under its laws as compared to what we should say and how we should say it while participating in a public discussion that we hope to be productive, critical, informative, and ongoing. As discussed in Chapters One and Two, the former questions about government actions rely mostly on judgements as to whether others are harmed, and not on the veracity, accuracy, or wisdom of the speech in question, whereas the latter necessarily involves such qualitative judgements.

Whether we are concerned about government infringements on the freedom of expression or public shaming of certain words or ideas, other distinctions need to come into play. For example, we need to consider whether the speech in question was made in public by someone as an individual; or whether it was made by someone in their capacity as the representative of an organization, such as a media commentator or politician; or whether it was made by a professor in their role as a professor with academic freedom. These considerations led me to propose that we distinguish constitutional principles of the freedom of expression when considering the Canadian Charter right from more general *ideals* of public discussion that include vibrant, open, critical, diverse, and inclusive discussion (which I have shortened to "critical and inclusive discussion"). Both concepts are also different from academic freedom.

I have argued that digital technology that has allowed the development of social media makes these distinctions even more important, but also more contested, as the very structure of our communication becomes increasingly dictated by private companies aimed at making profits.

This book has disambiguated distinct goals and principles so often conflated in the mainstream discussions of free expression. I have done this in part to ward off the danger of merely expanding an already vague idea of free speech to encompass what should be understood as different, and often contrary, principles. For example, numerous advocates of free speech have enlisted Martin Luther King, Jr. to their cause. Jacob Mchangama's *Free Speech: A History from Socrates to Social Media* extols King and his struggles for civil rights and anti-racism as if for him free speech was paramount.[1] This includes referring to King's "Letter from Birmingham Jail" while never addressing King's actual position concerning free speech beyond his famous comments about it in his speech, "I've Been to the Mountaintop": "But somewhere I read of the freedom of assembly . . . the freedom of speech . . . the freedom of press. Somewhere I read that the greatness of America is the right to protest for right."[2] But King here is calling out hypocrisy as he references civil disobedience practice; he is not endorsing a position that freedom of speech is the sole or best strategy to advance towards racial justice. Similarly, the Foundation for Individual Rights and Expression (FIRE) routinely celebrates King and attempts to present him as if he held their views on First Amendment free speech issues.[3] Yet such superficial treatments of King obscure his theorization of civil disobedience that rests on an implicit rejection of a faith that free expression and reason *alone* are sufficient to confront American racism. FIRE, and the other free speech advocates invoking King, somehow omit his thesis: "Always anchor our external *direct action* with the power of economic withdrawal." Of course, King's speech was given in support of striking sanitation workers.[4]

If all that was needed in response to racism was freedom of speech, civil disobedience (including breaking the law) would be unnecessary. King's strategy of civil disobedience is at odds with the belief that Justice Brandeis's "more speech" or Justice Holmes's "free marketplace of ideas," as discussed in Chapter Two, will herald progress against racism in the US. King's argument is that disobeying the law with overt action is required.[5] This is not the optimism in reason and free speech within the framework of law and order that is at the heart of the tradition running from Kant through to Mill and into current mantras about free speech absolutism. Of course, King supported freedom of speech, but to confuse that support with the arguments of Kant or Mill is misleading. King was under no illusion that those in power would relinquish their advantages upon hearing a better argument. Collective direct action and organization are central for King to struggle against the myriad defences of racism, colonialism, and white supremacy.

By presenting these different concepts and distinctions at the heart of different advocations of free expression, I do not hope to solve all of the controversies around free speech. Rather, my goal is to provide some tools so that free speech discussions can be more productive and refrain from repeating the same old oppositions with which we are so familiar: free speech absolutism versus cancel culture.

Moreover, since the most recent outbreak of carnage in the Israel-Palestine conflict, issues of free expression have entered perhaps a new phase. We should not understand this as merely the latest controversy as this is reductive of the life and death issues for thousands or millions of people. This conflict obviously began well before 7 October 2023, as does the struggle for the free expression of Palestinian protests against Israel and problems of antisemitism. I wrote the following section on free speech and the definition of antisemitism early in 2023 and have chosen to preserve its narrow focus. I hope this provides insight into the long-standing nature of these questions, and that debates over the very definition of antisemitism illustrate the complexity of these issues that are best addressed with more than one conceptual tool of free speech.

The Case of Antisemitism and Contested Definitions

My discussion in Chapter Two of the important cases — *Brandenburg v. Ohio* in the US and *R. v. Keegstra* in Canada — provides examples of the central role antisemitism plays in the history of free speech. These cases also highlight a key theme in this book: the critical differences between Canada and the US, including the matter of there being laws against hate speech that are constitutional in Canada, but not in the US. As I noted in the book's preface so as to illustrate this point, Liberal MPs of Canada sent letters to presidents of Canadian universities in December 2023, demanding responses from them that were based on the US legal context, not on Canada's.

In 2010, Canadian sociologists and activists Mary-Jo Nadeau and Alan Sears argued that "the Palestine test is becoming a crucial measure of commitment to freedom of expression, social justice, and academic freedom on North American campuses in the context of a silencing campaign to shut down Palestine solidarity work." They contend that there is a campaign to silence critics of the Israeli occupation of Palestine and the treatment of Palestinian people, including by Canadian politicians, university administrators, and others. They argue that it rests on the logic that "critics of Israeli policies are antisemitic."[6] I will put my framework of distinctions to this "Palestine test" with less than conclusive results precisely because I distinguish between freedom of expression as a legal/constitutional principle and that of academic freedom and social justice, which involves ideals of critical and inclusive discussion and political strategy. I will leave it to others to judge whether this framework passes Nadeau and Sears's Palestine test. Again, my hope for this work is that it generates a more nuanced understanding of the important free speech issues at stake. My own position is that Nadeau and Sears have persuasively demonstrated that such suppression of expression has clearly occurred and continues to this day. But the point of this book is to present a framework of distinctions that allow us to investigate this as a question. To highlight the distinctions concerning free speech articulated in this book, I will restrict my analysis to a specific debate about the definition of antisemitism.

The International Holocaust Remembrance Alliance (IHRA) is an intergovernmental organization founded in 1998 with thirty-five member states, including Canada, that "unites governments and experts to strengthen, advance and promote Holocaust education, research and remembrance."[7] As such, IHRA's actions should have little to do with the negative legal right protecting Canadians from the government of Canada's restriction on their free expression as guaranteed by the Charter. Rather, it is in the realm of the positive effort to foster specific speech involving Holocaust education and awareness.

In 2016, IHRA adopted a "non-legally binding working definition of antisemitism" that reads: "Antisemitism is a certain perception of Jews, *which may* be expressed as hatred toward Jews. Rhetorical and physical manifestations of antisemitism are directed toward Jewish or non-Jewish individuals and/or their property, toward Jewish community institutions and religious facilities" (emphasis added). IHRA added eleven examples of possible manifestations of such antisemitism.[8] Many Jewish organizations, human rights advocates, Palestinian activists, civil liberties groups, and academics have severely criticized the vagueness of the definition, the focus of many of the examples on Israel, and the campaign for its adoption by governments and organizations.[9]

Kenneth Stern, who was involved in drafting the definition, argues that even in its development, "starting in 2010, rightwing Jewish groups took the 'working definition'… and decided to weaponize it." This process, Stern contends, culminated in President Donald Trump's executive order to adopt the IHRA definition. According to Stern, this executive order is an "attack on academic freedom and free speech, and will harm not only pro-Palestinian advocates, but also Jewish students and faculty, and the academy itself."[10]

Regardless of whether one accepts Stern's position, his point can be examined from the tools that this book presents to arrive at a deeper understanding of the issue. Stern uses academic freedom and free speech without articulating any distinction, as well as describes a shift from this definition being offered for general public discussion of antisemitism to its weaponization. This, I argue, is a shift from discussing a definition in the sphere of critical and inclusive discussion to the constitutional or legal sphere of free expression protections. It is one thing to view the IHRA definition as part of public discussion and thus we should consider how critical and inclusive it is. In this context, we should also ask about the extent to which it fosters knowledge production and critical evaluation. Stern explains that the original intent of the IHRA definition was to help those collecting data and monitoring antisemitism, especially across borders. The criteria for such evaluations are ideals of open debate, and, where applicable, academic methodology. But as Stern indicates, the issue becomes quite different when it is moved into the legal arena where governments, along with their resources and coercive capacity, officially adopt such a definition. This is the realm of constitutional protections of freedom of expression but is complicated in this instance because IHRA — made up of government members and experts — labels this a "non-legally binding working definition."

Stern draws a parallel with other discussions of hate speech, noting: "There's no definition of anti-black racism that has the force of law.... If you were to craft one, would you include opposition to affirmative action? Opposing removal of Confederate statues?"[11] Of course, as noted above, hate speech is protected speech in the US under the First Amendment, but Stern's criticism concerns the effects of the government adopting this "non-legally-binding working definition." In places like Canada, where hate speech is a criminal act, such determinations are even more confusing, threatening the constitutional protection of the freedom of expression.

In terms of the ideals of critical and inclusive discussion, definitions are and should be continuously debated. Definitions are incredibly important yet often remain contentious. Even if a certain definition becomes dominant, other definitions remain in the discussion. What constitutes racism? What constitutes patriotism? What constitutes colonialism? What constitutes the state? What constitutes populism? What constitutes sexism, homophobia, or anti-trans statements? These are all debatable questions that are sometimes addressed by attempts at articulating clear definitions but rarely are any such definitions accepted by all or most participants in any discussion. Grappling with differing definitions is part of critical, diverse, and inclusive dialogue. Forcing groups to accept a specific definition, if actual governmental powers come into play, is no longer about critical and inclusive discussion.

In this case, it is a sign of vibrant, critical, and inclusive debate that another group of scholars in the fields of Holocaust history, Jewish studies, and Middle East studies countered the IHRA definition with their own definition. The "Jerusalem Declaration" attempts: "(1) to strengthen the fight against antisemitism by clarifying what it is and how it is manifested," and, "(2) to protect a space for an open debate about the vexed question of the future of Israel/Palestine." To fulfill these goals, they offer a definition that they argue will be more effective in the struggle against antisemitism: "Antisemitism is discrimination, prejudice, hostility or violence against Jews as Jews (or Jewish institutions as Jewish)."[12]

In contrast to this definition, the IHRA definition is very broad and difficult to understand, as critics have noted. For instance: "Antisemitism is a certain perception of Jews" is vague and unclear. What entails the "certain perception?" If someone comments that Jewish people make great food — that the Jewish community has a rich culinary history — is this stereotype antisemitic? The added non-restrictive clause, *which may include,* prior to this core part of the definition, *hatred towards Jews,* is very troubling. Hatred towards Jews is a key element, if not *the* basis, of many definitions of antisemitism, yet is rendered here as merely a *possible* manifestation of "a certain perception." It is no wonder some scholars worry about teaching prominent Jewish intellectuals, such as Hannah Arendt, Judith Butler, Isaiah Berlin, or Moses Maimonides, if the IHRA definition is the official one, with legal or disciplinary power behind it.[13] However, I argue that we need to distinguish free expression from academic freedom and that such scholarly points about teaching should not be lumped in with questions of free expression. It is one thing for someone to question in a public discussion if a stereotype about Jewish people — whether as seemingly innocuous as about food or more troubling concerning money — is antisemitic. It is another thing to do so in a forum where academic freedom holds sway, yet is not extended to protecting antisemitic expression or racism. Chapter Three explained how academic freedom does not protect a professor from confusing astrology and astronomy, but free expression does protect an individual from government censure due to such ignorance. This same distinction is operative in this case: ignorance about aspects of Judaism or Jewish culture is one thing when discussing government censorship and punishing crimes; another in informal conversation; and yet a third matter for a professor teaching in a university classroom.

The eleven examples attached to the IHRA definition have been the centre of even greater critical debate. In explaining these examples, IHRA states: "Manifestations might include the targeting of the state of Israel, conceived as a Jewish collectivity." This is followed by eleven examples, six of which reference the state of Israel. Proponents like Aidan Fishman, former director of B'nai Brith Canada's League for Human Rights, interpret the definition and examples to mean that the Boycott, Divestment and Sanctions (BDS) movements would constitute antisemitism if such supporters did not also call for similar actions against Iran.[14] Where Fishman favours the IHRA definition for this reason, many critics agree with him about the implication of the definition but reject it for this same reason. For them, this amounts to silencing important movements based on human rights and combatting injustice, including criticisms of the state of Israel and its policies by stipulating that all states who meet some vague notion of similar actions must be included. In many instances, BDS movements target the US or Canadian governments for supporting Israel, when they do not, for example, send aid or weapons to Iran. The statement of the Canadian Jewish Faculty Network — signed by over 150 members, many of whom are prominent scholars — specifically notes that one of their key worries about the IHRA definition is that it conflates antisemitism with criticisms of Israel in its relation to Palestine: "We recognize that the Boycott, Divestment and Sanctions (BDS) movement is a legitimate, non-violent form of protest. While not all of us endorse the BDS movement we oppose equating its support with antisemitism."[15]

My role here is not to judge the merit of the IHRA definition, the attached examples, or the debate that has ensued, although I strongly agree with the many critics. Rather my point is to illustrate how the legal principle of the freedom of expression can and should be distinguished from the value of critical and inclusive discussion and both should be distinguished from academic freedom.

I do not think it makes sense to explicitly challenge the IHRA definition on Charter grounds or the First Amendment. It is one definition among others and should be able to be expressed. It is fair, of course, to raise all the challenges noted above, especially that the definition closes down criticisms of Israel, including Palestinian perspectives on the Israel/Palestine conflict. That is, critics can challenge the extent to which this particular definition fails to live up to the ideals of critical and inclusive discussion. But to attempt to get governmental bodies to accept it introduces dangerous confusions that enter into questions of the suppression of the legal principle of free expression.

In terms of critical and open discussion, those who reject the IHRA definition, especially if they do so vehemently and categorically, should realize that its proponents will be unlikely to participate further in their discussions or work with them to alleviate antisemitism. Likewise, if those who endorse IHRA's position do not listen to and address their critics, they can hardly expect any dialogue to reach their goals of arriving at a greater understanding and apprehension of the truth, making progress towards a better society, or fulfilling the need for humans to express themselves, as we saw in Chapter One. But advocating or criticizing this definition or any definition is *not in itself* contrary to the ideals of critical and inclusive discussion unless it is presented as having the force of government or institutional policy behind it. The differences in definitions are likely rooted in deep disagreements about the history of Israel, the treatment of Palestinians, and other political values. One can idealistically hope that all sides continue to communicate and openly present their positions. In reality, this depends on some mutual goodwill and faith that such discussions can be productive. It is perfectly reasonable to decide that either those who disagree are not acting in good faith or that one's own moral and political starting premises are so divergent, that critical and inclusive dialogue is no longer possible. In this case, idealistic appeals to critical and inclusive continued discussion seem unlikely. This is one reason why we cannot hold up ideals of critical and inclusive dialogue as being the only avenue for progress and justice. My previous example of Martin Luther King, Jr., is another such example.

There are some parallels with public discussion concerning racism. Some argue that being critical of racism is most effective when we do not call individuals themselves racist.[16] Others disagree, arguing that calling individuals out as racist is necessary. Of course, no one can or should be *forced* to listen to or feel compelled to argue with those with radically different definitions and perspectives. The ideals of critical and inclusive discussion are just that, *ideals*. Laurie Penny has eloquently defended her refusal to debate white supremacists as she has no faith that the spectacles created by such debates are in any sense constructed as potentially fruitful and respectful dialogue. Indeed, as Penny asks, how can one have such a dialogue with those who hold white supremacist views?[17]

All these questions relate to issues raised in the Introduction concerning the 2020 *Harper's* Letter that calls for open and even "caustic" speech, decrying the "new set of moral attitudes and political commitments that tend to weaken our norms of open debate and toleration of differences in favor of ideological conformity."[18] However, they are distinguishable from the legal or constitutional questions of the freedom of expression and from academic freedom. Here, too, it matters whether one's primary goal is the search for truth and knowledge, as John Stuart Mill argued, in which case the focus would be on discovering the best definition for, or a deeper understanding of, antisemitism. And the limit would be determined, according to Mill, if this definition constituted harm or excited an angry mob. For those focused more on the human need for expression, as articulated by C. Edwin Baker, the focus would be on public discussion as a vehicle for such expression (including overtly antisemitic expression). If public discussion is a key venue for democratic participation, yet other considerations would come to the fore, one could argue that antisemitism, being based in hate, is akin to what Alexander Meiklejohn argued about sedition and treason: none is really about public good.[19]

Of course, the distinction between legal and constitutional protections of free expression and critical and inclusive discussion is not absolute. If speech in the realm of public discussion causes harm, whether it defames, infringes copyright, or provokes hate and violence, legal questions must kick in. IHRA defends its definition by arguing that antisemitic expression does harm, and most critics of IHRA agree with this position. But to my knowledge, no defenders of the IHRA definition contend that antisemitism, by this "non-legally binding working definition," constitutes legal defamation. And I have not seen any discussion that the US is a different case since hate speech is protected by the First Amendment, whereas in most countries, including Canada, hate speech laws are constitutional.

In the realm of critical and inclusive public discussion, we should ask if there is any evidence that the IHRA definition is more effective at combatting the harms of antisemitism than the other definitions. Specifically, are definitions of antisemitism actually more effective if they are not so vague and broad as IHRA's version? Would a definition that allows greater attention to building solidarity with Palestinian and anti-colonial struggles be more successful? In a sense, these are strategic questions.

While we need to consider free speech both in relation to the ideals of critical and inclusive discussion and the constitutional protections of free expression, as Stern describes, the situation changes categorically when the question is the adoption of the IHRA definition by national, provincial, or municipal governments. As discussed in the Introduction and Chapter Two, governments often take actions related to encouraging certain types of speech not related to the constitutional protections of freedom of expression. But were a government to withdraw funding from organizations, including universities, because they chose not to adopt the IHRA definition, or because they were deemed antisemitic solely based on this definition, it would certainly veer into the realm of obstructing the freedom of expression, and, in the case of universities, academic freedom.[20]

The Canadian government adopted the IHRA definition in 2019, as have many provincial and municipal governments. This is very problematic and creates confusion, especially as the definition is a "non-legally binding working definition." It becomes unclear how this definition is related to the Canadian Criminal Code which uses the term "antisemitism" but does not define it. Section 319 (2.1) states,

> Everyone who, by communicating statements, other than in private conversation, wilfully promotes antisemitism by condoning, denying or downplaying the Holocaust (a) is guilty of an indictable offence and liable to imprisonment for a term not exceeding two years; or (b) is guilty of an offence punishable on summary conviction.[21]

While not a definition per se, it qualifies antisemitism in relation to denying the reality of the Holocaust. If there is also a "non-legally binding working" definition of antisemitism that is much broader and some see as including many criticisms of Israel, and the government has adopted this definition, we have competing assessments of what "wilfully promot[ing] antisemitism" entails.

The Canadian government presents its adoption of the IHRA definition as part of its plan to strengthen Canadian hate speech laws in the Criminal Code.[22] This goes well beyond the type of positive encouragement that governments necessarily take part in that I discussed in Chapter Two. It clearly blurs the line between the ideals of critical and inclusive discussion (that even governments can play a part in) and the freedom of expression as a legal principle that should restrain government action from infringing on its citizens' ability to participate in a free exchange of ideas.

Similarly, in 2022, when the Manitoba provincial government adopted the IHRA definition, the Minister of Culture, Andrew Smith, stated, "By adopting this definition of antisemitism, we are empowering our policymakers, law enforcement agencies and community leaders with a critical framework they can use to identify, understand and combat contemporary forms of antisemitism in public life, the media, schools, workplaces and religious spheres."[23] To the extent that these are more than mere words, it would seem that as opposed to being a "non-legally binding wording definition," compatible with the ideals of critical and inclusive discussion, the IHRA definition is being incorporated into the legal realm and contravenes the freedom of expression.

Defining Antisemitism and Academic Freedom

While not invoking a distinction between academic freedom and free expression, Jeffrey Sachs, a political scientist at Acadia University, critiques the IHRA definition, arguing that:

This is about targeting critics of Israel and pro-Palestinian activists, especially those on university campuses. Supporters have been quite clear on this point, suggesting, for example, that universities should use the new definition to censure and silence popular campus events like Israel Apartheid Week and movements like Boycott, Divestment, and Sanctions (BDS)."[24]

Focusing more specifically on academic freedom, Abigail Bakan and her co-authors observe: "On campuses where this definition has been adopted, it's been used to intimidate and silence the work of unions, student groups, academic departments and faculty associations that are committed to freedom, equality and justice for Palestinians."[25] Both critiques are substantial, although I argue there is much to be gained by distinguishing more clearly the issues of academic freedom from the general questions of the freedom of expression, however much they often intermingle and overlap in the realm of extramural academic freedom (as discussed in Chapter Three).

A panel discussion entitled, "My Jerusalem," held at the University of Winnipeg in February 2018, illustrates how academic freedom can be infringed upon when a university adopts and uses the IHRA definition. The event was sponsored by a coalition of community groups, including Independent Jewish Voices–Winnipeg, the United Jewish People's Order–Winnipeg, and the Canadian Arab Association of Manitoba. Some of the participants were academics, and the Global College, a unit of the university, also sponsored the event. According to the official University of Winnipeg statement, the administration received complaints about the event being "anti-Israel."[26] The university has a "Respectful Workplace and Learning Environment" policy so that "members of the University community" can conduct their activities in a respectful environment, free of harassment and discrimination.[27] In addition to covering students, faculty, and staff, the policy applies to all visitors on campus. Following this policy, a committee made up of two administrators and one faculty member was struck to investigate the complaints. Its response explained: "For the purpose of the review analysis, the IHRA definition of anti-Semitism was applied. The review determined that certain statements made at the event could be considered anti-Semitic under this definition."[28] It did not acknowledge that the IHRA definition was supposed to be a "non-legally-binding working definition." The committee stated six "concerns," including that "speakers at the event made comments that were anti-Semitic." Another "concern" was that the Global College had "rebuffed suggestions by B'nai Brith Canada to include an authentic Jewish perspective," without explaining on what authority B'nai Brith might overrule the organizers' decisions about appropriate content for their event and what constitutes "an authentic Jewish perspective." This is particularly alarming given that the event's organizers included Independent Jewish Voices and the United Jewish People's Order. The committee made eight recommendations, and the university issued a public statement. One could argue that because the Charter does not apply to universities here, one is dealing only with ideals of critical and inclusive discussion and academic freedom for the professors involved. If this were the case, the complaint process was solely B'nai Brith (and perhaps others) voicing their perspectives. Use of the "Respectful Workplace and Learning Environment" policy, however, brings it into direct conflict with academic freedom, as that policy also governs the conduct of every professor working at the university. Moreover, critical and inclusive discussion does not take place through the type of complaint mechanism of the "Respectful Workplace and Learning Environment" policy. This situation seems similar to Stern's contention that the IHRA definition is being "weaponized," and is not contributing to the ideals of free expression as critical and inclusive discussion.

Proponents of the IHRA definition specifically reject the idea that it is an infringement on academic freedom:

> It's important to know that the IHRA definition does not, as is often alleged by its detractors, prohibit free speech and 'academic freedom.' People on campus are free to criticize any Israeli policy that they wish, just as we in Canada freely criticize our own government's policies. What IHRA does is provide a guideline for distinguishing between valid criticism and nefarious forms of demonization that can appropriately be characterized as antisemitic.[29]

Whether we agree the definition adequately clarifies that distinction, the point of academic freedom is that such guidelines are determined by academics, not university administrators, government officials, nor other external bodies.

Independent Jewish Voices Canada has collated a long list documenting how the IHRA definition has been used to "to cancel events or silence Palestine solidarity movements," including many hosted by universities.[30] The *Jewish Journal* finds that one in five universities in the UK have adopted the IHRA definition.[31] Thus, there is ample evidence that this definition is having an impact that both undermines critical and inclusive discussion, as well as curtails academic freedom. The Canadian Association of University Teachers (CAUT) has also found that the adoption of the IHRA definition of antisemitism by universities infringes on academic freedom. At a November 2021 meeting, the CAUT Council unanimously adopted a resolution:

> Be it resolved that CAUT opposes the adoption of IHRAWDA [International Holocaust Remembrance Alliance Working Definition of Antisemitism] at Canadian universities and colleges. CAUT supports the academic freedom of its members and recognizes the need to safeguard the rights of scholars to develop critical perspectives on all states, including the state of Israel, without fear of outside political influence, cuts to funding, censorship, harassment, threats, and intimidation.[32]

Part of its rationale was that:

> The IHRAWDA poses a significant threat to academic freedom at Canadian universities and colleges and has already been used on a number of occasions to censor and impede the academic freedom of teachers and researchers who have developed anti-racist and decolonial perspectives on the policies and practices of the state of Israel.

Some of those occasions are documented by Jasmine Zine, Greg Bird, and Sara Matthews in their article, "Criticizing Israel Is Not Antisemitic — It's Academic Freedom."[33]

In sum, by applying my distinctions regarding free expression as the ideals associated with critical and inclusive discussion, free expression as a legal or constitutional principle restraining government (or institutional) prohibition, and academic freedom to the case of the IHRA definition, one can see these are not simple concepts with watertight boundaries separating them. But the distinctions can still help. In the realm of critical and inclusive discussion, one must expect differing definitions and debates concerning any important concept, most especially one such as this one. To the extent that the disagreements have been so great that they have obstructed further discussion and potential cooperation (in this case, in fighting antisemitism), the ideals have failed. To the extent that collaboration and the increase of knowledge were possible prior to such breakdowns, it is regrettable, yet predictable and common, especially concerning such controversial political issues as this one.

When the same issue of defining antisemitism enters the realm of the legal or constitutional principle of freedom of expression, however, things are very different. In this case, such problems are exacerbated both by the self-declared status of being a "non-legally binding working definition," and by the adoption of it by governments, especially as it relates that adoption to legal and juridical procedures. In the latter case, it is difficult to see how its use is not an infringement on academic freedom.

Moving Forward:
Opening Free Speech to Truly New Ideas

In addition to providing conceptual tools to foster understanding of free speech controversies, this book engages in a more thorough rethinking of free expression. The rise of social media is one immediate reason for the need for this work, but equally important is whether our current understanding of free expression is meeting the goals for effectively advancing new and better ideas. Free expression has come to mean the freedom to repeat endlessly the same old arguments — whether they are racist, sexist, colonialist, or homophobic — without thoughtfully considering new and challenging ideas that may lead to a substantial increase in our understanding. This has led many to accept P.E. Moskovitz's assessment that free speech is an empty concept, only useful as a shield for regressive speech. My hope is to reinvigorate discussions of free speech at a deeper and more meaningful level.

This book has clung closely to the terrain of contemporary free speech debates with their historical roots in the modern "Western" tradition of Kant, Mill, and others. My rationale for this approach concerns the dominance and nature of free speech conceptions of this so-called Western tradition, and how they fit within structures of the Canadian Charter, academic freedom, and current social media. They have a powerful hold on how people think about free expression.

My approach, what can be called "immanent critique," has limits and disadvantages, as well as advantages. In focusing on the dominant ways free speech has been understood and discussed, this book can ironically obscure alternative perspectives. Indeed, I have not engaged with Indigenous, postcolonial, or any non-European traditions of critical and inclusive dialogue in this study. This is work that desperately needs doing.

To shake up and change the dominance of the European, American, and Canadian approaches to free speech, we need to work from both inside and outside of common-sense understandings of free speech. My hope is that this book constitutes the part of that project that acts from the inside of these debates — the immanent critique — by showing the cracks and fissures at the centre of the dominant tradition of free expression. I see this book as a small part of the wider movements that are more open to a variety of truly new, diverse, and challenging ideas. I have tried to uncover the dysfunctions in our conversations about free speech, whether they occur on social media or in the university classroom. The next step, in my view, is to look outside of the well-worn path of free speech discourse. For example, I have a lot to learn from the insights of Indigenous studies professor David Newhouse (Onondaga) who uses the metaphor of Teiakwanahstahsontéhrha′ — "extending the rafters" — to discuss academic freedom. When the Haudenosaunee longhouses could no longer contain the growing families, Newhouse recounts, the houses remained intact but the new family members would be integrated within it by extending the rafters. "Academic freedom," he explains, "is about the capacity of the system to welcome and create space for Indigenous speech and knowledge that has been excluded."[34]

Newhouse describes how he was guided by Chickasaw scholar Eber Hampton who himself had been guided by an Elders Advisory Committee at First Nation University of Canada (FNUNIV) when he was president there. The committee was struck to address concerns about academic freedom and it included Cree Elders who advised Hampton that faculty and academic staff at FNUNIV were tasked to tell the truth. From his own conversation with Hampton, who recounted this lesson, Newhouse notes how he has been guided "over the years" to "see academic freedom through this Cree lens: it's the responsibility to speak the truth." Newhouse explains:

> Speaking the truth also means making the grounds that I use for my truth claims visible so that it can be evaluated by others. The exercise of my responsibility also means that I have to make room for other truth claims. I don't have to agree with others' truths, but I have to respect them.

Perhaps most significantly, Newhouse highlights the importance of realizing that "engaging in a dialogue may result in the emergence of additional truths as we bring our minds together."[35]

Newhouse describes academic freedom from Indigenous perspectives in a way that could help us move beyond the difficulties of free speech debates, especially as they pertain to social media:

> Indigenous scholarship comes to the table with a central notion of "complex understanding." Complex understanding occurs when we begin to see phenomenon from various perspectives and to discern the relationships among these perspectives.... It allows for our understandings to change depending upon where we stand to see or upon the time that we look or who is doing the looking.[36]

Such complex understanding seems to be what is missing in our increasingly polarized public discussion. Just as Newhouse never claims that Cree or Onondaga understandings have some monopoly on the appreciation of diverse perspectives, so we too must accept this is true for the Western tradition, however defined.

Anishinaabe legal scholar John Borrows demonstrates how Indigenous law on Turtle Island, like most legal traditions, derives from different sources, including customary and positive law, but also deliberative law.[37] He explains how the Anishinaabe concept of dibenindizowin ("freedom") is closely related to that of mino-bimaadiziwin ("living well in this world"), and he describes the latter as focusing "on living well and giving expression to visions of life as we alone understand them, in responsible relationship with others."[38] While Borrows may not have been thinking of contemporary issues of free speech, his discussion of freedom is relevant:

> Dissent is a very important practice that can lead towards freedom, if its strength is directed towards the pursuit of a good life, or *mino-bimaadiziwin,* with its many paths and meanings.

However, unqualified dissent for its own sake, detached from context, and regarded as an absolute value, can ensnare people and nations in its conceptual grip.[39]

I want to be careful not to decontextualize Borrows's point here, but it seems to be an apt description of the current state of free speech discussions ensnared in a linear perspective judged by some boundary separating what should be allowed and what the government or public opinion should not allow. This captures much of my worry about the *Harper's* Letter, as described in the Introduction, concerning "caustic" speech.

There are two related points, neither of which I explored in this book. One concerns the non-Western roots of the current dominant traditions of free speech. John Mohawk has demonstrated how Haudenosaunee and other Indigenous peoples in North America "carried with other's differences of religion, of all those things which got attached to the [American] Bill of Rights."[40] More work needs to be done to show how the so-called Western tradition is far from hermetically sealed and we cannot define the problematic concept of the West through some circular reference to free speech, as evident in the work of scholars like Stephen A. Smith, Timothy Garton Ash, and Robert M. Hutchins, as I discussed in Chapter One.[41]

The second point that requires more work is for those like myself engaged in these dominant free speech debates to seek out and learn from diverse perspectives, especially from those people and traditions that have and continue to experience colonialism and racist oppression. It is for this reason that the ideals of truly critical and inclusive discussion have been a major focus of this book. Such dialogue needs to include a general diversity of perspectives and positions, and more specifically, it needs to include the viewpoints of people who have diverse experiences. The recent push towards what is labelled "viewpoint diversity" is a backlash that tries to obscure differences of experience and elevate conservative voices that feel unheard or unsuccessful in convincing others of their ideas. Thus, by "inclusive," I do not only mean that each of us as individuals needs to *feel* included, but that people who have been and continue to be discriminated against, oppressed, marginalized, and exploited need to have their perspectives taken seriously.

By critical, I mean that taken-for-granted ideas must be challenged, but also this needs to be done in a truly open and genuine way. The Anishinaabeg phrase, mino-bimaadiziwin, as noted by Borrows, or the

Cree one of mino-pimatisiwin, usually translated into English as "in a good way," "living well in this world," or "the good life,"[42] have started to be used more often in public spaces, becoming phrases heard at many public events that I have attended in Winnipeg. As I learn more about mino-bimaadiziwin, I think it has much to add to my understanding of approaching discussion "in a good way," as distinct from the call for "caustic speech" that I have discussed in reference to the *Harper's* Letter. This also includes not conducting discussions always as a win-or-lose debate, as a game or a battle, where the sentiments expressed are disconnected from the practices of people's lives and the effects of the debates. To reap the benefits from free expression in all its dimensions and meanings, we must learn to engage in a good way — in mino-bimaadiziwin.

NOTES

Preface

1. Tascha Shahriari-Parsa, "It's Time for Progressives to Recommit to Academic Freedom," *The Nation*, 25 June 2024. thenation.com/article/archive/progressives-academic-freedom-gaza-harvard-law-review/.
2. Alexandra Holyk, "Winnipeg MP Signs Letter Calling on University Presidents to Address Antisemitism on Campus," *CTV News*, 15 December 2023. winnipeg.ctvnews.ca/winnipeg-mp-signs-letter-calling-on-university-presidents-to-address-antisemitism-on-campus-1.6690022.
3. See Government of Canada, *Criminal Code*, RSC, 1985, c. C–46. laws-lois.justice.gc.ca/eng/acts/c-46/; and Mohamed Berrada, "Balancing Respect and Freedom in an Era of Global Tensions," *University Affairs/Affaires Universitaires*, 14 February 2024. universityaffairs.ca/features/feature-article/balancing-respect-and-freedom-in-an-era-of-global-tensions/.
4. See Colleen Flaherty, "Diversifying a Classic Humanities Course," *Inside Higher Ed*, 11 April 2018. insidehighered.com/news/2018/04/12/responding-student-criticism-its-foundational-humanities-course-too-white-reed.
5. Bryan Denson, "1998 Story: Legacy of a Hate Crime: Mulugeta Seraw's Death a Decade Ago Avenged," *The Oregonian*, 12 November 2014.
6. Denson, "1998 Story."
7. Rob London, "Sending a $12.5 Million Message to a Hate Group," *New York Times*, 26 October 1990. nytimes.com/1990/10/26/news/sending-a-12.5-million-message-to-a-hate-group.html.
8. Brianna Booker, "Mulugeta Seraw (1960–1988)," *BlackPast*, 30 August 2020. blackpast.org/african-american-history/mulugeta-seraw-1960-1988/.
9. Lee Romney, "Metzger Seized by Canadian Authorities After Speech," *LA Times*, 30 June 1992. latimes.com/archives/la-xpm-1992-06-30-me-1437-story.html.
10. Tess Riski and Aaron Mesh, "Kyle Brewster, Convicted in 1988 Killing of Mulugeta Seraw, Fought at Jan. 6 Pro-Trump Rally in Salem," *Willamette Week*, 17 January 2021. wweek.com/news/2021/01/17/kyle-brewster-convicted-in-1988-killing-of-mulugeta-seraw-fought-at-jan-6-pro-trump-rally-in-salem/.

Introduction

1. Bethany Lindsay, "B.C. Doctor Disciplined for 'Harmful' COVID-19 Misinformation Claims Free Speech Violations," *CBC News*, 7 July 2021. cbc.ca/news/canada/british-columbia/bc-stephen-malthouse-doctors-petition-college-1.6092437.

2   Madeline Smith, "Kenney Follows Ford's Push for Campus Free Speech," *Toronto Star*, 8 May 2019. thestar.com/calgary/2019/05/06/alberta-and-ontario-premiers-campus-free-speech-policies-a-dog-whistle-blow-for-the-right-expert.html.

3   Peter Ives and Eve Haque, "What is Québec's Bill 32 on Academic Freedom and Why Does it Matter," *The Conversation*, 1 June 2022. theconversation.com/what-is-quebecs-bill-32-on-academic-freedom-and-why-does-it-matter-183122.

4   Cecilia Kang, "What is Facebook's Oversight Board?" *New York Times*, 5 May 2021. nytimes.com/2021/05/05/technology/What-Is-the-Facebook-Oversight-Board.html.

5   The sense of line drawing is ubiquitous from a wide range of methodological and ideological perspectives; for example, see Stephen A. Smith, "Introduction: Welcome to the Conversation," in *Freedom of Expression* (Oxford: Oxbridge Research Associates, 2018), xvi; P.E. Moskowitz, *The Case Against Free Speech* (New York: Bold Type Book, 2019), 12–27; CBC Radio, "Free Speech On Campus: Where Should Universities Draw the Line?" 22 June 2018. cbc.ca/radio/outintheopen/free-speech-on-campus-where-should-universities-draw-the-line-1.4712119; Zach Beauchamp, "The 'Free Speech Debate' Isn't Really About Free Speech," *Vox*, 22 July 2020. vox.com/policy-and-politics/2020/7/22/21325942/free-speech-harpers-letter-bari-weiss-andrew-sullivan.

6   For an interesting discussion of the free speech absolutism of US Supreme Court Justice Hugo Black, see Scott Gerber, "The Politics of Free Speech," *Social Philosophy and Policy* 21, 2 (July 2004): 23–47. Gerber argues that even Black's free speech absolutism is not quite so absolute.

7   See Twitter's statement, "Sensitive Media Policy," help.twitter.com/en/rules-and-policies/media-policy. The role of pornography in the development of the internet is, of course, much more complex. See, for example, Wendy Hui Kyong Chun, "Screening Pornography," in *Control and Freedom* (Boston: MIT Press, 2008), 77–127.

8   See the podcast *Sway* where host Kara Swisher interviews George Farmer: "One Year After the Jan. 6 Attack, Parler's C.E.O. Grapples with Big Tech and Trump," 6 January 2022, produced by *New York Times*. nytimes.com/2022/01/06/opinion/sway-kara-swisher-george-farmer.html.

9   See Chapter Four and Shoshana Zuboff, *The Age of Surveillance Capitalism* (London: Profile Books, 2019).

10 Richard Moon, *The Constitutional Protection of Freedom of Expression* (Toronto: University of Toronto Press, 2000), 19.

11 Timothy Garton Ash, *Free Speech: Ten Principles for a Connected World* (New Haven: Yale University Press, 2016), 73. The American Civil Liberties Union (ACLU) lists three different reasons why free expression is essential: "self-fulfillment," "the attainment and advancement of knowledge, and the search for truth," and because it "gives the American people a 'checking function' against government excess and corruption." See ACLU, "Free Expression," 1 March 2002. aclu.org/documents/freedom-expression. See also Frederick Schauer, *Free Speech: A Philosophical Inquiry* (Cambridge: Cambridge University Press, 1982), 15.

12 Schauer, 85.

13 Jacob Mchangama, *Free Speech: From Socrates to Social Media* (New York: Basic Books, 2022).
14 Mchangama, *Free Speech*, 233–56; 147–69; and 10–11, 38–43, and 63–91.
15 Arlene Saxonhouse is one of the few scholars of free speech more keenly aware of the discrepancies between differing philosophical approaches to free speech, but ultimately, she too is searching for the congruence among Athenian "free speech" and rarified conceptions of philosophy and democracy; see Saxonhouse, *Free Speech and Democracy in Ancient Athens* (Cambridge: Cambridge University Press, 2006).
16 Schauer, 86.
17 Moskowitz, *The Case Against Free Speech*, 2, 44, 205–09. See also Anthony Leaker, *Against Free Speech* (Lanham, Maryland: Rowman & Littlefield), 2020.
18 Stanley Fish, *There's No Such Thing As Free Speech* (Oxford: Oxford University Press, 1994), 102. See also Stanley Fish, *The First: How to Think about Hate Speech, Campus Speech, Religious Speech, Fake News, Post-Truth, and Donald Trump* (New York: Atria, 2019).
19 Fish, *The First*, 52–59, 77.
20 Some readers may recognize an allusion here to Ludwig Wittgenstein's famous discussion of "language games" in *Philosophical Investigations*, trans. G.E.M. Anscombe (New York: Macmillan, 1953).
21 Garton Ash provides an interesting discussion, emphasizing the necessity of "positive freedom" of speech and arguing that all humans should be both free and *able* to express themselves. Garton Ash, *Free Speech*, 120.
22 BBC News Online, "Trump Sues Twitter, Google and Facebook Alleging 'Censorship,'" *BBC News*, 7 July 2021. bbc.com/news/world-us-canada-57754435.
23 Elizabeth A. Harris and Alexandra Alter, "Simon & Schuster Cancels Plans for Senator Hawley's Book," *New York Times*, 7 January 2021. nytimes.com/2021/01/07/books/simon-schuster-josh-hawley-book.html.
24 While there seems to be some evidence of intentional conflation and opportunism here, more often than not these ideas are presented in good faith, though from confused approaches, in my opinion. There are many on the left who also take such undifferentiated advocacy of all free expression, often with the argument that any restrictions on free expression will be used most vociferously against the marginalized and oppressed. See, for example, Samir Gandesha, "In Defense of Free Speech," *Canadian Dimension*, 13 March 2018. canadiandimension.com/articles/view/in-defense-of-free-speech.
25 Bhikhu Parekh has made a persuasive argument of the advantages of using "Western" and "Non-Western" to categorize approaches to political theory despite all its problems. See Bhikhu Parekh, "Non-Western Political Thought," in *The Cambridge History of Twentieth-Century Political Thought*, eds. Terence Ball and Richard Bellamy (Cambridge: Cambridge University Press, 2006), 553–78.
26 "A Letter on Justice and Open Debate," *Harper's Magazine*, 7 July 2020. harpers.org/a-letter-on-justice-and-open-debate/.
27 Of course, the context of Brandeis's legal judgement was government censorship and the First Amendment, not any vague ideal of open debate and critical culture.

28 Jeet Heer, "The Left Needs to Reclaim Free Speech," *The Nation*, 10 July 2020. thenation.com/article/society/left-free-speech-harpers/.
29 See Beauchamp, "The 'Free Speech Debate.'"
30 "Caustic" can also mean sarcastic which introduces other questions of how such speech is beneficial for open and critical debate if reason and mutual communication are presumed to be the basis of such debate.
31 For example, see Colby Cosh, "Is Neil Young's Stand Against Joe Rogan the Natural Outcome of 1960s Anti-Corporate Spirit?" *The National Post*, 28 January 2022. nationalpost.com/opinion/colby-cosh-is-neil-youngs-stand-against-joe-rogan-the-natural-outcome-of-1960s-anti-corporate-spirit; Kalin M. Williams, "Neil Young and Joni Mitchell are Destroying Free Speech," 29 January 2022. medium.com/the-riff/neil-young-and-joni-mitchell-are-destroying-free-speech-c92fdff6c732; or Zaid Jilani, "Heart of Scold," *City Journal*, 28 January 2022. city-journal.org/neil-young-v-joe-rogan-and-free-speech. Lost in most of these diatribes is the fact that Spotify had previously removed thousands of podcasts, including *The Joe Rogan Experience* episodes featuring interviews with white supremacists Gavin McInnes and Alex Jones. Eamonn Forde, "Rogan in the Free (Speech) World," *Forbes*, 25 January 2022. forbes.com/sites/eamonnforde/2022/01/25/rogan-in-the-free-speech-world-neil-young-wants-to-pull-music-from-spotify-over-podcast-host-controversy/?sh=1220be444fdd.
32 Neil Young Archives, "Spotify: More Songs and Less Sounds," 28 January 2022. neilyoungarchives.com/news/1/article?id=Spotify-More-Songs-Less-Sound.
33 Jilani, "Heart of Scold."
34 Conceptually, this is related to the key debate about whether boycotts are expression. See Laura Weinrib, *The Taming of Free Speech* (Cambridge, Mass.: Harvard University Press, 2016), 82–110.
35 As reported in Anastasia Tsioulcas, "David Crosby, Graham Nash and Stephen Stills Ask to Pull Their Content from Spotify," *NPR Music News*, 2 February 2022. npr.org/2022/02/02/1077653424/crosby-stills-nash-young-spotify.
36 Indeed, in March 2024, both Young and Mitchell returned to Spotify. See Laura Snapes, "Joni Mitchell Follows Neil Young in Returning Her Music to Spotify," *The Guardian*, 22 March 2024. theguardian.com/music/2024/mar/22/joni-mitchell-follows-neil-young-in-returning-her-music-to-spotify.
37 For a thorough analysis, see Ralph Wilson and Isaac Kamola, *Free Speech and Koch Money: Manufacturing a Campus Culture War* (London: Pluto Press, 2021).
38 Brian Leiter, "The Case Against Free Speech," *The Sydney Law Review* 38 (2016): 407–39.
39 For example, see Leonard Pitts, "Freedom of Speech Is Not Freedom from Consequences," *Times-Republican*, 24 March 2022. timesrepublican.com/opinion/columnists/2022/03/freedom-of-speech-is-not-freedom-from-consequences/; Scott Lemieux, "Free Speech Doesn't Mean Speech Free from all Consequences, Despite What Some Conservatives Argue," *NBC News, Think: Opinion, Analysis, Essays*, 6 July 2019. nbcnews.com/think/opinion/free-speech-doesn-t-mean-speech-free-all-consequences-despite-ncna1026911.

Chapter One

1   The examples are too many to list, but see: Stephen A. Smith, *Freedom of Expression*, v–vii; Jacob Mchangama, *Free Speech*; and, for a refreshing argument in favour of tracing free speech far back in history but from a critical perspective, see John Durham Peters, *Courting the Abyss: Free Speech and the Liberal Tradition* (Chicago: Chicago University Press, 2005).
2   Garton Ash, *Free Speech*, 75.
3   Garton Ash, *Free Speech*, 111.
4   Robert M. Hutchins as quoted in Stephen A. Smith, *Freedom of Expression*, v–vi.
5   For example, see Nico Perino and Dale E. Miller, "John Stuart Mill's 'On Liberty,'" in *So to Speak: The Free Speech Podcast,* FIRE: Foundation for Individual Rights in Education, 26 November 2019, podcast, MP3 Audio, 1:27:42. thefire.org/news/podcasts/so-speak-free-speech-podcast/john-stuart-mills-liberty; and "Essential Scholars," The Fraser Institute, accessed 26 August 2022. essentialscholars.org.
6   John Stuart Mill, *"On Liberty" and Other Writings*, ed. Stefan Collini (Cambridge: Cambridge University Press, 1989 [1859]), 7.
7   See, for example, Ivan Hare and James Weinstein, eds., *Extreme Speech and Democracy* (Oxford: Oxford University Press, 2014).
8   John Durham Peters, *Courting the Abyss: Free Speech and the Liberal Tradition* (Chicago: Chicago University Press, 2005), 156–57. Another example of a free speech slogan that has been misattributed is Mill coining the phrase "marketplace of ideas." See Ro Khanna, *Dignity in a Digital Age* (New York: Simon & Shuster, 2022), 208.
9   Peters, *Courting the Abyss*, 157.
10 For example, see Jane Stevenson, "Conservative Leader Pierre Poilievre Defends Jordan Peterson's Right to Free Speech," *Toronto Sun,* 7 January 2023. torontosun.com/news/national/conservative-leader-pierre-poilievre-defends-jordan-petersons-right-to-free-speech.
11 Voltaire, "Liberty of the Press," in *Freedom of Expression: Foundational Documents and Historical Arguments*, ed. Stephen A. Smith (Oxford: Oxbridge Research Associates, 2018), 123.
12 I retain the masculine language of this translation — "men" instead of "people" for the original "Mensch" — despite the argument that Kant may have been referring to all humans, because, as will be discussed, Kant did hold sexist assumptions that women did not have the same qualities as men, including those that would enable them to enlighten themselves. It seems likely that Kant was literally thinking only of men in this essay. See Robin May Schott, "The Gender of Enlightenment," in *Feminist Interpretations of Immanuel Kant*, ed. Robin May Schott (University Park, PA: University of Pennsylvania Press, 1997), 319–40.
13 Immanuel Kant, "An Answer to the Question: 'What is Enlightenment?'" in *Kant's Political Writings*, ed. Hans Reiss (Cambridge: Cambridge University Press, 1970), 54–55.
14 Charles W. Mills, *Black Rights/White Wrongs: The Critique of Racial Liberalism* (Oxford: Oxford University Press, 2017), 91–112.
15 Sankar Muthu, *Enlightenment Against Empire* (Princeton: Princeton University Press, 2003), 124.

16 Kant, "What is Enlightenment," 55.
17 Kant, "What is Enlightenment," 55.
18 Jürgen Habermas, *The Structural Transformation of the Public Sphere: An Inquiry into a Category of Bourgeois Society*, trans. Thomas McCarthy (Cambridge, Ma.: MIT Press, 1989).
19 Kant, "What is Enlightenment," 55.
20 My focus is on *On Liberty* because it is by far Mill's most influential work on our current discussions of free speech. But his other works, such as *Considerations on Representative Government,* show his consistent concern about the dangers of majority rule and nowhere does he follow the line of argumentation advanced by Alexander Meiklejohn that public or any collective deliberation is a suitable bulwark against tyranny of the majority.
21 Mill, *On Liberty,* 13.
22 Mill, *On Liberty,* 109.
23 Mill, *On Liberty*, 13–14.
24 For a full discussion, see Uday Singh Mehta, *Liberalism and Empire* (Chicago: University of Chicago Press, 1999).
25 See Domenico Losurdo, *Liberalism: A Counter-History*, trans. Gregory Elliot (London: Verso, 2011), 179.
26 There is considerable debate in the scholarship about the relationship between Chapter Two and the rest of *On Liberty*. For a recent summary of this debate, and a reiteration of a version of the standard interpretation that Chapter Two focuses on a distinct type of individual freedom but fits in with Mill's overall defence of liberty, see Dale Miller, "The Place of 'The Liberty of Thought and Discussion' in *On Liberty*," *Utilitas* (2021): 33, 133–49.
27 Mill, *On Liberty,* 20.
28 Mill, *On Liberty,* 14.
29 There is much scholarly debate on how to interpret Mill's version of utilitarianism in relation to his liberalism. The classic discussion is John Gray, *Mill on Liberty: A Defence,* 2nd ed. (London: Routledge, 1996).
30 Mill, *On Liberty,* 20.
31 Mill, *On Liberty,* 37.
32 Mill, *On Liberty,* 37–38.
33 Mill, *On Liberty,* 48.
34 Mill, *On Liberty,* 56. Piers Norris Turner uses terminology that he derives from other writings by Mill to discuss how expression, for Mill, can be restricted when words are "joined" with harmful acts. See Turner, "Introduction: Updating Mill on Free Speech," *Utilitas* 33, 2 (2021): 130.
35 Mill, *On Liberty,* 56–57.
36 Mill, *On Liberty,* 56–57. I should note the historical change in the meaning of the word "nuisance," derived from the French "for harm," which is closer to Mill's nineteenth-century usage than it is to our contemporary usage that is synonymous with "a bother" or "a trivial annoyance," as distinct from "a significant harm." See: *Oxford English Dictionary*, s.v. "nuisance," accessed 25 June 2022. oed.com/dictionary/nuisance_n#.
37 Melina Constantine Bell, "John Stuart Mill's Harm Principle and Free Speech," *Utilitas* 33 (2021): 162–79.
38 Bell, 163.

39 Mill, *On Liberty*, 64.
40 *Merriam-Webster Dictionary*, s.v. "sheeple," accessed 25 June 2022. merriam-webster.com/dictionary/sheeple.
41 This is an argument of omission when considering *On Liberty*, as Mill never discusses the need for free discussion in democratic governance. However, in *Considerations of Representative Government*, Mill describes in great detail his assessment of many facets of representative democracy and nowhere does he discuss a public deliberative process. His arguments that elected representatives should not be beholden to the voters but free to use their own reason distinguishes his approach to free speech and democracy from that of Meiklejohn. See Mill, *Considerations on Representative Government* (Atlanta: Cherokee, 2007).
42 Alexander Meiklejohn, *Free Speech and Its Relation to Self-Government* (New York: Harper & Brothers, 1948).
43 In a sense, Meiklejohn's approach to democracy and freedom is much more like that of Jean-Jacques Rousseau for whom we are free, despite perhaps stringent laws that we must obey, because we are part of "the people" who will the General Will. See Jean-Jacques Rousseau, *The Social Contract*, trans. Maurice Cranston (London: Penguin Classics, 1968). Where Rousseau and Meiklejohn part company is the role of language in this process. Rousseau argues that language in "civilized" countries has lost its original expressive capacity. See Jean-Jacques Rousseau, "On the Origin of Languages," in *First and Second Discourse, Together with Replies to the Critics and Essays on the Origin of Languages*, ed. and trans. Victor Gourevitch (New York: Harper Collins, 1986).
44 Meiklejohn, *Free Speech*, 63.
45 Meiklejohn, *Free Speech*, 17.
46 Meiklejohn, *Free Speech*, 24.
47 Meiklejohn, *Free Speech*, 26.
48 Meiklejohn, *Free Speech*, 96–97.
49 *Schenck v. United States*, 249 US 47 (1919). supreme.justia.com/cases/federal/us/249/47/. See Richard Parker, "Clear and Present Danger Test," in *The First Amendment Encyclopedia*, Free Speech Center, 7 August, 2023, last updated 18 February 2024. mtsu.edu/first-amendment/article/898/clear-and-present-danger-test.
50 C. Edwin Baker, *Human Liberty and Freedom of Speech* (Oxford: Oxford University Press, 1989), 5.
51 C. Edwin Baker, "Harm, Liberty and Free Speech," *Southern California Law Review* 70, 4 (1997): 997.
52 Baker, *Human Liberty*, 3–24.
53 C. Edwin Baker, "Autonomy and Hate Speech," in *Extreme Speech and Democracy*, eds. Ivan Hare and James Weinstein (Oxford: Oxford University Press, 2009), 139.
54 Baker, "Autonomy and Hate Speech," 142.
55 Baker, *Human Liberty*, 26.
56 Fish, *The First*, 31–62.
57 See Emmett Macfarlane's "Hate Speech, Harm, and Rights" in *The Dilemmas of Free Expression*, ed. Emmett Macfarlane (Toronto: University of Toronto Press, 2021), 35–55.

58 Baker, "Harm, Liberty," 1019.
59 Baker, "Autonomy and Hate Speech," 143.
60 Baker, "Autonomy and Hate Speech," 143. Baker never defends his position from the obvious consequences: that in order for the state to remain legitimate, it is the marginalized targets of racism, misogyny, antisemitism, transphobia, and the like who must suffer the harms.
61 Baker, "Autonomy and Hate Speech," 151.
62 Baker, "Autonomy and Hate Speech," 151.
63 This is a little tricky in that Mill tells of overcoming his "crisis" by turning to Romantic poetry and writings, and he quotes Wilhelm von Humboldt very favourably.
64 Charles Taylor, "Atomism," in *Philosophy and the Human Sciences* (Cambridge: Cambridge University Press, 1985), 187–210.
65 I have explored some of this tension within "Western" philosophy concerning language; see Peter Ives, "Language and Collective Identity: Theorizing Complexity," in *Language and Identity Politics,* ed. Christina Späti (Oxford: Berghann, 2016), 17–37.
66 Richard Moon, *The Constitutional Protection of Freedom of Expression* (Toronto: University of Toronto Press, 2000), 7.
67 Baker, "Harm, Liberty," 1008.
68 For example, Stanley Fish, *The First: How to Think about Hate Speech, Campus Speech, Religious Speech, Fake News, Post-Truth, and Donald Trump* (New York: Atria, 2019); and P.E. Moskowitz, *The Case Against Free Speech* (New York: Bold Type Book, 2019).

Chapter 2

1 Richard Moon, *The Constitutional Protection of Freedom of Expression* (Toronto: University of Toronto Press, 2000), 3.
2 Emmett Macfarlane, "Introduction: The Challenge and Controversy of Free Expression," in *The Dilemmas of Free Expression,* ed. Emmett Macfarlane (Toronto: University of Toronto Press, 2021), 4.
3 Emmett Macfarlane offers an excellent argument that governments and public institutions should take a "*Charter* values" approach to issues of hate speech, including positive action to enhance and protect the expressive freedom (in the positive sense) of oppressed groups who are often the target of speech often protected by the negative variation of the freedom of speech. My distinction is not at odds with his or other scholars who emphasize *the need* for our legal conception of free speech to move from primarily a negative freedom to include more positive aspects. Indeed, we have similar assessments of the current legal situation although Macfarlane's analysis highlights how my account here is quite static and descriptive of the status quo. See Emmett Macfarlane, "Beyond the Hate Speech Law Debate: A '*Charter* Values' Approach to Free Expression," *Review of Constitutional Studies / Revue d'études constitutionnelles* 26/27, 2/1 (2022): 145–68.
4 For a nuanced discussion of the limits of the negative/positive rights distinction in the context of the Canadian Charter, see Benjamin Oliphant, "Positive Rights, Negative Freedoms and Expressive Freedom," in *The Dilemmas of Free*

Expression, ed. Emmett Macfarlane (Toronto: University of Toronto Press, 2021), 130–50.
5   Brian Leiter, "The Case Against Free Speech," *The Sydney Law Review* 38 (2016): 407–39.
6   See *Irwin Toy Ltd v. Quebec (Attorney General)*, [1989] 1 S.C.R. 927. canlii.org/en/ca/scc/doc/1989/1989canlii87/1989canlii87.html.
7   That scholars like Jamie Cameron criticize court decisions because they argue the court abridges content neutrality demonstrates this principle. See Jamie Cameron, "Freedom of Expression and the Charter:1982–2022 (Part 3 of 5)," *Centre for Free Expression* (blog), 28 July 2022. cfe.torontomu.ca/blog/2022/07/freedom-expression-and-charter1982-2022-part-3-5.
8   The English–French language regime of Canada is increasingly challenged by multiculturalism and demands for recognition and support of Indigenous languages. See Eve Haque, *Multiculturalism Within a Bilingual Framework* (Toronto: University of Toronto Press, 2012); and Peter Ives, "Canadian Language Politics in Global and Theoretical Contexts," in *Language Politics and Policies,* ed. Thomas Ricento (Cambridge: Cambridge University Press, 2019), 78–94.
9   For a particularly good history of free speech in the US and the social forces at work in the revisionist interpretation of the First Amendment, see Laura Weinrib's *The Taming of Free Speech* (Cambridge, Mass.: Harvard University Press, 2016). Weinrib tracks the changes in free speech arguments at the beginning of the twentieth century when developed against property rights, especially by radicals in the labour movement for whom it included the right to picket, strike, and boycott, through changes in the ACLU's advocacy, ultimately leading to the late twenty-first century's articulation of free speech as the protection of property rights.
10 Moon, *The Constitutional Protection*; Macfarlane, "Beyond the Hate Speech Law Debate."
11 See, for example, Kent Greenawalt, *Fighting Words* (Princeton: Princeton University Press, 1995); Jeremy Waldron, *The Harm in Hate Speech* (Cambridge, Mass.: Harvard University Press, 2012).
12 There is some grey area in legal arguments that the US government colluded with or pressured social media companies to suppress users' speech, but in the Trump cases, these arguments were not substantiated.
13 These predictions seem to be proving correct. See Josh Gerstein, "Appeals Court Doubtful on Trump's Lawsuit Against Twitter," *Politico*, 4 October 2023. politico.com/news/2023/10/04/appeals-court-doubtful-on-trumps-lawsuit-against-twitter-00119981.
14 "Trump Sues Twitter, Google and Facebook Alleging 'Censorship,'" *BBC News*, 7 July 2021. bbc.com/news/world-us-canada-57754435.
15 See Kent Greenawalt, *Fighting Words* (Princeton: Princeton University Press, 1995), 80–81. As will be discussed in Chapter Four, there have been "fair reporting laws" and some discussion of Section 230 of the US Communications Act that provide private companies with public bandwidth, or categorization as an information carrier rather than a publisher, that make this example a little more complicated.

16 Shane Goldmacher, "Trump Sues Tech Firms for Blocking Him, and Fund-Raises Off It," *New York Times,* 7 July 2021. nytimes.com/2021/07/07/us/politics/trump-lawsuit-facebook-google-twitter.html.
17 Elizabeth A. Harris and Alexandra Alter, "Simon & Schuster Cancels Plans for Senator Hawley's Book," *New York Times,* 7 January 2021. nytimes.com/2021/01/07/books/simon-schuster-josh-hawley-book.html.
18 Stefan Braun, *Democracy Off Balance: Freedom of Expression and Hate Propaganda Law in Canada* (Toronto: University of Toronto Press, 2014), 39. The so-called "notwithstanding clause," Section 33 of the Canadian Charter, could also potentially limit Section 2(b)'s protection of free expression. See, for example, Greenawalt, *Fighting Words*, 13. It would theoretically allow the federal government to invoke it and pass legislation that violates the Fundamental Freedoms of the Charter — but this has never occurred and has very rarely been used by provinces in relation to Section 2(b)'s right to free expression.
19 Parker, "Clear and Present Danger Test."
20 For a detailed analysis of the development of First Amendment ideas of free speech, see Laura Weinrib, *The Taming of Free Speech* (Cambridge, Mass.: Harvard University Press, 2016).
21 As quoted in Parker, 2009.
22 Here, I am looking at the line between speech and action from only one direction. One should also be aware that the US Supreme Court has ruled that many actions — for example, flag burning (*Texas v. Johnson* 1989), cross burning (*R.A.V. v. St. Paul* 1992), and wearing a black armband (*Tinker v. Des Moines* 1969) — are protected by the First Amendment's free speech clause; in other words, they constitute speech (or perhaps the Canadian Charter chose the more appropriate term, "expression"), whereas burning one's draft card (*United States v. O'Brien* 1967) or crosses, in some circumstances (*Virginia v. Black* 2003), do not constitute speech protected by the First Amendment.
23 Jennifer Petersen takes this argument further, tracing out how the concept of "speech" has changed legally with the development of new technologies. She shows the reasoning for why silent movies were not protected speech in the early twentieth century, to why algorithmic outputs with no speaker are now understood as protected "speech." See Petersen, *How Machines Came to Speak: Media Technologies and the Freedom of Speech* (Durham: Duke University Press, 2022).
24 Ludwig Wittgenstein, *Philosophical Investigations*, 20.
25 J.L. Austin, *How to Do Things with Words* (Oxford: Clarendon Press, 1962).
26 Abrams v. United States, 250 US 616 (1919).
27 Many falsely attribute this analogy to Mill. See, for example, David Schultz, "The Marketplace of Ideas," in *The First Amendment Encyclopedia*, 1 January 2009, last updated 18 February 2024. mtsu.edu/first-amendment/article/999/marketplace-of-ideas; and Ro Khanna, *Dignity in a Digital Age* (New York: Simon & Shuster, 2022), 208. As an economist, Mill would likely find this analogy inaccurate regardless of his celebration of both free expression and free markets.
28 Indeed, only the most libertarian positions do not see a place for government to regulate products that are potentially harmful, not to mention problems of false advertising, monopolies, and unfair trading practices that riddle actual

discussions of market regulation. For example, see the work of one of the most influential pro-market thinkers ever, F.A. Hayek's *The Road to Serfdom*, ed. Bruce Caldwell (Chicago: University of Chicago Press, 2007), 85–88.
29 Robert Sparrow and Robert Goodin, "The Competition of Ideas: Market or Garden?" *Critical Review of International Social and Political Philosophy* 4, 2 (2001): 45–58.
30 Vincent Blasi, "Holmes and the Marketplace of Ideas," *The Supreme Court Review* (2004): 1–46, 6.
31 Anshuman Mondal, "The Shape of Free Speech," *Continuum* 32, 4 (2018): 503–17.
32 Gavan Titley, *Is Free Speech Racist?* (Cambridge: Polity Press, 2020), 17–18, and 21.
33 Nancy Leong and Kevin Whitfield, "The Marketplace of Racist Ideas," *Law, Culture and the Humanities,* 19 October 2020, 1–20, first published online. online first. doi.org/10.1177/1743872120959836.
34 Jared Schroeder, "Towards a Discursive Marketplace of Ideas," *First Amendment Studies* 52, 1–2 (2018): 38–60.
35 Philip Napoli, *Social Media and the Public Interest* (New York: Columbia University Press, 2019), 131.
36 James Belpedio, "*Whitney v. California (1927),*" in *The First Amendment Encyclopedia*, Free Speech Center, 1 January 2009, last updated 10 February 2024. mtsu.edu/first-amendment/article/263/whitney-v-california. Belpedio notes that Brandeis's reasoning is at odds with the Majority Opinion that upheld Whitney's conviction.
37 This irony is compounded by her being pardoned by the Governor of California who could not abide by having her suffer the conditions of prison, notwithstanding her militant advocacy of women's equality.
38 Napoli, *Social Media*, 84–106.
39 Richard Moon, "Does Freedom of Expression Have a Future?" in *Dilemmas of Free Expression*, ed. Emmett Macfarlane (Toronto: University of Toronto Press, 2021), 30.
40 Weinrib, *The Taming of Free Speech,* 323.
41 As I will discuss in Chapter Four, Alexander Meiklejohn made this criticism about free speech being abused for commercial profit. See *Free Speech and Its Relation to Self-Government* (New York: Harper & Brothers, 1948), 103–05.
42 *McKinney v. University of Guelph,* [1990] 3 S.C.R. 229. scc-csc.lexum.com/scc-csc/scc-csc/en/item/687/index.do.
43 See Criminal Code of Canada, R.S.C., 1985, c. C-46. laws-lois.justice.gc.ca/eng/acts/C-46/page-45.html#docCont.
44 *R. v Keegstra* [1990], 3 S.C.R. 697. scc-csc.lexum.com/scc-csc/scc-csc/en/item/695/index.do. See also Moon, *The Constitutional Protection*, 11.
45 *Saskatchewan (Human Rights Commission) v. Whatcott* [2013], 1 S.C.R. 467. scc-csc.lexum.com/scc-csc/scc-csc/en/item/12876/index.do.
46 Canadian Human Rights Act, 1985, Section 13, repealed 2013. laws-lois.justice.gc.ca/eng/acts/h-6/section-13-20021231.html.
47 *Citron v Zündel* (2002) also involved this section and the Court more explicitly applied it to hate speech on the internet, addressed in more detail in Chapter Four. This case should not be confused with *R. v Zundel* (1992)

whereby the Supreme Court of Canada struck down the law against false news concerning Ernst Zündel's Holocaust denial.
48 See Richard Moon, *Report to the Canadian Human Rights Commission*, 2008, 4. publications.gc.ca/site/eng/9.819307/publication.html.
49 John Mohawk, "The Indian Way Is a Thinking Tradition," in *Indian Roots of American Democracy*, ed. José Barreiro (Ithaca, N.Y.: Akwe:kon Press, 1992), 25.
50 See John Borrows, *Canada's Indigenous Constitution* (Toronto: University of Toronto Press, 2010); and John Borrows, *Freedom and Indigenous Constitutionalism* (Toronto: University of Toronto Press, 2016).

Chapter Three

1 See "Gender, Rights and Freedom of Speech," *The Agenda with Steve Paikin*, 26 October 2016. tvo.org/video/genders-rights-and-freedom-of-speech.
2 Senate, Government of Canada, "Bill-16: An Act to Amend the Canadian Human Rights Act and the Criminal Code," First Session, Forty-Second Parliament of Canada, First Reading, 17 May 2016. parl.ca/DocumentViewer/en/42-1/bill/c-16/first-reading; and Nina Dragicevic, "Canada's Gender Identity Rights Bill C-16 Explained," *CBC Docs POV*, n.d. cbc.ca/cbcdocspov/features/canadas-gender-identity-rights-bill-c-16-explained.
3 Lindsay Shepherd, *Diversity & Exclusion: Confronting the Campus Free Speech Crisis* (Bolton, ON.: Magna Carta, 2021), 23.
4 I am using the transcript as published in Lindsay Shepherd, *Diversity and Exclusion: Confronting the Campus Free Speech Crisis* (Bolton, ON.: Magna Carta, 2021), 36.
5 Kate Bueckert, "Laurier Professor, President Apologize to TA over Video Sanction," *CBC News*, 17 December 2017. cbc.ca/news/canada/kitchener-waterloo/laurier-lindsay-shepherd-apology-video-petersen-1.4424590; Global News Staff, "Full Text: Apology from Wilfrid Laurier Officials over Handling of Free Speech Controversy," *Global News*, 21 November 2017. globalnews.ca/news/3873319/apology-wilfrid-laurier-free-speech-text/.
6 Most of the public commentators seem to agree with Shepherd that this "surveillance" was undue and outrageous punishment or sanction, despite the fact that it is common practice in many universities for professors to ask TAs working under their supervision to provide such lesson plans (many professors even dictate the lesson plans themselves leaving little leeway for the TAs to design their own). For the course professor to sit in on such tutorials or classes is also common practice. It allows the professor to provide guidance for first time TAs like Shepherd. It can also show the students that the professor supports the TA. Finally, it can be important so that the professor can write substantive letters of recommendation based on such visits.
7 Christie Blatchford, "Thought Police Strike Again as Wilfrid Laurier Grad Student Is Chastised for Showing Jordan Peterson Video," *National Post*, 10 November 2017. nationalpost.com/opinion/christie-blatchford-thought-police-strike-again-as-wilfrid-laurier-grad-student-is-chastised-for-showing-jordan-peterson-video.
8 Rick Mercer, "Rick's Rant: University Censorship," *Rick Mercer Report*, 28 November 2017, video, 1:32. youtube.com/watch?v=JCy-nLzlTKs.; *Maclean's*

Magazine has run many articles on this issue including the opinion piece; for instance, see Stephen Maher, "Jordan Peterson and the Big Mistake of University Censors," *Maclean's*, 17 November 2017. macleans.ca/news/canada/jordan-peterson-and-the-big-mistake-of-university-censors/; "Globe Editorial: Why Are We Killing Critical Thinking on Campus?" *The Globe and Mail*, 16 November 2017. theglobeandmail.com/opinion/editorials/globe-editorial-why-are-we-killing-critical-thinking-on-campus/article37008714/.

9   National Assembly of Québec, Forty-Second Legislature, Second Session, 7 June 2022. publicationsduquebec.gouv.qc.ca/dynamicSearch/telecharge.php?type=5&file=2022C21A.PDF; see also Peter Ives and Eve Haque, "What is Québec's Bill 32 on Academic Freedom and Why Does it Matter," *The Conversation*, 1 June 2022. theconversation.com/what-is-quebecs-bill-32-on-academic-freedom-and-why-does-it-matter-183122.

10 For example, see Thomas O. Hueglin, "There's a Difference Between Freedom of Expression and Academic Freedom," *The Record*, 23 March 2018. therecord.com/opinion/contributors/2018/03/23/there-s-a-difference-between-freedom-of-expression-and-academic-freedom.html; Aadita Chaudhury, "The WLU/Lindsay Shepherd Controversy Was Never about Free Speech," *Medium*, 28 November 2017. medium.com/@thylacinereport/the-WLU-lindsay-shepherd-controversy-was-never-about-free-speech-9fe3442d-a3c3; Shannon Dea, "First Dispatch: Academic Freedom and the Mission of the University," *University Affairs/Affaires Universitaires*, 5 September 2018. universityaffairs.ca/opinion/dispatches-academic-freedom/first-dispatch-academic-freedom-and-the-mission-of-the-university/; and Alex Usher, "Has Everybody Lost Their Damn Mind?" *Higher Education Strategy Associates*, 27 November 2017, higheredstrategy.com/everybody-lost-damn-mind/

11 Andrew Russell, "Wilfrid Laurier TA Happy School Apologized but Wants Long-Term Changes to Protect Free Speech," *Global News*, 22 November 2017. globalnews.ca/news/3874929/wilfrid-laurier-freedom-of-speech-lindsay-shepherd-apology-change/; Blair Crawford, "Laurier Free Speech Advocate Lindsay Shepherd Honoured in Ottawa, *The Ottawa Citizen*, 13 May 2018. ottawacitizen.com/news/local-news/laurier-free-speech-advocate-lindsay-shepherd-honoured-in-ottawa; Moira McDonald, "Free Speech on Campus: The Age-Old Debate Rages On," *University Affairs/Affaires Universitaires*, 3 October 2018. universityaffairs.ca/features/feature-article/free-speech-the-age-old-debate-rages-on/; Paul Stanway, "Lindsay Shepherd Tells All," *C2C Journal*, 9 April 2021. c2cjournal.ca/2021/04/lindsay-shepherd-tells-all/.

12 Committee on Freedom of Expression at the University of Chicago, "Report of the Committee on Freedom of Expression," 2014. freeexpression.uchicago.edu/

13 Sigal Ben-Porath, *Free Speech on Campus* (Philadelphia: University of Pennsylvania Press, 2017).

14 Joan Wallach Scott, *Knowledge, Power, and Academic Freedom* (New York: Columbia University Press, 2019), 95.

15 Shannon Dea, "The Evolving Social Purpose of Academic Freedom," *Kennedy Institute of Ethics Journal* 31, 2 (2021): 201.

16 Stanley Fish, *The First* (New York: Atria, 2020), 67–68.

17 Shepard, *Diversity and Exclusion*, 39. This sentence is from her transcript of the recorded conversation. There is, of course, much irony here in terms of

those who accept this form of epistemological relativism as appropriate but then decry postmodernism for being relativistic.

18 Michael Bérubé and Jennifer Ruth, "When Professors' Speech Is Disqualifying," *The New Republic,* 21 March 2022. newrepublic.com/article/165649/professors-speech-disqualifying. See also Michael Bérubé and Jennifer Ruth, *It's Not Free Speech: Race, Democracy, and the Future of Academic Freedom* (Baltimore: Johns Hopkins University Press, 2022).

19 For general overviews see, Matthew Finkin and Robert Post, *For the Common Good: Principles of American Academic Freedom* (New Haven: Yale University Press, 2009); Michael Horn, *Academic Freedom in Canada: A History* (Toronto: University of Toronto Press, 1999); James Turk, "Understanding Academic Freedom in Canada," Occasional Paper, 29 March 2022, Centre for Free Expression. cfe.torontomu.ca/news/understanding-academic-freedom-canada-cfes-newest-publication.

20 National Assembly of Québec, Forty-Second Legislature, Second Session, 7 June 2022. publicationsduquebec.gouv.qc.ca/dynamicSearch/telecharge.php?type=5&file=2022C21A.PDF; see also Peter Ives and Eve Haque, "What is Québec's Bill 32 on Academic Freedom and Why Does it Matter," *The Conversation,* 1 June 2022. theconversation.com/what-is-quebecs-bill-32-on-academic-freedom-and-why-does-it-matter-183122.

21 See Government of Manitoba, "The Advanced Education Administration Act," Role of the Minister, 2(1)(d): "respects the appropriate autonomy of educational institutions and the recognized principles of academic freedom." web2.gov.mb.ca/laws/statutes/ccsm/_pdf.php?cap=a6.3. Thanks to Lisa McGifford for bringing this to my attention.

22 Finkin and Post, *For the Common Good,* 39.

23 Dax D'Orazio, "Deplatforming in Theory and Practice," in *The Dilemmas of Free Expression,* ed. Emmett Macfarlane (Toronto: University of Toronto Press, 2021), 275.

24 Ian Angus, *Love the Questions* (Winnipeg: Arbeiter Ring, 2009), 22.

25 Eve Haque, "The Singular Freedom of Academic Freedom," *Journal of Historical Sociology,* 29, 1 (2016): 120. See also Julia Schleck, *Dirty Knowledge: Academic Freedom in the Age of Neoliberalism* (Lincoln: University of Nebraska Press, 2023).

26 For a good discussion of the many issues involved in what Shannon Dea calls the cluster of freedoms that make up academic freedom in the Canadian context, see her limited series of articles in *University Affairs/Affaires Universitaires,* "Dispatches on Academic Freedom," 5 September 2018 to 16 December 2021. universityaffairs.ca/opinion/dispatches-academic-freedom/. (See especially "A Brief History of Academic Freedom," 9 October 2018.) Refer also to Dea, "The Evolving Social Purpose of Academic Freedom." For a general history of academic freedom in Canada, see the classic work, Michael Horn, *Academic Freedom in Canada: A History* (Toronto: University of Toronto Press, 1999).

27 Scott, *Knowledge,* 18.

28 Scott, *Knowledge,* 50.

29 Fish, *The First,* 15. Of course, if an employer fires someone because her dislike of what they say is due to discrimination, one can claim wrongful dismissal, but this has nothing to do the one's right to free expression.

30 Greg Wyshynski, "Hockey Icon Don Cherry Fired for Immigrant Comments," ESPN, 11 November 2019. espn.com/nhl/story/_/id/28059815/hockey-icon-don-cherry-fired-immigrant-comments. Tacitly acknowledging the point that most of the media discussion missed concerning the Shepherd affair, Cherry said, "To keep my job, I cannot be turned into a tamed robot."
31 Wendy Mesley, "I made mistakes. But my departure wasn't the solution to the CBC's problem with racism," *The Globe and Mail*, 7 July 2021. theglobeandmail.com/opinion/article-the-cbcs-issues-with-systemic-racism-go-beyond-the-two-worst-moments/.
32 The place where this line gets more complicated is the "extramural" expression of academics. Michael Bérubé and Jennifer Ruth argue that "a historian who is a Holocaust denier is obviously unfit, whereas an electrical engineer who is a Holocaust denier is just a crank. This position makes perfect sense, though few people realize that it entails the unsettling corollary that professors enjoy *greater* protection for extramural speech when they have no idea what they're talking about than for speech within the areas of their research and teaching." Although my caveat would be that we need to keep a clear distinction — that yes, both individuals would be subject to the same potential legal hate speech proscriptions, but the historian could also face consequences from their university in ways the engineer would not. See Michael Bérubé and Jennifer Ruth, "When Professors' Speech is Disqualifying," *The New Republic*, 21 March 2022. newrepublic.com/article/165649/professors-speech-disqualifying.
33 Scott, *Knowledge*, 6.
34 Michael Bérubé and Jennifer Ruth, "When Professors' Speech is Disqualifying."
35 Shannon Dea, "Learning to Say Good Bye to Academic Freedom," *University Affairs/Affaires Universitaires* 14 September 2020. universityaffairs.ca/opinion/dispatches-academic-freedom/learning-to-say-goodbye-to-academic-freedom/.
36 *McKinney v. University of Guelph*, [1990]. The Supreme Court of Canada expanded its reasoning on this point in *Eldridge v. British Columbia* [1997] in its decision that the lack of sign language interpretation in hospitals is subject to the Charter, laying out a three-part test; the two key points for universities are that they are not exercising delegated statutory authority nor implementing specific government "policies, programs or objectives." See scc-csc.lexum.com/scc-csc/scc-csc/en/item/1552/index.do; and James Turk, "Universities, the *Charter*, Doug Ford, and Campus Free Speech," *Constitutional Forum constitutionnel* 29, 2 (2020): 31–44. journals.library.ualberta.ca/constitutional_forum/index.php/constitutional_forum/article/view/29398.
37 Turk, "Universities," 40–41.
38 *Wilson v University of Calgary* [2014]. jccf.ca/wp-content/uploads/2014/04/Wilson-v-U-of-Calgary-April-2014-Judgment.pdf. See also Turk, 2020, 41.
39 *Pridgen v University of Calgary* (2010). canlii.org/en/ab/abqb/doc/2010/2010abqb644/2010abqb644.html; see also Turk, 2020, 41; and Haque, "The Singular Freedom," 116–17.
40 Emma Davie, "Dalhousie Student Faces Disciplinary Action over Canada 150 Post," *CBC*, 17 October 2017. cbc.ca/news/canada/nova-scotia/masuma-khan-dalhousie-student-disciplinary-action-facebook-post-1.4364586. See also Kaitlyn Swan, "Dalhousie Grad Gets Long-Awaited Apology from

University via Tweet," *CBC*, 25 October 2019. cbc.ca/news/canada/nova-scotia/masuma-khan-dalhousie-university-apology-1.5335599.
41 See Haque, "The Singular Freedom," 116–17.
42 P.E. Moskowitz, *The Case Against Free Speech* (New York: Bold Type Books, 2019), 44.
43 *UAlberta Pro-Life v. Governors of the University of Alberta* (2020). See Atrisha S. Lewis, et al, "Free Speech on Campus Is Subject to the Charter — But Only in Alberta," *McCarthy Tétrault*, 15 January 2020. mccarthy.ca/en/insights/blogs/canadian-appeals-monitor/free-speech-campus-subject-charter-only-alberta; and Jeffrey Sachs, "Faculty Free Speech in Canada," in *Dilemmas of Free Expression*, ed. Emmett Macfarlane (Toronto: University of Toronto Press, 2021), 244–46.
44 Turk, "Universities," 40–42. See also Sachs, "Faculty Free Speech," 244–46.
45 Turk, "Universities," 38–43.
46 Shannon Dea, "First Dispatch: Academic Freedom and the Mission of the University," *University Affairs/Affaires Universitaires*, 5 September 2018. universityaffairs.ca/opinion/dispatches-academic-freedom/first-dispatch-academic-freedom-and-the-mission-of-the-university/.
47 In California, since the passing of the so-called Leonard Law in 1992, First Amendment protections of speech have been applied to private universities, colleges, and even high schools. But California is unique in this instance. See Kate Selig, "California's Leonard Law: What it Means for Campus Speakers," *The Daily Stanford*, 20 May 2020. stanforddaily.com/2020/05/20/californias-leonard-law-what-it-means-for-campus-speakers/. But many private universities accept these standards regardless of it not being a legal requirement.
48 The absence of hate speech legislation in the US is another difference, although arguably the implications move in the opposite direction. The First Amendment protections of free speech could be deemed to protect hate speech even in the university classroom; however, no case law has developed on this point.
49 See Laura Weinrib, *The Taming of Free Speech*, 146–82.
50 Walter Metzger, "Profession and Constitution: Two Definitions of Academic Freedom in America," *Texas Law Review* 66 (1988): 1286.
51 *Adler v. Board of Education of the City of New York,* 342 US 485 (1952). law.cornell.edu/supremecourt/text/342/485; see also Metzger, "Profession and Constitution."
52 *Sweezy v. New Hampshire,* 354 US 234 (1957). tile.loc.gov/storage-services/service/ll/usrep/usrep354/usrep354234/usrep354234.pdf.
53 See, for example, Emilie Kraft, "Academic Freedom," in *The First Amendment Encyclopedia*, 10 August 2023, last updated 2 June 2024. mtsu.edu/first-amendment/article/17/academic-freedom.
54 Sachs, "Faculty Free Speech," 244. Sachs does not make the clear distinctions I have employed concerning free speech, so I do not think by "free speech" here he means just "extra-mural academic freedom," but rather his claim is that there is greater freedom for Canadian academics in general than in the US.
55 Wilfrid Laurier University, Values, Vision, Mission. Approved by the Board of Governors, 20 November 2008. WLU.ca/about/discover-laurier/values-vision-mission.html

56 The University of Winnipeg, The University, updated 26 May 2022. uwinnipeg.ca/academics/calendar/docs/the-university.pdf.
57 The Wilfrid Laurier University Act, 1973, as Amended, 2001 and 2016. WLU.ca/about/governance/assets/resources/wilfrid-laurier-university-act.html.
58 For further discussion see Shannon Dea, "Academic Freedom in a Non-Ideal World," 19 November 2018, "Two Kinds of Academic Freedom? Lessons from a Scholar Who Fled Turkey," 11 February 2019, and "Students and the Freedom to Learn," *University Affairs/Affaires Universitaires*. universityaffairs.ca/opinion/dispatches-academic-freedom/.
59 Section 7.4. WLU.ca/about/working-at-laurier/assets/resources/collective-agreement-WLUfa-full-time-faculty-and-librarians.html.
60 I should note that my former colleague, Dr. Matt Gibbs, a classicist conducts research on beer brewing in Ancient Rome. I have not asked him whether he discusses this when he teaches introductory Classics courses, but he could make a better case than I, that such topics belong in his course. All such discussions can occur in terms of academic freedom but are unrelated to the types of considerations of free expression as discussed in Chapters One and Two.
61 Dea, "The Evolving Social Purpose of Academic Freedom," 212–14.
62 Michael Lynk, "Academic Freedom, Canadian Labour Law and the Scope of Intra-Mural Expression," *Constitutional Forum constitutionnel* 29, 2 (2020): 45–64. Thanks to Mark Gabbert for bringing this to my attention.
63 Shepherd, *Diversity and Exclusion*, 22.
64 CAUT Policy Statement, Academic Freedom, approved by CAUT Council November 2018. caut.ca/about-us/caut-policy/lists/caut-policy-statements/policy-statement-on-academic-freedom.
65 Shannon Dea, "Students and the Freedom to Learn," *University Affairs/Affaires Universitaires,* 30 October 2020. universityaffairs.ca/opinion/dispatches-academic-freedom/students-and-the-freedom-to-learn/; Dea, "The Evolving Social Purpose of Academic Freedom," 215–16.
66 The University of Winnipeg, The University, updated 26 May 2022. uwinnipeg.ca/academics/calendar/docs/the-university.pdf.
67 Greg Mercer, "Laurier President Promises Change after Shepherd Affair," *The Record,* 18 December 2017. therecord.com/news/waterloo-region/2017/12/18/laurier-president-promises-change-after-shepherd-affair.html.
68 Scott, *Knowledge*, 117.
69 Blatchford, "Thought Police Strike Again." She then compares the discussion with a TA to Mao's "struggle sessions" and, like many others, was outraged at the "discipline" that Shepherd faced — allowing the professor to review prior to the class her preparation notes and perhaps sitting in on some sessions, activities that are hardly "discipline" but often regular procedures for TAs working under the supervision of a professor who is responsible for the course. Many TAs welcome such procedures for, among other reasons, it enables the professor to write more thorough letters of recommendation in the future. Indeed, professors and program directors are not allowed to discipline TAs. Such decisions need to go through the academic or non-academic misconduct procedures. The only "discipline" was that her supervisors tried to mentor Shepherd so that her tutorial sessions would not create the type of exchanges commonly found on Twitter, Facebook, and other social media.

70 Deborah MacLatchy, "Not Merely Free Speech, But Better Speech Needs to be Protected on Campus," *The Globe and Mail*, 31 July 2018. theglobeandmail.com/opinion/article-not-merely-free-speech-but-better-speech-needs-to-be-protected-on/.
71 "Statement on Freedom of Expression," approved by the Wilfrid Laurier University Senate, 29 May 2018. wlu.ca/about/discover-laurier/freedom-of-expression/statement.html.
72 Ben-Porath, *Free Speech on Campus,* 23.
73 Ben-Porath, *Free Speech on Campus,* 34.
74 As quoted in Parker, 2009.
75 Jeremy Waldron has developed this idea of how hate speech undermines the victimized groups' participation in a democratic society, including a discussion that relates "members in good standing" with the concept of dignity, which Ben-Porath draws on. See Jeremy Waldron, *The Harm of Hate Speech* (Cambridge, Mass.: Harvard University Press, 2012), especially Chapter 5. Ben-Porath notes, however, that "Sensitivity to inclusion in all its forms should not be enacted through an attack on freedom; it should not be pursued as a matter of course by calling for limits on freedom of speech." See Ben-Porath, *Free Speech,* 34.
76 David Newhouse, "Teiakwanahstahsontéhrha' – We Extend the Rafters," in *Dilemmas of Free Expression,* ed. Emmett Macfarlane (Toronto: University of Toronto Press, 2021), 222–35.
77 See Turk, "Universities," 33–34.
78 Office of the Premier, "Upholding Free Speech on Ontario University and College Campuses," 30 August 2018. news.ontario.ca/en/backgrounder/49950/upholding-free-speech-on-ontarios-university-and-college-campuses; Madeline Smith, "Kenney Follows Ford's Push for Campus Free Speech. But Critics Say It's a Dog Whistle for Far-Right Voters," *Toronto Star,* 6 May 2019. thestar.com/calgary/2019/05/06/alberta-and-ontario-premiers-campus-free-speech-policies-a-dog-whistle-blow-for-the-right-expert.html.
79 Geoffrey R. Stone, et al., "Report of the Committee on Freedom of Expression," 2014. provost.uchicago.edu/sites/default/files/documents/reports/FOECommitteeReport.pdf.
80 Sigal Ben-Porath, "Against Endorsing the Chicago Principles," *Inside Higher Ed,* 11 December 2018. insidehighered.com/views/2018/12/11/what-chicago-principles-miss-when-it-comes-free-speech-and-academic-freedom-opinion.
81 Shama Rangwala, "The Real Free-Speech Crisis on Alberta's Campuses Might Not Be What You Think It Is," *The Globe and Mail,* 31 August 2019. theglobeandmail.com/opinion/article-the-real-free-speech-crisis-on-albertas-campuses-might-not-be-what/.
82 Shama Rangwala, "Free Speech and the University: A Closer Look at the Chicago Principles," *Pyriscence*, 30 May 2019. pyriscence.ca/home/2019/5/30/chicagoprinciples. See also Rangwala quoted on Facebook: "The Chicago Principles have enough ambiguity to sound like 'common sense.' In practice, however, the kinds of meanings that are ultimately attached to the vague language are hardly those championing critiques of power: governments, administrators, and other groups benefitting from and supporting existing systems of power get to decide what counts as 'free speech,' and have the means to

shut down critique." Shama Rangwala quoted on Pyriscence Facebook page, 31 May 2019. facebook.com/Pyriscence.
83 Dea, "The Evolving Social Purpose of Academic Freedom," 199–200.
84 Rangwala, "Free Speech and the University"; James Turk, "Universities, the *Charter*, Doug Ford, and Campus Free Speech," *Constitutional Forum constitutionnel* 29, 2 (2020): 31–44. journals.library.ualberta.ca/constitutional_forum/index.php/constitutional_forum/article/view/29398; and Madeline Smith, "Kenney Follows Ford's Push for Campus Free Speech. But Critics Say It's a Dog Whistle for Far-Right Voters," *Toronto Star,* 6 May 2019. thestar.com/calgary/2019/05/06/alberta-and-ontario-premiers-campus-free-speech-policies-a-dog-whistle-blow-for-the-right-expert.html.
85 Turk, "Universities," 31.
86 Turk, "Universities," 33.
87 Dax D'Orazio, "How and Why the Chicago Principles Came to Canada," *American Review of Canadian Studies* 51, 4 (2021): 533–53.
88 Turk, "Universities," 42.
89 Mark Gabbert, "Academic Freedom: Freedom of Expression's Vulnerable Child," *CAUT Journal* (2021): 13, 2. journal.caut.ca/index.php/caut-journal/article/view/5.
90 Haque, "The Singular Freedom," 123.
91 Dea, "The Evolving Social Purpose of Academic Freedom," 207–08, 216.
92 Rick Mercer, "Rick's Rant: University Censorship," *Rick Mercer Report,* 28 November 2017, video, 1:32. youtube.com/watch?v=JCy-nLzlTKs.
93 For example, see Ben-Porath, *Free Speech on Campus*, 23.
94 As quoted in Scott, *Knowledge,*" 100.

Chapter Four

1 A.J. Liebling, "Do You Belong in Journalism," *The New Yorker*, 14 May 1960. newyorker.com/magazine/1960/05/14/do-you-belong-in-journalism.
2 There are, of course, many other preconditions to such global communication, especially in the early days of the internet; for example, consider the massive spread of the English language across the globe that facilitated the initial spread of social media prior to the increase in linguistic diversity on the internet. See David Crystal, *Language and the Internet* (Cambridge: Cambridge University Press, 2001); Peter Ives, "Cosmopolitanism and Global English," *Political Studies* 58, 3 (2010): 516–35. General literacy, computer literacy, typing skills, and the like are other preconditions that should not be neglected.
3 As quoted in Paul Wallich, "Turf Wars in Cyberspace," *Scientific American*, 24 June 1996. scientificamerican.com/article/turf-wars-in-cyberspace/.
4 American Civil Liberties Union, "ACLU Lauds Judges' Ruling Protecting Free Speech in Cyberspace," 12 June 1996. aclu.org/press-releases/aclu-lauds-judges-ruling-protecting-free-speech-cyberspace. The following year, the Supreme Court struck down much of the Communications Decency Act but again left Section 230 in place. See *Reno v ACLU* (1997). supreme.justia.com/cases/federal/us/521/844/.
5 Anshuman Mondal, "The Shape of Free Speech," *Continuum* 32, 4 (2018): 503. Also, see Chapter Three.

6   According to Shahram Azhar, Facebook quickly made the Fortune 500 list and its revenues increased by 18,000 percent between 2008–2019. Shahram Azhar, "Consumption, Capital, and Class in Digital Space: The Political Economy of Pay-per-Click Business Models," *Rethinking Marxism* 33, 2 (2021): 196–216.

7   As Bollinger and Stone emphasize, Justice Holmes's ground-breaking, dissenting opinion in *Abrams* (1919) described his interpretation of the freedom of speech as an experiment. See Lee Bollinger and Geoffrey Stone, "Dialogue," in *The Free Speech Century*, eds. Lee Bollinger and Geoffrey Stone (New York: Oxford University Press, 2019), 4–5.

8   Keith N. Hampton, Inyoung Shin, and Weixu Lu, "Social Media and Political Discussion: When Online Presence Silences Offline Conversation," *Information, Communication & Society*, 20:7 (2017): 1090–1107; Knight Foundation, "The Future of Tech Policy: American Views," 16 June 2020. knightfoundation.org/reports/the-future-of-tech-policy-american-views/; Kalev Leetaru, "Has Social Media Killed Free Speech?" *Forbes*, 31 October 2016. forbes.com/sites/kalevleetaru/2016/10/31/has-social-media-killed-free-speech/?sh=4109b69046b1.

9   Jacob Mchangama, *Free Speech*, 369. Mchangama does discuss research studies that find only an incredibly small portion of internet content is "fake news," and that polarization, filter bubbles, and echo chambers are exaggerated. But he too refers vaguely to "the darker side of free speech" and celebrates that "activists are developing tools to combat the dark side of the Internet . . . ." (378).

10 Jonathan Haidt, "Why the Last Ten Years of American Life Have Been Uniquely Stupid," *The Atlantic*, 11 April 2022. theatlantic.com/magazine/archive/2022/05/social-media democracy-trust-babel/629369/.

11 Kalev Leetaru, "The Death of Internet Freedom: Mourning the Demise of a 20-Year-Old Dream," *Forbes*, 17 February 2016. forbes.com/sites/kalevleetaru/2016/02/17/the-death-of-internet-freedom-mourning-the-demise-of-a-20-year-old-dream/?sh=1759cbf3d519.

12 See for example, Bill Baer and Caitlin Chin-Rothman, "Addressing Big Tech's Power Over Speech," *The Regulatory Review*, 1 June 2021. theregreview.org/2021/06/01/baer-chin-addressing-big-techs-power-over-speech/; Janna Anderson and Lee Rainie, "Many Tech Experts Say Digital Disruption Will Hurt Democracy," *Pew Research Center* 21 February 2020. pewresearch.org/internet/2020/02/21/many-tech-experts-say-digital-disruption-will-hurt-democracy/; Konrad von Finckenstein and Peter Menzies, "Social Media Responsibility and Free Speech," Macdonald-Laurier Institute, February 2022. macdonaldlaurier.ca/mli-files/pdf/Feb2022_Social_media_responsibility_and_free_speech_Finckenstein_Menzies_PAPER_FWeb.pdf.

13 Michael Bérubé and Jennifer Ruth, *It's Not Free Speech: Race, Democracy, and the Future of Academic Freedom* (Baltimore: John Hopkins University Press, 2022), 5.

14 Damien Gayle, "Facebook Aware of Instagram's Harmful Effects on Teenage Girls, Leak Reveals," *The Guardian*, 14 September 2021. theguardian.com/technology/2021/sep/14/facebook-aware-instagram-harmful-effect-teenage-girls-leak-reveals; Rosemary Sedgwick, et al., "Social Media, Internet Use and Suicide Attempts in Adolescents," *Current Opinion in Psychiatry* 32, 6 (November 2019): 534–41. doi.org/ 10.1097/YCO.0000000000000547.

15 Nicholas Confessore, "Cambridge Analytica and Facebook: The Scandal and the Fallout So Far," *New York Times,* 4 April 2018. nytimes.com/2018/04/04/us/politics/cambridge-analytica-scandal-fallout.html; Kari Paul, "A brutal year: how the 'techlash' caught up with Facebook, Google and Amazon," *The Guardian* 28 December 2019. theguardian.com/technology/2019/dec/28/tech-industry-year-in-review-facebook-google-amazon; The Knight Foundation, "Techlash? Americans Growing Concern with Major Technology Companies," Gallup, Inc., 11 March 2020. knightfoundation.org/wp-content/uploads/2020/03/Gallup-Knight-Report-Techlash-Americas-Growing-Concern-with-Major-Tech-Companies-Final.pdf.
16 Dan Milmo, "Rohingya Sue Facebook for 150bn Over Myanmar Genocide," *The Guardian* 6 December 2021. theguardian.com/technology/2021/dec/06/rohingya-sue-facebook-myanmar-genocide-us-uk-legal-action-social-media-violence; Natasha Lomas, "Meta Urged to Pay Reparations for Facebook's Role in Rohingya Genocide," *Tech Crunch,* 29 September 2022. techcrunch.com/2022/09/29/amnesty-report-facebook-rohingya-reparations/.
17 Jason Proctor, "Award-Winning Documentary Maker Accuses Twitter of Muzzling Speech Critical of Corporations," *CBC,* 25 July 2021. cbc.ca/news/canada/british-columbia/twitter-corporation-free-speech-lawsuit-1.6113724; Joel Bakan, "Twitter Gone Rogue: Who Governs Content in Canada?" *Newswire,* 19 July 2021. newswire.ca/news-releases/twitter-gone-rogue-who-governs-content-in-canada-lawsuit-from-joel-bakan-and-sujit-choudhry-argues-canadian-democracy-is-under-assault-by-big-tech-policies-804751879.html.
18 Tom Blackwell, "Canadian Lawyers Accusing Twitter of Stifling Free Speech Score First Victory in Novel Lawsuit," *The National Post,* 17 January 2023. nationalpost.com/news/lawsuit-twitter-free-speech.
19 For example, Julia Angwin, "Facebook's Secret Censorship Rules Protect White Men from Hate Speech but not Black Children," *ProPublica,* 28 June 2017. perma.cc/7F9M-A8HF.
20 Ro Khanna, *Dignity in a Digital Age* (New York: Simon & Schuster, 2022), 186. For example, see works as diverse as Steve Davis, Larry Elin, and Grant Reeher, *Click on Democracy: The Internet's Power to Change Political Apathy into Civic Action* (New York: Routledge, 2002); and Manuel Castells, *Networks of Outrage and Hope: Social Movements in the Internet Age* (Cambridge: Polity, 2012).
21 Ronald Deibert, *Reset: Reclaiming the Internet for Civil Society* (Toronto: Anansi, 2020), 5.
22 Government of Canada, "Proposed Bill to Address Online Harms," accessed 1 March 2024. canada.ca/en/canadian-heritage/services/online-harms.html; David Ljunggren, "Canada Unveils Plans to Make Online Hate Speech a Crime," *Reuters,* 23 June 2021. reuters.com/world/americas/canada-unveils-plans-make-online-hate-speech-crime-2021-06-23/; Alex Hern, "What Is the GDPR and How Will It Affect You?" *The Guardian,* 21 May 2018. theguardian.com/technology/2018/may/21/what-is-gdpr-and-how-will-it-affect-you.
23 For a detailed analysis including the argument that technology has changed how we define "speech," see Jennifer Petersen, *How Machines Came to Speak: Media Technologies and Freedom of Speech* (Durham: Duke University Press, 2022).

24 Petersen, *How Machines Came*, 194.
25 See the podcast interview, Kara Swisher and Jason Miller, "How Jason Miller Is Trying to Get Trump Back on the Internet," 19 August 2021, in *Sway*, produced by *New York Times*, MP3audio. nytimes.com/2021/08/19/opinion/sway-kara-swisher-jason-miller.html; see also Meridith McGraw, Tina Nguyen and Cristiano Lima, "Team Trump Quietly Launches New Social Media Platform," *Politico*, 1 July 2021. politico.com/news/2021/07/01/gettr-trump-social-media-platform-497606.
26 See "Terms," GETTR, accessed 20 August 2021. GETTR.COM/TERMS.
27 Billy Perrigo, "Facebook and Twitter Finally Locked Donald Trump's Accounts. Will They Ban Him Permanently?" *Time Magazine*, 7 January 2021. time.com/5927398/facebook-twitter-trump-suspension-capitol/.
28 See "Social Truth Guidelines," TRUTH Social, accessed 11 April 2022. help.truthsocial.com/community-guidelines-page. These guidelines twice reference the US First Amendment, invoking its spirit and concept of "value-neutral" regulation. As discussed in Chapter Two, this is an odd reference in that the First Amendment limits the actions of the US government not private companies. For a general assessment, see Edward Helmore's "Harsh Truth: Trump's Social Media App Follows Long Line of Failed Products," *The Guardian*, 9 April 2022. theguardian.com/us-news/2022/apr/09/truth-social-trump-app-failed-products.
29 Josh Halliday, "Twitter's Tony Wang: 'We Are the Free Speech Wing of the Free Speech Party,'" *The Guardian*, 22 March 2012. theguardian.com/media/2012/mar/22/twitter-tony-wang-free-speech.
30 Even the gamer-oriented platform Discord, known for white-supremacist content, cancelled accounts of right-wing racist users. April Glaser, "White Supremacists Still Have a Safe Space Online," *Slate*, 9 October 2018. slate.com/technology/2018/10/discord-safe-space-white-supremacists.html. Signal and Telegram may seem to be exceptions, but they are messaging apps, which leaves Gab as coming closer to allowing any content that is legal, yet they too go further than this: they retain the right of using sole discretion to terminate accounts that they suspect of spreading "junk mail," "spam," and content that they deem might harm Gab, and they determine what they think may be against the law rather than leaving it to law enforcement (gab.com/about/tos). Even 4chan and Reddit have moderators and the latter can be seen as an interesting experiment in users moderating content by voting on posts.
31 Jack M. Balkin, "The Future of Free Expression in a Digital Age," *Pepperdine Law Review*, Vol. 36, 2 (2009): 427. digitalcommons.pepperdine.edu/plr/vol36/iss2/9.
32 Richard Moon, "Does Freedom of Expression Have a Future?" in *Dilemmas of Free Expression,* ed. Emmett Macfarlane (Toronto: University of Toronto Press), 30.
33 Philip Napoli, *Social Media and the Public Interest* (New York: Columbia University Press, 2019), 28.
34 Timothy Wu, "Is the First Amendment Obsolete," in *The Free Speech Century*, eds. Lee Bollinger and Geoffrey Stone. New York: Oxford University Press, 2019, 285. See also James Williams, *Stand Out of Our Light: Freedom and Resistance in the Attention Economy* (Cambridge: Cambridge University Press, 2018).

35 While this is an implicit assumption in many positions, for a well-thought-out argument, see David Hudson, "In the Age of Social Media, Expand the Reach of the First Amendment," *The Human Rights Magazine* (American Bar Association), 43, 4 (October 2018). americanbar.org/groups/crsj/publications/human_rights_magazine_home/the-ongoing-challenge-to-define-free-speech/in-the-age-of-socia-media-first-amendment/. Of course, Chapters Two and Three demonstrate how any such position runs the risk of confusing the constitutional goal of limiting the government and creates a myriad of murky questions, including how the law decides which non-governmental organizations and individuals are infringing on the speech rights of others and how such infringements are not themselves expression — as in the case of boycotts, strikes, and protests.

36 Monika Bickert, "Defining the Boundaries of Free Speech on Social Media," in *The Free Speech Century,* eds. Lee Bollinger and Geoffrey Stone (New York: Oxford University Press, 2019), 254. Later in this essay, Bickert admits, "Despite those critics, technology companies necessarily play a critical role in content governance," but for her, this is distinguishable from content creation (257). Facebook's general position on this issue is more murky and perhaps duplicitous; see Sam Levin, "Is Facebook a Publisher? In Public It Says No, But in Court It Says Yes," *The Guardian,* 3 July 2018. theguardian.com/technology/2018/jul/02/facebook-mark-zuckerberg-platform-publisher-lawsuit.

37 Khanna, *Dignity in a Digital Age,* 194. Konrad von Fickenstein and Peter Menzies also maintain that social media companies are not like publishers: "they do not select content for 'publication' or 'broadcast.' Content is generated by users whose activity/data is then monetized by the platform." I will draw on analyses below that show how this monetization process necessitates "curation" performed by secret algorithms without which Facebook, X, and YouTube could not generate the profits that define them. See von Finckenstein and Menzies, "Social Media Responsibility and Free Speech," Macdonald-Laurier Institute, February 2022, 17. macdonaldlaurier.ca/files/pdf/Feb2022_Social_media_responsibility_and_free_speech_Finckenstein_Menzies_PAPER_FWeb.pdf.

38 *Stratton Oakmont, Inc. v. Prodigy Servs.*, WL 323710, 1995 N.Y., accessed 18 April 2022. casetext.com/case/stratton-oakmont-inc-v-prodigy-servs. The Court distinguished this case from *Cubby, Inc. v Compuserv* (1991), because Compuserv made no attempt at any moderation and thus, the Court argued, it was not a publisher.

39 "47 US Code Section 230 - Protection for Private Blocking and Screening of Offensive Material." law.cornell.edu/uscode/text/47/230.

40 See Betsy Klein, "White House Reviewing Section 230 Amid Efforts to Push Social Media Giants to Crack Down on Misinformation," CNN, 21 July 2021. cnn.com/2021/07/20/politics/white-house-section-230-facebook/index.html.

41 Abram Brown, "What Is Section 230—And Why Does Trump Want to Change It?" *Forbes*, 28 May 2020. forbes.com/sites/abrambrown/2020/05/28/what-is-section-230-and-why-does-trump-want-to-change-it/?sh=4036ebaa389d; Betsy Klein, "White House reviewing Section 230 amid efforts to push social media giants to crack down on misinformation," CNN, 20 July 2021. cnn.com/2021/07/20/politics/white-house-section-230-facebook/index.html.

42 Mason Walker and Katerina Eva Matsu, "News Consumption Across Social Media in 2021," *Pew Research Center*, 21 September 2021. pewresearch.org/journalism/2021/09/20/news-consumption-across-social-media-in-2021/. I will address the issue of the quality of this "news" below.

43 Emily Bell, "The Unintentional Press: How Technology Companies Fail as Publishers," in *The Free Speech Century*, eds. Lee Bollinger and Geoffrey Stone (New York: Oxford University Press, 2019), 235. See also Philip Napoli and Robyn Caplan, "Why Media Companies Insist They're Not Media Companies, Why They Are Wrong, and Why it Matters," *First Monday*, 22, 5 (2017). journals.uic.edu/ojs/index.php/fm/article/view/7051/6124; and Philip Napoli, *Social Media and the Public Interest* (New York: Columbia University Press, 2019), 5–14.

44 "Canada–United States–Mexico Agreement," Chapter 19.1, Digital Trade, Government of Canada, accessed 20 April 2022. international.gc.ca/trade-commerce/trade-agreements-accords-commerciaux/agr-acc/cusma-aceum/text-texte/19.aspx?lang=eng; Daniel Tsai, "Online Platforms Must Be Made Liable for Third-Party Hate Content — and It Might Happen Soon," *Toronto Star*, 30 October 2020. thestar.com/business/opinion/2020/10/30/online-platforms-must-be-made-liable-for-third-party-hate-content.html; Hugh Stephen, "Thank You Professor! 'Explaining' Section 230 to Canadians," *Hugh Stephen's Blog*, (blog), 4 October 2021. hughstephensblog.net/2021/10/04/thank-you-professor-explaining-section-230-to-canadians%EF%BF%BC/.

45 Mark Zuckerberg's response to Senator Orrin Hatch's question during a Senate committee's hearings during the fall out of the Cambridge Analytica scandal, as quoted in Emily Stewart, was: "Lawmakers seem confused about what Facebook does — and how to fix it." In *Vox*, 10 April 2018. vox.com/policy-and-politics/2018/4/10/17222062/mark-zuckerberg-testimony-graham-facebook-regulations.

46 Shoshana Zuboff, *The Age of Surveillance Capitalism* (New York: Hachette, 2019), 71.

47 Zuboff, *The Age of Surveillance*, 63–82.

48 Victor Luckerson, "Here's Why Facebook Won't Put Your News Feed in Chronological Order," *Time Magazine*, 9 July 2015. time.com/3951337/facebook-chronological-order/.

49 Will Oremus, "Why Facebook Won't Let You Control Your Own News Feed," *The Washington Post*, 13 November 2021. washingtonpost.com/technology/2021/11/13/facebook-news-feed-algorithm-how-to-turn-it-off/.

50 Diane Bartz and Nandita Bose, "Facebook, Google CEOs Suggest Ways to Reform Key Internet Law," *Reuters* 24 March 2021. reuters.com/article/usa-socialmedia-congress/facebook-google-ceos-suggest-ways-to-reform-key-internet-law-idINKBN2BH0AF/; see also Monika Bickert, "Charting Our Way Forward," *Meta*, 17 February 2020. about.fb.com/news/2020/02/online-content-regulation/.

51 See Eric Goldman, "Five Things to Know about Section 230," Centre for International Governance Innovation (8 July 2021). papers.ssrn.com/sol3/papers.cfm?abstract_id=3871507#.

52 Cory Doctorow, *The Internet Con: How to Seize the Means of Computation* (London: Verso, 2023), 33–34.

53 Diana Bossio, "Canada's Online News Act May Let Meta and Google Decide the Winners and Losers in the Media Industry," *The Conversation*, 26 June 2023. theconversation.com/canadas-online-news-act-may-let-meta-and-google-decide-the-winners-and-losers-in-the-media-industry-208088.
54 "The Online News Act," Government of Canada (website). canada.ca/en/canadian-heritage/services/online-news.html.
55 Daniel Thibault, et al, "Federal Government Reaches Deal with Google on Online News Act," *CBC News*, 29 November 2023. cbc.ca/news/politics/google-online-news-act-1.7043330.
56 Mickey Djuric, "Conservatives Ran on Similar Media Policy as Liberals, But Now Claim It's Censorship," *CBC News*, 2 August 2023. cbc.ca/news/politics/conservatives-policy-tech-giants-online-news-1.6925990.
57 Zuboff, *The Age*, 86–87.
58 Peter Zimonjic, "Federal Government Names Organizations that Will Help Spend $600M Journalism Fund," *CBC News*, 24 May 2019. cbc.ca/news/politics/journalism-support-fund-panel-1.5144282.
59 Jürgen Habermas, *The Structural Transformation of the Public Sphere: An Inquiry into a Category of Bourgeois Society*, trans. Thomas McCarthy (Cambridge, Ma.: MIT Press, 1989).
60 Habermas, *The Structural Transformation*, 42.
61 See, for example, Nick Crossley and John Michael Roberts, eds., *After Habermas: New Perspectives on the Public Sphere* (Oxford: Blackwell, 2004).
62 Nancy Fraser, *Unruly Practices: Power, Discourse and Gender in Contemporary Social Theory* (Minneapolis: University of Minnesota Press, 1989), especially Chapter 6, 113–44.
63 There are many extensive criticisms of Habermas's faith in reason and free expression. My own critique can be found in Chapter Four of my work, *Gramsci's Politics of Language: Engaging the Bakhtin Circle and the Frankfurt School* (Toronto: University of Toronto Press, 2004), 134–71. This critique does not detract from Habermas's main insight that it matters how the public sphere is structured.
64 Ives, *Gramsci's Politics of Language*, 134–71.
65 See, among other works, Marshall McLuhan, *The Gutenberg Galaxy* (Toronto: University of Toronto Press, 1962); Marshall McLuhan, *Understanding Media* (New York: McGraw-Hill, 1964); Harold Innis, *Empire and Communication* (Oxford: Clarendon Press, 1950).
66 Neil Postman, *Amusing Ourselves to Death* (New York: Viking, 1985).
67 Jason Hannan, *Trolling Ourselves to Death: Democracy in the Age of Social Media* (Oxford: Oxford University Press, 2023), 28.
68 Arlene Saxonhouse makes the interesting claim that those political theorists working from the insights of Jürgen Habermas, such as Joshua Cohen and Seyla Benhabib, "are in many ways the unacknowledged heirs to Meiklejohn . . . ." See Saxonhouse, *Free Speech and Democracy in Ancient Athens* (Cambridge: Cambridge University Press, 2006), 26 n.19.
69 Alexander Meiklejohn, *Free Speech and Its Relation to Self-Government*, 103–04.
70 Meiklejohn, *Free Speech*, 104–05.
71 As quoted in Ann Blair, "Information Overload, The Early Years," *The Boston*

Globe, 28 November 2010. http://archive.boston.com/bostonglobe/ideas/articles/2010/11/28/information_overload_the_early_years/?page=2.
72   Nick Srnicek, *Platform Capitalism* (Cambridge: Polity, 2017), 43.
73   Timothy Garton Ash, *Free Speech*; see also Moon, "Does Freedom of Expression Have a Future?" 15–34, 27–29.
74   A more critical label also pertinent to social media may be that of "pseudo-public spaces." See Jack Shenker, "Revealed: The Insidious Creep of Pseudo-Public Space in London," *The Guardian*, 24 July 2017. theguardian.com/cities/2017/jul/24/revealed-pseudo-public-space-pops-london-investigation-map. Shenker's description of land developers matches many criticisms of social media: "Under existing laws, public access to pseudo-public spaces remains at the discretion of landowners who are allowed to draw up their own rules for 'acceptable behaviour' on their sites and alter them at will. They are not obliged to make these rules public."
75   Philip Napoli, *Social Media and the Public Interest* (New York: Columbia University Press, 2019).
76   Petersen, 201.
77   Wendy Hui Kyong Chun, *Discriminating Data: Correlation, Neighborhoods, and the New Politics of Recognition* (Boston: MIT Press, 2024).
78   Mark Sweney, "Facebook Outage Highlights Global Over-Reliance on Its Services," *The Guardian*, 5 October 2021. theguardian.com/technology/2021/oct/05/facebook-outage-highlights-global-over-reliance-on-its-services; Alexandra Posadzki, "How a Coding Error Caused Rogers Outage that Left Millions Without Service," *The Globe and Mail*, 25 July 2022. theglobeandmail.com/business/article-how-a-coding-error-caused-rogers-outage-that-left-millions-without/.
79   See "Facebook News Feed Algorithm History," Wallaroo, accessed 29 December 2022. wallaroomedia.com/facebook-newsfeed-algorithm-history/#four.
80   See Derek Hrynyshyn, "Imagining Platform Socialism," in *The Socialist Register 57: Beyond Digital Capitalism*, eds. Leo Panitch and Greg Albo (London: Merlin, 2021), 150.
81   K. Sabeel Rahman and Zephyr Teachout, "From Private Bads to Public Goods: Adapting Public Utility Regulation for Informational Infrastructure," Knight First Amendment Institute, 4 February 2020, 19. knightcolumbia.org/content/from-private-bads-to-public-goods-adapting-public-utility-regulation-for-informational-infrastructure. Richard Moon also argues for regulation of "direct, individualized marketing." See Moon, "Does Freedom of Speech Have a Future?" 30.
82   Rahman and Teachout, 19.
83   This issue has come to prominence recently as it is one of the possible changes the Elon Musk has proposed with his purchase of Twitter. See Jillian York, Gennie Gebhart, Jason Kelley, and David Greene, "Twitter has a New Owner. Here's What He Should Do," The Electronic Frontier Foundation, 25 April 2022. eff.org/deeplinks/2022/04/twitter-has-new-owner-heres-what-he-should-do.
84   Jack Balkin and Jonathan Zittrain, "A Grand Bargain to Make Tech Companies Trustworthy," *The Atlantic*, 3 October 2016. theatlantic.com/technology/archive/2016/10/information-fiduciary/502346/.

85 Steve Lohr, "He Created the Web. Now He's Out to Remake the Digital World," *New York Times*, 10 January 2021. nytimes.com/2021/01/10/technology/tim-berners-lee-privacy-internet.html; see also Berners-Lee's organization, "World Wide Web Foundation." webfoundation.org/our-work/.
86 Doctorow, 31–73.
87 See Open Media website: openmedia.org/.
88 Konrad von Finckenstein and Peter Menzies, "Social Media Responsibility and Free Speech: A New Approach to Regulating Internet Harms," Macdonald-Laurier Institute, February 2022. macdonaldlaurier.ca/mlifiles/pdf/Feb2022_Social_media_responsibility_and_free_speech_Finckenstein_Menzies_PAPER_FWeb.pdf.
89 See Konrad von Finckenstein and Peter Menzies, "Webinar Panel Video: Protecting Free Speech in the Age of Social Media," Macdonald-Laurier Institute, 5 April 2022. macdonaldlaurier.ca/webinar-panel-video-protecting-free-speech-in-the-age-of-social-media/.
90 Chris Hughes, "It's Time to Break Up Facebook," *New York Times*, 9 May 2019. nytimes.com/2019/05/09/opinion/sunday/chris-hughes-facebook-zuckerberg.html.
91 For a more thorough argument in favour of breaking up the big social media platforms, specifically for reasons of free expression, see Andrea Prat, "Measuring and Protecting Media Plurality in the Digital Age: A Political Economy Approach," First Amendment Institute at Columbia University, 10 August 2020. knightcolumbia.org/content/measuring-and-protecting-media-plurality-in-the-digital-age.
92 Sara Morrison, "Elizabeth Warren's Plan to Break Up Big Everything," *Vox*, 5 April 2022. vox.com/recode/23003056/elizabeth-warren-big-tech-mergers; see also, Elizabeth Warren, "Break Up Big Tech," 2020 Presidential Campaign Website. 2020.elizabethwarren.com/toolkit/break-up-big-tech. Warren is in favour of various proposals to better regulate social media, especially those aimed at combating disinformation and voter suppression. See: elizabethwarren.com/plans/fighting-digital-disinformation.
93 Bernie Sanders, "Op-Ed: Bernie Sanders on His Plan for Journalism," *Columbia Journalism Review*, 26 August 2019. cjr.org/opinion/bernie-sanders-media-silicon-valley.php.
94 Neil Chilson and Casey Mattox, "[The] Breakup Speech: Can Antitrust Fix the Relationship Between Platforms and Free Speech Values?" Knight First Amendment Institute, 5 March 2020. knightcolumbia.org/content/the-breakup-speech-can-antitrust-fix-the-relationship-between-platforms-and-free-speech-values.
95 Rahman and Teachout, "From Private Bads to Public Goods," 19.
96 Rahman and Teachout, "From Private Bads," 15–17.
97 Nick Srnicek, *Platform Capitalism* (Cambridge: Polity Press, 2017), 128.
98 See Derek Hrynyshyn, "Imagining Platform Socialism," in *The Socialist Register 57: Beyond Digital Capitalism*, eds. Leo Panitch and Greg Albo (London: Merlin, 2021), 137–52; James Muldoon, *Platform Socialism: How to Reclaim our Digital Future from Big Tech* (London: Pluto, 2021). See also Ben Tarnoff, *Internet for the People: The Fight for our Digital Future* (London: Verso, 2022).

99 Trebor Scholz, "Platform Cooperativism: Challenging the Corporate Sharing Economy," New York, Rosa Luxemburg Stiftung, 2016. rosalux.nyc/wp-content/uploads/2020/11/RLS-NYC_platformcoop.pdf; and see "Platform Cooperativism Consortium, website. platform.coop/.
100 Hrynyshyn, "Imagining Platform Socialism," 144.
101 Rahman and Teachout, "From Private Bads to Public Goods," 6–7.
102 Hrynyshyn, "Imagining Platform Socialism," 147.
103 Hrynyshyn, "Imagining Platform Socialism," 149.
104 Khanna, *Dignity in a Digital Age*, 203.
105 Khanna, *Dignity in a Digital Age*, 203. Also, see, for example, the website for Nextdoor: ca.nextdoor.com/.
106 See fediverse website: fediverse.party/.
107 Robert Gehl, "Citizens' Social Media Can Provide an Antidote to Propaganda and Disinformation," *The Conversation*, 22 October 2022. theconversation.com/citizens-social-media-can-provide-an-antidote-to-propaganda-and-disinformation-192491.
108 Khanna, *Dignity in a Digital Age*, 203–04.

Conclusion

1 Martin Luther King, Jr. as quoted in Jacob Mchangama, *Free Speech*, 252, 298–300.
2 King, Jr., Martin Luther. "I've Been to the Mountaintop." 3 April 1968. afscme.org/about/history/mlk/mountaintop.
3 See Robert Shibley, "Martin Luther King, Free Speech, and the Albany Movement," *FIRE*, 16 January 2017. thefire.org/news/martin-luther-king-free-speech-and-albany-movement.
4 Martin Luther King, Jr., "I've Been to the Mountaintop," 3 April 1968. afscme.org/about/history/mlk/mountaintop.
5 Martin Luther King, Jr., "Letter from Birmingham Jail," in *Twentieth Century Political Theory: A Reader,* ed. Stephen Eric Bronner (New York: Routledge, 1997), 291–302.
6 Mary-Jo Nadeau and Alan Sears, "The Palestine Test: Countering the Silencing Campaign," *Studies in Political Economy* 85, 1 (2010): 7–33. doi.org/10.1080/19187033.2010.11675033.
7 "Who We Are," *International Holocaust Remembrance Alliance*, accessed 15 August 2022. holocaustremembrance.com/who-we-are.
8 "Working Definition of Antisemitism," International Holocaust Remembrance Alliance, accessed 15 August 2022. holocaustremembrance.com/resources/working-definitions-charters/working-definition-antisemitism.
9 See Corey Balsam, "Who's Against Adopting the IHRA Antisemitism Definition?" *Times of Israel*, 9 December 2020. blogs.timesofisrael.com/whos-against-adopting-the-IHRA-antisemitism-definition/; Jasmine Zine, Greg Bird, and Sara Matthews, "Criticizing Israel is Not Antisemitic — It's Academic Freedom," *The Conversation*, 15 November 2020. theconversation.com/criticizing-israel-is-not-antisemitic-its-academic-freedom-148864
10 Kenneth Stern, "I Drafted the Definition of Antisemitism. Rightwing Jews Are Weaponizing It," *The Guardian*, 13 December 2020. theguardian.com/

commentisfree/2019/dec/13/antisemitism-executive-order-trump-chilling-effect?fbclid=IwAR3o_RVfoJXieaRFooXktpzSCDqjP2InYqfxcTNHUY-HaMUW5DuXhARupEA.
11 Stern, "I Drafted the Definition."
12 "The Jerusalem Declaration on Antisemitism," *The Jerusalem Declaration on Antisemitism*, convened by the Van Leer Jerusalem Institute, 25 March 2021. jerusalemdeclaration.org/
13 Jasmine Zine, Greg Bird, and Sara Matthews, "Criticizing Israel Is Not Antisemitic — It's Academic Freedom," *The Conversation*, 15 November 2020. theconversation.com/criticizing-israel-is-not-antisemitic-its-academic-freedom-148864.
14 See Maura Forrest, "There's A Debate Over Canada's New Definition of Anti-Semitism, and It Might Sound Strangely Familiar," *National Post,* 27 June 2019. nationalpost.com/news/politics/theres-a-debate-over-canadas-new-definition-of-anti-semitism-and-it-might-sound-strangely-familiar.
15 "Jewish Faculty Against the IHRA Working Definition of Antisemitism," *Jewish Faculty Network,* accessed 28 December 2022. jewishfaculty.ca/jewish-faculty-against-the-IHRA-defn/.
16 For example, see Eduardo Bonilla-Silva, "Want to Beat Racism? Stop Labeling People as Racists, and Start Asking Better Questions," *Scalawag Magazine,* 17 February 2017. scalawagmagazine.org/2017/02/want-to-beat-racism-stop-labeling-people-as-racists-and-start-asking-better-questions/; see also Eduardo Bonilla-Silva, *Racism without Racists,* 4th ed. (Lanham: Rowman & Littlefield, 2013).
17 Laurie Penny, "No, I Will Not Debate You," *Long Reads*, 18 September 2018. longreads.com/2018/09/18/no-i-will-not-debate-you/#more-113762.
18 "A Letter on Justice and Open Debate," *Harper's Magazine,* 7 July 2020. harpers.org/a-letter-on-justice-and-open-debate/.
19 Alexander Meiklejohn, *Free Speech and Its Relation to Self-Government* (New York: Harper & Brothers, 1948), 18.
20 See the overview from the Independent Jewish Voices (IJV/VJI), 4 September 2020. ijvcanada.org/IHRA-definition-at-work/.
21 Section 319, Criminal Code (R.S.C., 1985, c. C-46). laws-lois.justice.gc.ca/eng/acts/c-46/section-319.html.
22 Government of Canada, "Canada's Pledges on Holocaust Remembrance and Combatting Antisemitism," updated 25 October 2021. canada.ca/en/canadian-heritage/services/canada-holocaust/canada-pledges.html.
23 "Manitoba Adopts Definition of Antisemitism," *Winnipeg Free Press*, 27 October 2022. winnipegfreepress.com/breakingnews/2022/10/27/manitoba-adopts-definition-of-antisemitism.
24 Jeffrey Sachs, "Canada's New Definition of Anti-Semitism Is a Threat to Campus Free Speech," *University Affairs/Affaires Universitaires*, 10 September 2019. universityaffairs.ca/opinion/in-my-opinion/canadas-new-definition-of-anti-semitism-is-a-threat-to-campus-free-speech./
25 Abigail Bakan, Alejandro Paz, Anna Zalik and Deborah Cowen, "Jewish Scholars Defend the Right to Academic Freedom on Israel/Palestine," *The Conversation*, 11 April 2021. theconversation.com/jewish-scholars-defend-the-right-to-academic-freedom-on-israel-palestine-157674.

26 University of Winnipeg, "Statement on Comments at 'My Jerusalem' Panel Discussion," 6 March 2018. news.uwinnipeg.ca/statement-on-comments-at-my-jerusalem-panel-discussion/. Accessed 20 July 2024.
27 University of Winnipeg, "Respectful Workplace and Learning Environment Policy," 1 June 2013. uwinnipeg.ca/policies/docs/policies/respectful-working-and-learning-environment-policy.pdf.
28 See University of Winnipeg, "Final Review Summary," 3 October 2018. news.uwinnipeg.ca/wp-content/uploads/2018/03/Final-review-summary-October-3-18.pdf. Accessed 20 July 2024.
29 Michael Mostyn, Stuart Kamenetsky, and Howard Tenenbaum, "University of Toronto must act now to uproot antisemitism," *Toronto Star*, 2 February 2021. thestar.com/opinion/contributors/2021/02/02/university-of-toronto-must-act-now-to-uproot-antisemitism.html.
30 Independent Jewish Voices Canada, "The IHRA Definition at Work," 4 September 2020. ijvcanada.org/IHRA-definition-at-work/#Canada.
31 Aaron Bandler, "1 in 5 British Universities Have Adopted the IHRA Definition of Anti-Semitism, Survey Says," *The Jewish Journal*, 30 September 2020. jewishjournal.com/news/worldwide/322348/1-in-5-british-universities-have-adopted-IHRA-definition-of-anti-semitism-survey-says/.
32 CAUT, Motions, 25–26 November 2021, CAUT Council Meeting. council.caut.ca/sites/default/files/motions_resolutions_for_caut_council_website-en.pdf. Accessed 20 July 2024.
33 Jasmine Zine, Greg Bird, and Sara Matthews, "Criticizing Israel Is Not Antisemitic — It's Academic Freedom," *The Conversation*, 15 November 2020. theconversation.com/criticizing-israel-is-not-antisemitic-its-academic-freedom-148864.
34 David Newhouse, "Teiakwanahstahsontéhrha´ — We Extend the Rafters," in *Dilemmas of Free Expression,* ed. Emmett Macfarlane (Toronto: University of Toronto Press, 2021), 223.
35 Newhouse, "Teiakwanahstahsontéhrha´," 233.
36 Newhouse, "Teiakwanahstahsontéhrha´," 230.
37 John Borrows, *Canada's Indigenous Constitution* (Toronto: University of Toronto Press, 2010).
38 John Borrows, *Freedom and Indigenous Constitutionalism* (Toronto: University of Toronto Press, 2016), 181.
39 Borrows, *Freedom*, 12.
40 John Mohawk, "The Indian Way Is a Thinking Tradition," in *Indian Roots of American Democracy*, ed. José Barreiro (Ithaca, N.Y.: Akwe:kon Press, 1992), 25.
41 Stephen A. Smith, *Freedom of Expression*, v–vii; Timothy Garton Ash, *Free Speech*, 111.
42 See Borrows, *Freedom and Indigenous Constitutionalism*, especially 6–7, and 181. See also Winona LaDuke, "Minobimaatisiiwin: The Good Life," *Cultural Survival*, 16 March 2010. culturalsurvival.org/publications/cultural-survival-quarterly/minobimaatisiiwin-good-life.

BIBLIOGRAPHY

Ackerman, Elliot, et al. "A Letter on Justice and Open Debate," *Harper's Magazine*, 7 July 2020. https://harpers.org/a-letter-on-justice-and-open-debate/.

American Civil Liberties Union (ACLU), "Free Expression," https://www.aclu.org/other/freedom-expression, accessed 15 January 2022.

Anderson, Janna and Lee Rainie, "Many Tech Experts Say Digital Disruption Will Hurt Democracy," *Pew Research Center* 21 February, 2020. https://www.pewresearch.org/internet/2020/02/21/many-tech-experts-say-digital-disruption-will-hurt-democracy/, accessed 15 April 2022.

Angus, Ian. *Love the Questions.* Winnipeg: Arbeiter Ring, 2009.

Angwin, Julia. "Facebook's Secret Censorship Rules Protect White Men From Hate Speech But Not Black Children," *ProPublica*, 28 June 2017. https://perma.cc/7F9M-A8HF, accessed 20 April 2022.

Austin, J.L. *How To Do Things With Words.* Oxford: Clarendon Press, 1962.

Azhar, Shahram, "Consumption, Capital, and Class in Digital Space: The Political Economy of Pay-per-Click Business Models," *Rethinking Marxism* 33, 2 (2021), 196-216.

Baer, Bill and Caitlin Chin, "Addressing Big Tech's Power Over Speech," *The Regulatory Review,* 1 June 2021. https://www.theregreview.org/2021/06/01/baer-chin-addressing-big-techs-power-over-speech/, accessed 15 April, 2022.

Bakan, Abigail, Alejandro Paz, Anna Zalik and Deborah Cowen, "Jewish scholars defend the right to academic freedom on Israel/Palestine," *The Conversation*, 11 April 2021. https://theconversation.com/jewish-scholars-defend-the-right-to-academic-freedom-on-israel-palestine-157674.

Bakan, Joel. "Twitter Gone Rogue: Who governs content in Canada?," *Newswire*, 19 July 2021. https://www.newswire.ca/news-releases/twitter-gone-rogue-who-governs-content-in-canada-lawsuit-from-joel-bakan-and-sujit-choudhry-argues-canadian-democracy-is-under-assault-by-big-tech-policies-804751879.html, accessed 10 March 2022.

Baker, C. Edwin. *Human Liberty and Freedom of Speech*. Oxford: Oxford University Press, 1989.

Baker, C. Edwin. "Harm, Liberty and Free Speech," *Southern California Law Review* 70, 4 1997, 979-1020.

Baker, C. Edwin. "Autonomy and Hate Speech," in *Extreme Speech and Democracy*, Ivan Hare and James Weinstein, eds. Oxford: Oxford University Press, 2009, 139-57.

Balkin, Jack M. "The Future of Free Expression in a Digital Age," *Pepperdine Law Review*, Vol. 36, 2 (2009), 427-444. https://digitalcommons.pepperdine.edu/plr/vol36/iss2/9.

Balkin, Jack and Jonathan Zittrain, "A Grand Bargain to Make Tech Companies Trustworthy," *The Atlantic*, 3 October 2016. https://www.theatlantic.com/technology/archive/2016/10/information-fiduciary/502346/.

Balsam, Corey. "Who's against adopting the IHRA antisemitism definition?," *Times of Israel*, 9 December 2020. https://blogs.timesofisrael.com/whos-against-adopting-the-ihra-antisemitism-definition/.

Bandler, Aaron. "1 in 5 British Universities have Adopted the IHRA Definition of Anti-Semitism, Survey Says," *The Jewish Journal*, 30 September 2020. https://jewishjournal.com/news/worldwide/322348/1-in-5-british-universities-have-adopted-ihra-definition-of-anti-semitism-survey-says/.

Bartz, Diane and Nandita Bose, "Facebook, Google CEOs suggest ways to reform key internet law," *Reuters* 24 March 2021. https://www.reuters.com/article/us-usa-socialmedia-congress/facebook-google-ceos-suggest-ways-to-reform-key-internet-law-idUSKBN2BG29D.

Beauchamp, Zach. "The 'free speech debate' isn't really about free speech," *Vox*, 22 July 2020. https://www.vox.com/policy-and-politics/2020/7/22/21325942/free-speech-harpers-letter-bari-weiss-andrew-sullivan.

Bell, Emily. "The Unintentional Press: How Technology Companies Fail as Publishers," in *The Free Speech Century*, Lee Bollinger and Geoffrey Stone, eds. New York: Oxford University Press, 2019, 235-53.

Bell, Melina Constantine. "John Stuart Mill's Harm Principle and Free Speech," *Utilitas* 33, 2021, 162-79.

Belpedio, James. "*Whitney v. California (1927),*" in *The First Amendment Encyclopedia*, 2009, https://www.mtsu.edu/first-amendment/article/263/whitney-v-california.

Ben-Porath, Sigal. *Free Speech on Campus*. Philadelphia: University of Pennsylvania Press, 2017.

Ben-Porath, Sigal. "Against Endorsing the Chicago Principles," *Inside Higher Ed*, 11 December 2018, https://www.insidehighered.com/views/2018/12/11/what-chicago-principles-miss-when-it-comes-free-speech-and-academic-freedom-opinion.

Berrada, Mohamed. "Balancing respect and freedom in an era of global tensions," *University Affairs/Affaires Universitaires*, 14 February 2024, https://universityaffairs.ca/features/feature-article/balancing-respect-and-freedom-in-an-era-of-global-tensions/.

Bérubé, Michael and Jennifer Ruth, "When Professors' Speech is Disqualifying," *The New Republic*, 21 March 2022, https://newrepublic.com/article/165649/professors-speech-disqualifying.

Bérubé, Michael and Jennifer Ruth, *It's Not Free Speech: Race, Democracy, and the Future of Academic Freedom*. Baltimore: Johns Hopkins University Press, 2022.

Bickert, Monika. "Defining the Boundaries of Free Speech on Social Media," in *The Free Speech Century*, Lee Bollinger and Geoffrey Stone, eds. New York: Oxford University Press, 2019, 254-71.

Bickert, Monika "Charting Our Way Forward," *Meta* 17 February, 2020. https://about.fb.com/news/2020/02/online-content-regulation/, accessed 18 March 2023.

Binkley, Collin. "As a new generation rises, tension between free speech and inclusivity on college campuses simmers," *The Hill*, 13 January 2024, https://thehill.com/homenews/ap/ap-u-s-news/ap-as-a-new-generation-rises-tension-between-free-speech-and-inclusivity-on-college-campuses-simmers/.

Blackwell, Tom. "Canadian lawyers accusing Twitter of stifling free speech score first victory in novel lawsuit," *The National Post*, 17 January, 2023, https://nationalpost.com/news/lawsuit-twitter-free-speech.

Blasi, Vincent. "Holmes and the Marketplace of Ideas," *The Supreme Court Review* (2004), 1-16, 6. https://www-journals-uchicago-edu.uwinnipeg.idm.oclc.org/doi/epdf/10.1086/scr.2004.3536967.

Blatchford, Christie. "Thought police strike again as Wilfrid Laurier grad student is chastised for showing Jordan Peterson video," *National Post*, 10 November 2017, https://nationalpost.com/opinion/christie-blatchford-thought-police-strike-again-as-wilfrid-laurier-grad-student-is-chastised-for-showing-jordan-peterson-video.

Bollinger, Lee and Geoffrey Stone, eds. *The Free Speech Century*, New York: Oxford University Press, 2019.

Bonilla-Silva, Eduardo. *Racism without Racists,* 4th ed. Lanham: Rowman & Littlefield, 2013.

Bonilla-Silva, Eduardo. "Want to beat racism? Stop labeling people as racists, and start asking better questions," *Scalawag Magazine,* 17 February 2017. https://scalawagmagazine.org/2017/02/want-to-beat-racism-stop-labeling-people-as-racists-and-start-asking-better-questions/.

Booker, Brianna. "Mulugeta Seraw (1960-1988)," *Blackpast*, August 30, 2020. https://www.blackpast.org/african-american-history/mulugeta-seraw-1960-1988/.

Borrows, John. *Canada's Indigenous Constitution*. Toronto: University of Toronto Press, 2010.

Borrows, John. *Freedom and Indigenous Constitutionalism*. Toronto: University of Toronto Press, 2016.

Bossio, Diana. "Canada's Online News Act may let Meta and Google decide the winners and losers in the media industry," *The Conversation*, 26 June, 2023, https://theconversation.com/canadas-online-news-act-may-let-meta-and-google-decide-the-winners-and-losers-in-the-media-industry-208088.

Braun, Stefan. *Democracy Off Balance: Freedom of Expression and Hate Propaganda Law in Canada*. Toronto: University of Toronto Press, 2014.

Brown, Abram. "What Is Section 230—And Why Does Trump Want To Change It?" *Forbes*, 28 May 2020, https://www.forbes.com/sites/abrambrown/2020/05/28/what-is-section-230-and-why-does-trump-want-to-change-it/?sh=4036ebaa389d.

Bueckert, Kate. "Laurier professor, president apologize to TA over video sanction," *CBC,* 17 December 2017. https://www.cbc.ca/news/canada/kitchener-waterloo/laurier-lindsay-shepherd-apology-video-petersen-1.4424590.

Cameron, Jamie. "Freedom Of Expression and the Charter:1982-2022 (Part 3 of 5)," Centre for Free Expression, blog, 28 July, 2022, https://cfe.torontomu.ca/blog/2022/07/freedom-expression-and-charter1982-2022-part-3-5.

Canadian Heritage, "Proposed Bill to address Online Harms," https://www.canada.ca/en/canadian-heritage/services/online-harms.html, accessed 1 March 2024.

CBC Out in the Open, "Free Speech On Campus: Where Should Universities Draw the Line?," 22 June 2018, https://www.cbc.ca/radio/outintheopen/free-speech-on-campus-where-should-universities-draw-the-line-1.4712119.

Chaudhury, Aadita. "The WLU/Lindsay Shepherd controversy was never about free speech," *Medium,* 28 November 2017. https://medium.com/@thylacinereport/the-wlu-lindsay-shepherd-controversy-was-never-about-free-speech-9fe3442da3c3.

Chilson, Neil and Casey Mattox, "[The] Breakup Speech: Can Antitrust Fix the Relationship Between Platforms and Free Speech Values?," Knight First Amendment Institute, 5 March 2020. https://knightcolumbia.org/content/the-breakup-speech-can-antitrust-fix-the-relationship-between-platforms-and-free-speech-values, accessed 19 April 2022.

Chun, Wendy Hui Kyong. *Control and Freedom.* Boston: MIT Press, 2008.

Chun, Wendy Hui Kyong. *Discriminating Data: Correlation, Neighborhoods, and the New Politics of Recognition.* Boston: MIT Press, 2024.

Committee on Freedom of Expression at the University of Chicago, "Report of the Committee on Freedom of Expression," 2014, https://freeexpression.uchicago.edu/

Confessore, Nicholas. "Cambridge Analytica and Facebook: The Scandal and the Fallout So Far," *The New York Times* 4 April 2018. https://www.nytimes.com/2018/04/04/us/politics/cambridge-analytica-scandal-fallout.html.

Cosh, Colby. "Is Neil Young's stand against Joe Rogan the natural outcome of 1960s anti-corporate spirit?" *The National Post,* 28 January 2022. https://nationalpost.com/opinion/colby-cosh-is-neil-youngs-stand-against-joe-rogan-the-natural-outcome-of-1960s-anti-corporate-spirit.

Court of Appeal of Alberta, *UAlberta Pro-Life v. Governors of the University of Alberta* (2020), https://canliiconnects.org/en/commentaries/73370.

Court of Queen's Bench of Alberta, *Pridgen v University of Calgary* (2010). https://www.canlii.org/en/ab/abqb/doc/2010/2010abqb644/2010abqb644.html.

Court of Queen's Bench of Alberta, *Wilson v University of Calgary* (2014), https://www.jccf.ca/wp-content/uploads/2014/04/Wilson-v-U-of-Calgary-April-2014-Judgment.pdf.

Crawford, Blair. "Laurier free speech advocate Lindsay Shepherd honoured in Ottawa, *The Ottawa Citizen,* 13 May 2018. https://ottawacitizen.com/news/local-news/laurier-free-speech-advocate-lindsay-shepherd-honoured-in-ottawa.

Crossley, Nick and John Michael Roberts, ed., *After Habermas: New Perspectives on the Public Sphere.* Oxford: Blackwell, 2004.

Crystal, David. *Language and the Internet.* Cambridge: Cambridge University Press, 2001.

Davie, Emma. "Dalhousie student faces disciplinary action over Canada 150 post," *CBC,* 17 October 2017, https://www.cbc.ca/news/canada/nova-scotia/masuma-khan-dalhousie-student-disciplinary-action-facebook-post-1.4364586.

Dea, Shannon. "First Dispatch: Academic Freedom and the Mission of the University," *University Affairs/Affaires Universitaires,* 5 September 2018. https://www.universityaffairs.ca/opinion/dispatches-academic-freedom/first-dispatch-academic-freedom-and-the-mission-of-the-university/.

Dea, Shannon, "A Brief History of Academic Freedom," *University Affairs/Affaires Universitaires*. October 9, 2018, https://universityaffairs.ca/opinion/dispatches-academic-freedom/a-brief-history-of-academic-freedom/.

Dea, Shannon. "Learning to Say Good Bye to Academic Freedom," *University Affairs/Affaires Universitaires*. 14 September, 2020, https://www.universityaffairs.ca/opinion/dispatches-academic-freedom/learning-to-say-goodbye-to-academic-freedom/.

Dea, Shannon. "Dispatches on Academic Freedom," *University Affairs/Affaires Universitaires* 5 September 2018 to 20 September 2022. https://www.universityaffairs.ca/opinion/dispatches-academic-freedom/.

Dea, Shannon. "The Evolving Social Purpose of Academic Freedom," *Kennedy Institute of Ethics Journal* 31, 2 (2021), 199-222.

Deibert, Ronald. *Reset: Reclaiming the Internet for Civil Society*. Toronto: Anansi, 2020.

Denson, Bryan. "1998 story: Legacy of a hate crime: Mulugeta Seraw's death a decade ago avenged," *The Oregonian*, 12 November, 2014. https://www.oregonlive.com/portland/2014/11/1998_story_legacy_of_a_hate_cr.html.

Doctorow, Cory. *The Internet Con: How to Seize the Means of Computation*. London: Verso, 2023.

D'Orazio, Dax. "How and Why the Chicago Principles Came to Canada," *American Review of Canadian Studies* 51, 4 (2021), 533-53.

D'Orazio, Dax. "Deplatforming in Theory and Practice," in *The Dilemmas of Free Expression*, Emmett Macfarlane, ed. Toronto: University of Toronto Press, 2021, 269-98.

Dummitt, Christopher. "Oh look, the progressive left suddenly cares about free speech," *The National Post*, 16 November 2023, https://nationalpost.com/opinion/christopher-dummitt-oh-look-the-progressive-left-suddenly-cares-about-free-speech.

Dragicevic, Nina. "Canada's Gender Identity Rights Bill C-16 Explained," CBC, n.d., https://www.cbc.ca/cbcdocspov/features/canadas-gender-identity-rights-bill-c-16-explained.

Djuric, Mickey. "Conservatives ran on similar media policy as Liberals, but now claim it's censorship," *CBC News*, 2 August, 2023, https://www.cbc.ca/news/politics/conservatives-policy-tech-giants-online-news-1.6925990.

Feldman, Noah. "Israel-Hamas War Tests Left's Views on Cancel Culture," *The Washington Post*, 25 October 2023, https://www.washingtonpost.com/business/2023/10/25/israel-hamas-war-tests-left-s-views-on-cancel-culture/86ba918e-7336-11ee-936d-7a16ee667359_story.html.

Finckenstein, Konrad Von and Peter Menzies, "Social Media Responsibility and Free Speech," Macdonald-Laurier Institute, February 2022. https://macdonaldlaurier.ca/mli-files/pdf/Feb2022_Social_media_responsibility_and_free_speech_Finckenstein_Menzies_PAPER_FWeb.pdf, accessed 10 April 2022.

Finkin, Matthew and Robert Post, *For the Common Good: Principles of American Academic Freedom*. New Haven: Yale University Press, 2009.

Fish, Stanley. *There's No Such Thing As Free Speech*. Oxford: Oxford University Press, 1994.

Fish, Stanley. *The First: How to Think about Hate Speech, Campus Speech, Religious Speech, Fake News, Post-Truth, and Donald Trump*. New York: Atria, 2019.

Flaherty, Colleen. "Diversifying a Classic Humanities Course," *Inside Higher Ed,* 11 April 2018, https://www.insidehighered.com/news/2018/04/12/responding-student-criticism-its-foundational-humanities-course-too-white-reed.

Forde, Eamonn. "Rogan in the Free (Speech) World," *Forbes,* 25 January 2022. https://www.forbes.com/sites/eamonnforde/2022/01/25/rogan-in-the-free-speech-world-neil-young-wants-to-pull-music-from-spotify-over-podcast-host-controversy/?sh=1220be444fdd.

Forrest, Maura. "There's a debate over Canada's new definition of anti-Semitism, and it might sound strangely familiar," *National Post,* 27 June 2019, https://nationalpost.com/news/politics/theres-a-debate-over-canadas-new-definition-of-anti-semitism-and-it-might-sound-strangely-familiar.

Fraser Institute, Student Centre, Essential Scholars, accessed 26 August 2022, https://www.fraserinstitute.org/education-programs/west/student-centre.

Fraser, Nancy. *Unruly Practices: Power, Discourse and Gender in Contemporary Social Theory.* Minneapolis: University of Minnesota Press, 1989.

Gabbert, Mark. "Academic Freedom: Freedom of Expression's Vulnerable Child," *CAUT Journal de l'ACPPU,* 2021, https://journal.caut.ca/index.php/caut-journal/article/view/5.

Gandesha, Samir. "In Defense of Free Speech," *Canadian Dimension,* 13 March 2018, https://canadiandimension.com/articles/view/in-defense-of-free-speech.

Garton Ash, Timothy. *Free Speech: Ten Principles for a Connected World.* New Haven: Yale University Press, 2016.

Gayle, Damien. "Facebook Aware of Instagram's Harmful Effects on Teenage Girls, Leak Reveals," *The Guardian* 14 September, 2021. https://www.theguardian.com/technology/2021/sep/14/faccbook-aware-instagram-harmful-effect-teenage-girls-leak-reveals, accessed 23 March 2022.

Gehl, Robert. "Citizens' social media can provide an antidote to propaganda and disinformation," *The Conversation,* 22 October 2022. https://theconversation.com/citizens-social-media-can-provide-an-antidote-to-propaganda-and-disinformation-192491.

Gerber, Scott. "The Politics of Free Speech," *Social Philosophy and Policy* 21, 2 (July 2004), 23-47.

Gerstein, Josh. "Appeals court doubtful on Trump's lawsuit against Twitter," *Politico,* 4 October 2023, https://www.politico.com/news/2023/10/04/appeals-court-doubtful-on-trumps-lawsuit-against-twitter-00119981.

Glaser, April. "White Supremacists Still Have A Safe Space Online," *Slate,* 9 October 2018. https://slate.com/technology/2018/10/discord-safe-space-white-supremacists.html.

Globe and Mail Editors. "Why are we killing critical thinking on campus?," *Globe and Mail,* 16 November 2017. https://www.theglobeandmail.com/opinion/editorials/globe-editorial-why-are-we-killing-critical-thinking-on-campus/article37008714/.

Goldmacher, Shane. "Trump Sues Tech Firms for Blocking Him, and Fund-Raises Off it," *New York Times,* 7 July 2021. https://www.nytimes.com/2021/07/07/us/politics/trump-lawsuit-facebook-google-twitter.html.

Government of Canada, Criminal Code, (R.S.C., 1985), c. C-46, https://laws-lois.justice.gc.ca/eng/acts/c-46/section-318.html.

Government of Canada, The Online News Act, https://www.canada.ca/en/canadian-heritage/services/online-news.html, accessed 15 January 2024.

Government of Manitoba, "The Advanced Education Administration Act," https://web2.gov.mb.ca/laws/statutes/ccsm/a006-3e.php, accessed 22 February, 2022.

Gray, John. *Mill on Liberty: A Defense,* 2nd Ed. London: Routledge, 1996.

Greenawalt, Kent. *Fighting Words.* Princeton: Princeton University Press, 1995.

Habermas, Jürgen. *The Structural Transformation of the Public Sphere,* translated by Thomas McCarthy. Cambridge, Mass.: MIT Press, 1989.

Haidt, Jonathan. "Why the Last Ten Years of American Life Have Been Uniquely Stupid," *The Atlantic,* 11 April 2022, https://www.theatlantic.com/magazine/archive/2022/05/social-media-democracy-trust-babel/629369/.

Halliday, Josh. "Twitter's Tony Wang: 'We are the free speech wing of the free speech party," *The Guardian,* 22 March 2012. https://www.theguardian.com/media/2012/mar/22/twitter-tony-wang-free-speech.

Hampton Keith N., Inyoung Shin & Weixu Lu, "Social media and political discussion," *Information, Communication & Society,* 20:7 (2017), 1090-1107.

Haque, Eve. *Multiculturalism Within a Bilingual Framework.* Toronto: University of Toronto Press, 2012.

Haque, Eve. "The Singular Freedom of Academic Freedom," *Journal of Historical Sociology,* 29, 1 (March 2016), 112-25.

Hare, Ivan and James Weinstein, eds., *Extreme Speech and Democracy.* Oxford: Oxford University Press, 2014.

Hannan, Jason. *Trolling Ourselves to Death: Democracy in the Age of Social Media.* Oxford: Oxford University Press, 2023.

Harris Elizabeth A. and Alexandra Alter, "Simon & Schuster Cancels Plans for Senator Hawley's Book," *New York Time,* January 7, 2021, https://www.nytimes.com/2021/01/07/books/simon-schuster-josh-hawley-book.html.

Hayek, F.A. *The Road to Serfdom,* Bruce Caldwell, ed. Chicago: University of Chicago Press, 2007.

Heer, Jeet. "The Left Needs to Reclaim Free Speech," *The Nation,* 10 July 2020. https://www.thenation.com/article/society/left-free-speech-harpers/.

Helmore, Edward. "Harsh Truth: Trump's Social Media App Follows Long Line of Failed Products," *The Guardian* 9 April, 2022. https://www.theguardian.com/us-news/2022/apr/09/truth-social-trump-app-failed-products.

Hern, Alex. "What is the GDPR and how will it affect you?" *The Guardian,* 21 May 2018. https://www.theguardian.com/technology/2018/may/21/what-is-gdpr-and-how-will-it-affect-you.

Holyk, Alexandra. "Winnipeg MP signs letter calling on university presidents to address antisemitism on campus," *CTV News,* 15 December 2023, https://winnipeg.ctvnews.ca/winnipeg-mp-signs-letter-calling-on-university-presidents-to-address-antisemitism-on-campus-1.6690022.

Horn, Michael. *Academic Freedom in Canada: A History.* Toronto: University of Toronto Press, 1999.

Hrynyshyn, Derek. "Imagining Platform Socialism," in *The Socialist Register 57: Beyond Digital Capitalism,* Leo Panitch and Greg Albo, eds., London: Merlin, 2021, 137-52.

Hudson, David. "In the Age of Social Media, Expand the Reach of the First Amendment," *The Human Rights Magazine.* American Bar Association, 43, 4

(October 2018), https://www.americanbar.org/groups/crsj/publications/human_rights_magazine_home/the-ongoing-challenge-to-define-free-speech/in-the-age-of-socia-media-first-amendment/, accessed 20 April 2022.

Hughes, Chris. "It's Time to Break Up Facebook," *The New York Times*, 9 May 2019. https://www.nytimes.com/2019/05/09/opinion/sunday/chris-hughes-facebook-zuckerberg.html.

Independent Jewish Voices Canada, "The IHRA Definition at Work," 4 September 2020. https://www.ijvcanada.org/ihra-definition-at-work/#Canada.

Innis, Harold. *Empire and Communication*. Oxford: Clarendon Press, 1950.

International Holocaust Remembrance Alliance. https://www.holocaustremembrance.com/resources/working-definitions-charters/working-definition-antisemitism accessed 15 August 2022.

Ives, Peter. *Gramsci's Politics of Language: Engaging the Bakhtin Circle and the Frankfurt School*. Toronto: University of Toronto Press, 2004.

Ives, Peter. "Cosmopolitanism and Global English," *Political Studies* 58, 3 (2010), 516-35.

Ives, Peter. "Language and Collective Identity: Theorizing Complexity," in *Language and Identity Politics,* ed. Christina Späti. Oxford: Berghann, 2016, 17-37.

Ives, Peter. "Canadian Language Politics in Global and Theoretical Contexts," in *Language Politics and Policies*, Thomas Ricento, ed. Cambridge: Cambridge University Press, 2019, 78-94.

Ives, Peter and Eve Haque, "What is Québec's Bill 32 on Academic Freedom and Why Does it Matter," *The Conversation*, 1 June 2022. https://theconversation.com/what-is-quebecs-bill-32-on-academic-freedom-and-why-does-it-matter-183122.

"Jerusalem Declaration on Antisemitism," *The Jerusalem Declaration on Antisemitism*, convened by the Van Leer Jerusalem Institute, 25 March 2021, https://jerusalemdeclaration.org/, accessed 15 March 2023.

"Jewish Faculty Against the IHRA Working Definition of Antisemitism," *Jewish Faculty Network,* https://jewishfaculty.ca/jewish-faculty-against-the-ihra-defn/, accessed 28 December 2022.

Jilani, Zaid. "Heart of Scold," *City Journal*, 28 January 2022. https://www.city-journal.org/neil-young-v-joe-rogan-and-free-speech.

Kang, Cecilia. "What is Facebook's Oversight Board?" *The New York Times*, 5 May 2021. https://www.nytimes.com/2021/05/05/technology/What-Is-the-Facebook-Oversight-Board.html.

Kant, Immanuel. "An Answer to the Question: 'What is Enlightenment?'" in Hans Reiss, ed. *Kant's Political Writings*. Cambridge: Cambridge University Press, 1970.

Khanna, Ro. *Dignity in a Digital Age*. New York: Simon & Shuster, 2022.

King, jr, Martin Luther. "I've Been to the Mountaintop," 3 April, 1968, https://www.afscme.org/about/history/mlk/mountaintop.

King, jr, Martin Luther. "Letter from Birmingham Jail," in *Twentieth Century Political Theory: A Reader,* Stephen Eric Bronner, ed. New York: Routledge, 1997, 291-302.

Klein, Betsy. "White House Reviewing Section 230 Amid Efforts to Push Social Media Giants to Crack Down on Misinformation," *CNN,* 21 July 2021, https://www.cnn.com/2021/07/20/politics/white-house-section-230-facebook/index.html.

Knight Foundation, "Techlash? Americans Growing Concern with Major Technology Companies," 11 March 2020. https://knightfoundation.org/wp-content/uploads/2020/03/Gallup-Knight-Report-Techlash-Americas-Growing-Concern-with-Major-Tech-Companies-Final.pdf, accessed 18 April 2022.

Knight Foundation, "The Future of Tech Policy: American Views," 16 June 2020. https://knightfoundation.org/reports/the-future-of-tech-policy-american-views/ accessed 4 April 2022.

Kohn, Daniel. "Neil Young on Joe Rogan, Spotify Spat," *Spin,* 28 January 2022. https://www.spin.com/2022/01/neil-young-joe-rogan-spotify-2/.

Kraft, Emilie. "Academic Freedom," *The First Amendment Encyclopedia*, updated June 2017. https://www.mtsu.edu/first-amendment/article/17/academic-freedom.

LaDuke, Winona. "Minobimaatisiiwin: The Good Life," *Cultural Survival*, 16 March 2010. https://www.culturalsurvival.org/publications/cultural-survival-quarterly/minobimaatisiiwin-good-life.

Leaker, Anthony. *Against Free Speech*. Lanham, Maryland: Rowman & Littlefield, 2020.

Leetaru, Kalev. "Has Social Media Killed Free Speech?" *Forbes*, 31 October 2016. https://www.forbes.com/sites/kalevleetaru/2016/10/31/has-social-media-killed-free-speech/?sh=4109b69046b1.

Leiter, Brian. "The Case Against Free Speech," *The Sydney Law Review* 38, 2016, pp.407-39.

Lemieux, Scott. "Free speech doesn't mean speech free from all consequences, despite what some conservatives argue," *NBCNews, Think: Opinion, Analysis, Essays,* 6 July 2019, https://www.nbcnews.com/think/opinion/free-speech-doesn-t-mean-speech-free-all-consequences-despite-ncna1026911.

Leong, Nancy & Kevin Whitfield, "The Marketplace of Racist Ideas," *Law, Culture and the Humanities,* October 19, 2020.

Levin, Sam. "Is Facebook a Publisher? In Public It Says No, but in Court it says Yes," *The Guardian,* 3 July, 2018. https://www.theguardian.com/technology/2018/jul/02/facebook-mark-zuckerberg-platform-publisher-lawsuit.

Lewis, Atrisha, et al, "Free speech on campus is subject to the Charter — but only in Alberta," *McCarthyTetrault,* 15 January 2020, https://www.mccarthy.ca/en/insights/blogs/canadian-appeals-monitor/free-speech-campus-subject-charter-only-alberta, accessed 15 March 2023.

Lindsay, Bethany. "B.C. Doctor Disciplined for 'Harmful' COVID-19 Misinformation Claims Free Speech Violations," *CBC News,* 7 July 2021. https://www.cbc.ca/news/canada/british-columbia/bc-stephen-malthouse-doctors-petition-college-1.6092437.

Ljunggren, David. "Canada Unveils Plans to Make Online Hate Speech a Crime," *Reuters,* 23 June 2021, https://www.reuters.com/world/americas/canada-unveils-plans-make-online-hate-speech-crime-2021-06-23/.

Lohr, Steve "He Created the Web. Now He's Out to Remake the Digital World," *The New York Times*, 10 January 2021. https://www.nytimes.com/2021/01/10/technology/tim-berners-lee-privacy-internet.html.

Lomas, Natasha. "Meta Urged to Pay Reparations for Facebook's Role in Rohingya Genocide," *Tech Crunch,* 29 September, 2022, https://techcrunch.com/2022/09/29/amnesty-report-facebook-rohingya-reparations/.

London, Rob. "Sending a $12.5 Million Message to a Hate Group," *New York Times,* 26 October 1990, 56. https://www.nytimes.com/1990/10/26/news/sending-a-12.5-million-message-to-a-hate-group.html.

Losurdo, Domenico. *Liberalism: A Counter-History,* trans. By Gregory Elliot. London: Verso, 2011.

Luckerson, Victor. "Here's Why Facebook Won't Put Your News Feed in Chronological Order," *Time Magazine,* 9 July 2015. https://time.com/3951337/facebook-chronological-order/.

Lynk, Michael. "Academic Freedom, Canadian Labour Law and the Scope of Intra-Mural Expression," *Constitutional Forum constitutionnel* 29, 2 (2020), 45-64.

Maher, Stephen. "Jordan Peterson and the Big Mistake of University Censors," *Maclean's,* 17 November, 2017, https://www.macleans.ca/news/canada/jordan-peterson-and-the-big-mistake-of-university-censors/.

Macfarlane, Emmett, ed. *The Dilemmas of Free Expression.* Toronto: University of Toronto Press, 2021.

Macfarlane, Emmett. "Hate Speech, Harm, and Rights," in *The Dilemmas of Free Expression,* Emmett Macfarlane, ed. Toronto: University of Toronto Press, 2021, 35-55.

Macfarlane, Emmett. "Beyond the Hate Speech Law Debate: A '*Charter* Values' Approach to Free Expression," *Review of Constitutional Studies / Revue d'études constitutionelles* 26, 2/27, 1 (2022), 145-168.

MacLatchy, Deborah. "Not merely free speech, but better speech needs to be protected on campus," *The Globe and Mail,* 31 July 2018. https://www.theglobeandmail.com/opinion/article-not-merely-free-speech-but-better-speech-needs-to-be-protected-on/.

McDonald, Moira. "Free speech on campus: The age old debate rages on," *University Affairs/Affaires Universitaires,* 3 October 2018, https://www.universityaffairs.ca/features/feature-article/free-speech-the-age-old-debate-rages-on/

McGraw, Meridith, Tina Nguyen and Cristiano Lima, "Team Trump quietly launches new social media platform," *Politico,* 1 July 2021. https://www.politico.com/news/2021/07/01/gettr-trump-social-media-platform-497606.

Mchangama, Jacob. *Free Speech: From Socrates to Social Media.* New York: Basic Books, 2022.

McLuhan, Marshall. *The Gutenberg Galaxy.* Toronto: University of Toronto Press, 1962.

McLuhan, Marshall, *Understanding Media.* New York: McGraw-Hill, 1964.

Mehta, Uday Singh. *Liberalism and Empire.* Chicago: University of Chicago Press, 1999.

Meiklejohn, Alexander. *Free Speech and Its Relation to Self-Government.* New York: Harper & Brothers, 1948.

Mercer, Greg. "Laurier president promises change after Shepherd affair," *The Record,* December 18, 2017, https://www.therecord.com/news/waterloo-region/2017/12/18/laurier-president-promises-change-after-shepherd-affair.html.

Mercer, Rick. "Rick's Rant: University Censorship," 28 November 2017. https://www.youtube.com/watch?v=JCy-nLzlTKs, accessed July 20, 2021.

Mesley, Wendy. "I made mistakes. But my departure wasn't the solution to the CBC's problem with racism," *The Globe & Mail*, 7 July 2021, https://www.theglobeandmail.com/opinion/article-the-cbcs-issues-with-systemic-racism-go-beyond-the-two-worst-moments/.

Metzger, Walter. "Profession and Constitution: Two Definitions of Academic Freedom in America," *Texas Law Review* 66 (1988), 1286-1322.

Mill, John Stuart. *On Liberty and Other Writings*, Stefan Colini, ed. Cambridge: Cambridge University Press, 1989 [1859].

Mill, John Stuart. *Considerations on Representative Government.* Atlanta: Cherokee, 2007.

Miller, Dale. "The Place of 'The Liberty of Thought and Discussion' in *On Liberty*," *Utilitas* (2021), 33, 133–149.

Mills, Charles W. *Black Rights / White Wrongs: A Critique of Racial Liberalism*. Oxford: Oxford University Press, 2017.

Milmo, Dan. "Rohingya Sue Facebook for 150bn Over Myanmar Genocide," *The Guardian* 6 December, 2021. https://www.theguardian.com/technology/2021/dec/06/rohingya-sue-facebook-myanmar-genocide-us-uk-legal-action-social-media-violence.

Mohawk, John. "The Indian Way Is a Thinking Tradition," in *Indian Roots of American Democracy*, José Barreiro, ed. Ithaca, N.Y.: Akwe:kon Press, 1992, 20-29.

Mondal, Anshuman. "The Shape of Free Speech," *Continuum* 32, 4 (2018), 503-17.

Moon, Richard. *The Constitutional Protection of Freedom of Expression.* Toronto: University of Toronto Press, 2000.

Moon, Richard. *Report to the Canadian Human Rights Commission*, 2008, 4. https://publications.gc.ca/site/eng/9.819307/publication.html.

Moon, Richard. "Does Freedom of Expression Have a Future?" in *Dilemmas of Free Expression*, Emmett Macfarlane, ed. Toronto: University of Toronto Press, 2021.

Morrison, Sara. "Elizabeth Warren's plan to break up Big Everything," *Vox*, 5 April 2022. https://www.vox.com/recode/23003056/elizabeth-warren-big-tech-mergers.

Moskowitz, P.E. *The Case Against Free Speech.* New York: Bold Type Book, 2019.

Mostyn, Michael, Stuart Kamenetsky, and Howard Tenenbaum, "University of Toronto must act now to uproot antisemitism," *The Toronto Star*, 2 February, 2021. https://www.thestar.com/opinion/contributors/2021/02/02/university-of-toronto-must-act-now-to-uproot-antisemitism.html.

Muldoon, James. *Platform Socialism: How to Reclaim our Digital Future from Big Tech,* London: Pluto, 2021.

Muthu, Sankar. *Enlightenment Against Empire*. Princeton: Princeton University Press, 2003.

Nadeau, Mary-Jo and Alan Sears, "The Palestine Test: Countering the Silencing Campaign," *Studies in Political Economy* 85, 1 (2010), 7-33. https://doi.org/10.1080/19187033.2010.11675033.

Napoli, Philip. *Social Media and the Public Interest*. New York: Columbia University Press, 2019.

Napoli, Philip and Robyn Caplan, "Why Media Companies Insist They're Not Media Companies, Why They Are Wrong, and Why it Matters," *First Monday*, Volume 22, Number 5, 1 May 2017. https://journals.uic.edu/ojs/index.php/fm/article/view/7051/6124, accessed 5 April 2022.

National Assembly of Québec, Forty-Second Legislature, Second Session, 7 June, 2022, http://www2.publicationsduquebec.gouv.qc.ca/dynamicSearch/telecharge.php?type=5&file=2022C21A.PDF.

Newhouse, David. "Teiakwanahstahsontéhrha' – We Extend the Rafters," in *Dilemmas of Free Expression,* Emmett Macfarlane, ed. Toronto: University of Toronto Press, 2021, 222-35.

New York State Supreme Court, *Stratton Oakmont, Inc. v. Prodigy Services Co.* (1995), https://h2o.law.harvard.edu/cases/4540.

Office of the Premier of Ontario. "Upholding Free Speech on Ontario University and College Campuses," 30 August 2018. https://news.ontario.ca/en/backgrounder/49950/upholding-free-speech-on-ontarios-university-and-college-campuses.

O'Hueglin, Thomas. "There's a difference between freedom of expression and academic freedom," *The Record,* 23 March, 2018, https://www.therecord.com/opinion/contributors/2018/03/23/there-s-a-difference-between-freedom-of-expression-and-academic-freedom.html.

Oladipo, Gloria. "Supporters Rally Around Rashida Tlaib After Censure While Whitehouse Denounces Use of Slogan," *The Guardian,* 8 November 2023, https://www.theguardian.com/us-news/2023/nov/08/rashida-tlaib-censure-vote-palestine-support-congress.

Oliphant, Benjamin. "Positive Rights, Negative Freedoms and Expressive Freedom," in *The Dilemmas of Free Expression,* Emmett Macfarlane, ed. Toronto: University of Toronto Press, 2021, 130-50.

Oremus, Will. "Why Facebook Won't Let you Control Your Own News Feed," *The Washington Post,* 13 November 2021. https://www.washingtonpost.com/technology/2021/11/13/facebook-news-feed-algorithm-how-to-turn-it-off/.

Paikin, Steve and Jordan Peterson, "Gender, Rights and Freedom of Speech," TVO *The Agenda,* 26 October 2016. https://www.tvo.org/video/genders-rights-and-freedom-of-speech.

Parekh, Bhikhu. "Non-Western Political Thought," in *The Cambridge History of Twentieth-Century Political Thought,* eds. Terence Ball and Richard Bellamy. Cambridge: Cambridge University Press, 553-78.

Parker, Richard. "Clear and Present Danger Test," in *The First Amendment Encyclopedia,* 2009, https://www.mtsu.edu/first-amendment/article/898/clear-and-present-danger-test.

Paul, Kari. "A brutal year: how the 'techlash' caught up with Facebook, Google and Amazon," *The Guardian* 28 December 2019, https://www.theguardian.com/technology/2019/dec/28/tech-industry-year-in-review-facebook-google-amazon.

Penny, Laurie. "No I will Not Debate You," *Long Reads,* 18 September 2018, https://longreads.com/2018/09/18/no-i-will-not-debate-you/#more-113762, accessed 5 March 2023.

Perino, Nico and Dale E. Miller, "John Stuart Mill's *On Liberty,*" 26 November 2019, *So To Speak: The Free Speech Podcast, Episode 99,* produced by FIRE (Foundation For Individual Rights in Education), MP3 Audio, 1:27.30, https://www.thefire.org/news/podcasts/so-speak-free-speech-podcast/john-stuart-mills-liberty.

Perrigo, Billy. "Facebook and Twitter Finally Locked Donald Trump's Accounts. Will They Ban Him Permanently?," *Time Magazine.* 7 January 2021, https://time.com/5927398/facebook-twitter-trump-suspension-capitol/.

Peters, John Durham. *Courting the Abyss: Free Speech and the Liberal Tradition.* Chicago: Chicago University Press, 2005.

Petersen, Jennifer. *How Machines Came to Speak: Media Technologies and the Freedom of Speech.* Durham: Duke University Press, 2022.

Pits, Leonard. "Freedom of Speech is not Freedom from Consequences," *Times-Republican*, 24 March 2022. https://www.timesrepublican.com/opinion/columnists/2022/03/freedom-of-speech-is-not-freedom-from-consequences/.

Posadski, Alexandra. "How a coding error caused Rogers outage that left millions without service," *The Globe & Mail*, 25 July 2022. https://www.theglobeandmail.com/business/article-how-a-coding-error-caused-rogers-outage-that-left-millions-without/.

Postman, Neil. *Amusing Ourselves to Death.* New York: Viking, 1985.

Prat, Andrea. "Measuring and Protecting Media Plurality in the Digital Age," First Amendment Institute at Columbia University, 10 August 2020. https://knightcolumbia.org/content/measuring-and-protecting-media-plurality-in-the-digital-age, accessed 20 April 2022.

Proctor, Jason. "Award-winning documentary maker accuses Twitter of muzzling speech critical of corporations," *CBC*, 25 July 2021. https://www.cbc.ca/news/canada/british-columbia/twitter-corporation-free-speech-lawsuit-1.6113724.

Rahman, Sabeel and Zephyr Teachout, "From Private Bads to Public Goods: Adapting Public Utility Regulation for Informational Infrastructure," Knight First Amendment Institute, 4 February 2020, 19. https://knightcolumbia.org/content/from-private-bads-to-public-goods-adapting-public-utility-regulation-for-informational-infrastructure, accessed 14 April 2022.

Rangwala, Shama. "The real free-speech crisis on Alberta's campuses might not be what you think it is," *Globe & Mail*, 31 August, 2019, https://www.theglobeandmail.com/opinion/article-the-real-free-speech-crisis-on-albertas-campuses-might-not-be-what/.

Rangwala, Shama. "Free Speech and the University: A Closer Look at the Chicago Principles," *Pyrisense*, 30 May, 2019, https://www.pyriscence.ca/home/2019/5/30/chicagoprinciples, accessed 18 February, 2022.

Riski, Tess and Aaron Mesh, "Kyle Brewster, Convicted in 1988 Killing of Mulugeta Seraw, Fought at Jan. 6 Pro-Trump Rally in Sale," *Willamette Week*, 17 January 2021. https://www.wweek.com/news/2021/01/17/kyle-brewster-convicted-in-1988-killing-of-mulugeta-seraw-fought-at-jan-6-pro-trump-rally-in-salem/.

Romney, Lee. "Metzger Seized by Canadian Authorities After Speech," *LA Times*, 30 June 1992. https://www.latimes.com/archives/la-xpm-1992-06-30-me-1437-story.html.

Rousseau, Jean-Jacques. *The Social Contract.* London: Penguin Classics, 1968.

Rousseau, Jean-Jacques. *First and Second Discourse, Together with Replies to the Critics and Essays on the Origin of Languages.* New York: Harper Collins, 1986.

Russell, Andrew. "Wilfrid Laurier TA happy school apologized but wants long-term changes to protect free speech," *Global News*, 22 November, 2017, https://globalnews.ca/news/3874929/wilfrid-laurier-freedom-of-speech-lindsay-shepherd-apology-change/.

Sachs, Jeffrey. "Canada's new definition of anti-Semitism is a threat to campus free speech," *University Affairs/Affaires Universitaires*, 10 September 2019.

https://www.universityaffairs.ca/opinion/in-my-opinion/canadas-new-definition-of-anti-semitism-is-a-threat-to-campus-free-speech/.

Sachs, Jeffrey. "Faculty Free Speech in Canada," in *Dilemmas of Free Expression*, Emmett Macfarlane, ed. Toronto: University of Toronto Press, 2021, 236-51.

Sanders, Bernie. "Op-Ed: Bernie Sanders on his plan for journalism," *Columbia Journalism Review*, 26 August 2019. https://www.cjr.org/opinion/bernie-sanders-media-silicon-valley.php.

Saxonhouse, Arlene. *Free Speech and Democracy in Ancient Athens*. Cambridge: Cambridge University Press, 2006.

Schauer, Frederick. *Free Speech: A Philosophical Inquiry*. Cambridge: Cambridge University Press, 1982.

Schleck, Julia. *Dirty Knowledge: Academic Freedom in the Age of Neoliberalism*. Lincoln: University of Nebraska Press, 2023.

Scholz, Trebor. "Platform Cooperativism: Challenging the Corporate Sharing Economy," Rosa Luxemburg Stiftung, New York, 2016. https://rosalux.nyc/wp-content/uploads/2020/11/RLS-NYC_platformcoop.pdf, accessed 20 April 2022.

Schott, Robin May. "The Gender of Enlightenment," in Robin May Schott, ed., *Feminist Interpretations of Immanuel Kant*. University Park, PA: University of Pennsylvania Press, 1997, 319-340.

Schroeder, Jared. "Towards a Discursive Marketplace of Ideas," *First Amendment Studies* 52, 1-2 (2018), 38-60.

Schultz, David. "The Marketplace of Ideas," in *The First Amendment Encyclopedia*, 2009, https://www.mtsu.edu/first-amendment/article/999/marketplace-of-ideas.

Scott, Joan Wallach. *Knowledge, Power, and Academic Freedom*. New York: Columbia University Press, 2019.

Sedgwick, Rosemary et al., "Social media, internet use and suicide attempts in adolescents," *Current Opinion in Psychiatry* 32, 6 (November 2019), pp.534-41, https://journals.lww.com/co-psychiatry/Fulltext/2019/11000/Social_media,_internet_use_and_suicide_attempts_in.12.aspx.

Selig, Kate. "California's Leonard Law: What it means for campus speakers," *The Daily Stanford*, 20 May, 2020, https://stanforddaily.com/2020/05/20/californias-leonard-law-what-it-means-for-campus-speakers/.

Shenker, Jack. "Revealed: The Insidious Creep of Pseudo-Public Space in London," *The Guardian*, 24 July 2017, https://www.theguardian.com/cities/2017/jul/24/revealed-pseudo-public-space-pops-london-investigation-map.

Shepherd, Lindsay. *Diversity & Exclusion: Confronting the Campus Free Speech Crisis*. Bolton, ON.: Magna Carta, 2021.

Shibley, Robert. "Martin Luther King, Free Speech, and the Albany Movement," Fire Newsdesk, 16 January 2017. https://www.thefire.org/news/martin-luther-king-free-speech-and-albany-movement, accessed 15 March 2023.

Smith, Madeline. "Kenney Follows Ford's Push for Campus Free Speech," *The Toronto Star*, 8 May 2019. https://www.thestar.com/calgary/2019/05/06/alberta-and-ontario-premiers-campus-free-speech-policies-a-dog-whistle-blow-for-the-right-expert.html.

Smith, Stephen A. *Freedom of Expression*. Oxford: Oxbridge Research Associates, 2018.

Snapes, Laura "Joni Mitchell follows Neil Young in returning her music to Spotify," *The Guardian* 22 March, 2024, https://www.theguardian.com/music/2024/mar/22/joni-mitchell-follows-neil-young-in-returning-her-music-to-spotify.

Sparrow, Robert and Robert Goodin, "The Competition of Ideas: Market or Garden?" *Critical Review of International Social and Political Philosophy* 4, 2 (2001), 45-58.

Srnicek, Nick. *Platform Capitalism.* Cambridge: Polity, 2017.

Stanway, Paul. "Lindsay Shepherd Tells All," *C2C Journal,* 9 April 2021. https://c2cjournal.ca/2021/04/lindsay-shepherd-tells-all/.

Stern, Kenneth. "I drafted the definition of antisemitism. Rightwing Jews are weaponizing it," *The Guardian,* 13 December 2020, https://www.theguardian.com/commentisfree/2019/dec/13/antisemitism-executive-order-trump-chilling-effect?fbclid=IwAR3o_RVfoJXieaRFooXktpzSCDqjP2InYqfxcTNHUYHaMUW5DuXhARupEA.

Stevenson, Jane. "Conservative Leader Pierre Poilievre defends Jordan Peterson's right to free speech," *The Toronto Sun,* 7 January 2023, https://torontosun.com/news/national/conservative-leader-pierre-poilievre-defends-jordan-petersons-right-to-free-speech.

Stone, Geoffrey R., et al., "Report of the Committee on Freedom of Expression," University of Chicago, 2014, https://provost.uchicago.edu/sites/default/files/documents/reports/FOECommitteeReport.pdf.

Supreme Court of Canada, *Irwin Toy Ltd. v. Quebec,* 1989, https://www.canlii.org/en/ca/scc/doc/1989/1989canlii87/1989canlii87.html.

Supreme Court of Canada, *McKinney v. University of Guelph,* 1990, https://scc-csc.lexum.com/scc-csc/scc-csc/en/item/687/index.do.

Supreme Court of Canada, *R. v Keegstra,* 1990, https://scc-csc.lexum.com/scc-csc/scc-csc/en/item/695/index.do.

Supreme Court of Canada, *Eldridge v. British Columbia* (1997), https://scc-csc.lexum.com/scc-csc/scc-csc/en/item/1552/index.do.

Supreme Court of Canada, *Saskatchewan (Human Rights Commission) v. Whatcott,* 2013, https://scc-csc.lexum.com/scc-csc/scc-csc/en/item/12876/index.do.

Supreme Court of the United States, *Schenck v. United States,* 249 U.S. 47 (1919), https://supreme.justia.com/cases/federal/us/249/47/.

Supreme Court of the United States, *Adler v. Board of Education of the City of New York* (1952), https://www.law.cornell.edu/supremecourt/text/342/485.

Supreme Court of the United States, *Sweezy v. New Hampshire* (1957), https://tile.loc.gov/storage-services/service/ll/usrep/usrep354/usrep354234/usrep354234.pdf.

Swan, Kaitlyn. "Dalhousie grad gets long-awaited apology from university via tweet," *CBC,* 25 October 2019, https://www.cbc.ca/news/canada/nova-scotia/masuma-khan-dalhousie-university-apology-1.5335599.

Sweney, Mark. "Facebook outage highlights global over-reliance on its services," *The Guardian,* 5 October, 2021. https://www.theguardian.com/technology/2021/oct/05/facebook-outage-highlights-global-over-reliance-on-its-services.

Swisher, Kara and Jason Miller, "How Jason Miller Is Trying to Get Trump Back on the Internet," 19 August 2021, in Podcast *Sway,* produced by The New York Times, MP3 audio. https://www.nytimes.com/2021/08/19/opinion/sway-kara-swisher-jason-miller.html.

Tarnoff, Ben. *Internet for the People: The Fight for our Digital Future.* London: Verso, 2022.

Taylor, Charles. "Atomism," in *Philosophy and the Human Sciences*. Cambridge: Cambridge University Press, 1985, 187-210.

Titley, Gavin. *Is Free Speech Racist?* Cambridge: Polity Press, 2020.

Thibault, Daniel et al, "Federal government reaches deal with Google on Online News Act," *CBC News*, 29 November, 2023, https://www.cbc.ca/news/politics/google-online-news-act-1.7043330.

Tsai, Daniel. "Online platforms must be made liable for third-party hate content — and it might happen soon," *The Toronto Star*, 30 October 2020. https://www.thestar.com/business/opinion/2020/10/30/online-platforms-must-be-made-liable-for-third-party-hate-content.html.

Tsioulcas, Anastasia. "David Crosby, Graham Nash and Stephen Stills ask to Pull Their Content from Spotify," NPR Music News, 2 February 2022. https://www.npr.org/2022/02/02/1077653424/crosby-stills-nash-young-spotify.

Turk, James. "Universities, the *Charter,* Doug Ford, and Campus Free Speech," *Constitutional Forum constitutionnel* 29, 2 (2020), 31-44, https://journals.library.ualberta.ca/constitutional_forum/index.php/constitutional_forum/article/view/29398.

Turk, James. "Understanding Academic Freedom in Canada," Occasional Paper, March 2022, Centre for Free Expression, https://cfe.torontomu.ca/news/understanding-academic-freedom-canada-cfes-newest-publication, accessed 15 February 2024.

Turner, Piers Norris. "Introduction – Updating Mill on Free Speech," *Utilitas* (2021), 125-32.

University of Winnipeg, "Statement on comments at 'My Jerusalem' panel discussion," 6 March 2018. https://news.uwinnipeg.ca/statement-on-comments-at-my-jerusalem-panel-discussion/, accessed 25 March 2024.

University of Winnipeg, "The University Calendar," updated 26 May 2022. https://www.uwinnipeg.ca/academics/calendar/docs/the-university.pdf.

Usher, Alex. "Has Everybody Lost Their Damn Mind?" *Higher Education Strategy Associates* blog post, 27 November 2017, https://higheredstrategy.com/everybody-lost-damn-mind/, accessed 15 March 2023.

Voltaire, "Liberty of the Press," in Stephen A. Smith, *Freedom of Expression: Foundational Documents and Historical Arguments*. Oxford: Oxbridge Research Associates, 2018.

Waldron, Jeremy. *The Harm in Hate Speech*. Cambridge, Mass.: Harvard University Press, 2012.

Walker, Mason and Katerina Eva Matsu, "News Consumption Across Social Media in 2021," *Pew Research Center*, 21 September 2021. https://www.pewresearch.org/journalism/2021/09/20/news-consumption-across-social-media-in-2021/.

Weinrib, Laura. *The Taming of Free Speech*. Cambridge, Mass.: Harvard University Press, 2016.

Wilfrid Laurier University, "Values, Vision, Mission." Approved by the Board of Governors, 20 November 2008. https://www.wlu.ca/about/discover-laurier/values-vision-mission.html, accessed 15 March 2023.

Wilfrid Laurier University Senate "Statement on Freedom of Expression," 29 May 2018. https://www.wlu.ca/about/discover-laurier/freedom-of-expression/statement.html, accessed 15 June 2023.

Williams, James. *Stand Out of Our Light: Freedom and Resistance in the Attention Economy.* Cambridge: Cambridge University Press, 2018.

Williams, Kalin M. "Neil Young and Joni Mitchell are Destroying Free Speech," *The Medium,* 29 January 2022. https://medium.com/the-riff/neil-young-and-joni-mitchell-are-destroying-free-speech-c92fdff6c732, accessed 15 March 2023.

Wittgenstein, Ludwig. *Philosophical Investigations,* G.E.M. Anscombe, trans. New York: Macmillan, 1953.

Wu, Timothy. "Is the First Amendment Obsolete," in *The Free Speech Century,* Lee Bollinger and Geoffrey Stone, eds. New York: Oxford University Press, 2019, 272-91.

Wyshynski, Greg. "Hockey icon Don Cherry fired for immigrant comments," *ESPN,* 11 November 2019, https://www.espn.com/nhl/story/_/id/28059815/hockey-icon-don-cherry-fired-immigrant-comments.

York, Jillian, Gennie Gebhart, Jason Kelley, and David Greene, "Twitter has a New Owner. Here's What He Should Do," The Electronic Frontier Foundation, 25 April 2022. https://www.eff.org/deeplinks/2022/04/twitter-has-new-owner-heres-what-he-should-do accessed 29 December 2022.

Zemonjic, Peter. "Federal government names organizations that will help spend $600M journalism fund," CBC News, 24 May 2019. https://www.cbc.ca/news/politics/journalism-support-fund-panel-1.5144282.

Zine, Jasmine, Greg Bird, and Sara Matthews, "Criticizing Israel is Not Antisemitic – It's Academic Freedom," *The Conversation,* 15 November, 2020, https://theconversation.com/criticizing-israel-is-not-antisemitic-its-academic-freedom-148864.

Zuboff, Shoshana. *The Age of Surveillance Capitalism.* London: Profile Books, 2019.

INDEX

Abrams v. United States, 56, 58, 169n7
absolutism, free speech, 20
    adherents to, 9–10, 12, 27, 32, 92, 133
    censorship versus, 8, 99, 133
    criticisms of, 2, 101, 104
    moderate views versus, 9–10, 32–4, 90
    notions of, 10, 41, 44–7, 151n6
    shifting positions on, 1, 7
academia, 23
    goals of, 9, 11–12, 85
    see also universities
academic freedom, 114
    academic disciplines/rigour and, 76, 78–9, 83–4, 128
    "better speech" and, 87–8, 92
    Chicago Principles in Canada, 90, 94–5
    collective agreements with faculty/unions and, 74, 79, 81–5
    concept/principles of, 72–5, 83–5, 89–91, 96, 131–2
    conflation with free speech, 14, 23, 70–5, 78–80, 90, 95–6
    extramural/intramural expression and, 73, 78, 81, 91, 142, 164n32
    free speech versus, 2–3, 14–15, 86–8, 100, 145
    Indigenous perspectives on, 145–7
    legalities in Canada versus US, 23, 71, 79, 81–2, 88–95, 134
    legislation/policies defining, 8, 71, 73–4, 79–81, 90–5
    Palestine/antisemitism and, 134–5, 137–45
    quality of expression and, 75–6, 94–5, 130–1
    shielding racism, 95–6
    teaching assistants and, *see* teaching assistants (TAs)
    university speech limits created on, 9, 24–5, 72–6
action versus speech, *see* speech/action distinction
advocacy, free speech, 1, 21, 97
    absolutist, *see* absolutism, free speech
    addressing reasons for, 12–13, 152n24
    apocryphal statements for, 29–30, 71
    limitations on, 31, 100, 128, 131
    social media, 103–4, 110, 122–3
    varying concepts of free speech in, 47–8, 78, 132–3
AdWords (Google), 109
Alberta,
    hate speech case in, 64–6
    notions of free expression in, 8, 71, 79–80, 89–91, 94
American Civil Liberties Union (ACLU), 4, 62, 81, 106, 151n11
Ancient Athenian society, 12, 28, 37, 152n15
Ancient Greek society, 27–8
Angus, Ian, 75
Anishinaabe, influence of, 6, 68, 147–9
anti-colonial movements, 36, 140
anti-racism, 4, 8, 36, 132
antisemitism, 2
    cases involving, 56–7, 64–5, 133–45
    critiques of IHRA definition of, 134–40, 142–5
    free speech versus accusations of, 14, 133–5

197

increasing, 5, 133
see also International Holocaust Remembrance Alliance (IHRA) antisemitism definition
antitrust law, 122–5
Ash, Timothy Garton, 11, 27–8, 117, 148, 152n21
attention economy, 105, 110
Austin, J.L., 40, 57
Australia, 112
authoritarianism, 42, 47, 74

Bakan, Abigail, 142
Bakan, Joel, 100
Baker, C. Edwin, 50, 131
   absolutism of, 44–7
   on civility rules, 46–7
   free speech as self-evident right, 23, 44–8, 119, 139
   on hate speech, 44–6
   individualism of, 44–6
   other Western political philosophers versus, 19, 25–7, 32, 35, 39, 46
Balkin, Jack, 104–5, 120
Bell, Emily, 108
Bell, Melina Constantine, 39–40
Belpedio, James, 61
Ben-Porath, Sigal, 92, 96, 167n75
   on inclusive freedom, 71, 88–91
Bentham, Jeremy, 37
Berlin, Isaiah, 10, 137
Berners-Lee, Tim, 120–1
Bérubé, Michael, 72, 78, 100, 164n32
Bickert, Monika, 106–7
big tech, 118
   critiques of, 100, 126
   monopolies, 115, 119, 121–3
Blasi, Vincent, 59
Blatchford, Christie, 70, 87
B'nai Brith Canada, 137, 143
Borrows, John, 68, 147–9
Boycott, Divestment and Sanctions (BDS) movement, 137–8, 142
Brandeis, Louis, 5, 20, 54, 56, 61, 132
Brandenburg v. Ohio, 43, 56, 90, 133
Brewster, Kyle, 3, 5

British Columbia, 66, 80–1
Brown, Brené, 22

Cambridge Analytica, 100, 173n45
Canada,
   academic freedom legalities in, 23, 71, 79, 81–2, 88–95, 134
   Chicago Principles in, 90, 94–5
   constitution of, 53–4
   freedom of expression court cases in, 54–5, 63–5, 79–81
   free speech protection in, 3, 7, 24, 54, 67, 157n3, 159n18
   hate speech law in, 2, 41, 52, 55, 88, 133–6
   see also Supreme Court of Canada
Canada (Human Rights Commission) v. Taylor, 66
Canadian Association of University Teachers (CAUT), 75, 144
Canadian Human Rights Act (CHRA), 2, 66, 69
cancel culture, 7–8, 22, 35, 45, 133
CBC, 70, 77–8, 101
censorship,
   absence of government, 13, 22, 105
   academic/institutional, 74, 78, 137
   claimed spreading of, 20
   concepts of, 10–11, 22
   content moderation versus, 10–11, 103–4
   counter-speech, versus, 62, 144
   criticisms of, 29–30, 144
   free speech absolutism versus, 1, 5, 8
   press, 12, 74
   of pro-Palestinian protestors, 1, 7, 133–4, 136, 142, 144
   restrictions on state, 17, 49–50, 74, 89, 100, 123, 137
   social media, 103–5, 123, 126
Charter of Rights and Freedoms, 138
   academic freedom versus, 83–4, 88, 95–6
   court cases involving, 63–6, 69–71, 79–80, 102
   curtailing of government

infringement in, 16, 49, 63
First Amendment versus, 25, 54–5, 63
free speech protection in, 3, 7, 24, 54, 67, 157n3, 159n18
non-applicability to Canadian universities, 15, 63–4, 71–6, 79–81, 94, 143
"reasonable limits" in, 54–6, 74–5, 134
scholarship on, 52, 145
social media and, 122, 131
workplaces versus academia, 73–9, 84
Cherry, Don, 77–8
Chicago Principles, 8, 25, 71, 89
in Canada, 90, 94–5
Statement of, 91–3
Citizens United v. Federal Election Committee, 62
clear-and-present-danger test, 43–4, 55–6
Coalition Avenir Québec (CAQ), 73–4
colonialism, 136
anti-, *see* anti-colonial movements
free speech as cover for, 14, 127, 145
post-, *see* post-colonial studies
struggles against, 80, 133, 148
Western tradition and, 19, 28, 36
see also decolonial perspectives
Communications Decency Act, 97, 168n4
section 230: 105–13, 121–2, 124, 158n15
communitarianism, 43, 46–7
constitutions, Canadian versus American, 53–4
content moderation, online, 10–11, 104, 111, 124
copyright,
infringement, 9, 111, 140
law, 58, 111–13, 121
counter-speech, 7, 53
caustic, 20, 38, 139, 148–9
doctrine, 5, 20, 53, 58, 61–3, 67
courts, 97, 158n7

differences in Canadian versus American, 4–5, 51–4, 67, 82
freedom of expression cases in Canadian, 54–5, 63–5, 79–81
presence/regulation of free speech in, 16–17, 23–4, 50, 56, 74, 130
"reasonable limits" on free expression in, 54–6, 64–5, 74
university decision-making versus, 93–4, 102
see also Supreme Court of Canada; Supreme Court, US
COVID-19: 8, 48
Cree, 6, 146–7, 149
Criminal Code, 2, 122
on hate speech and, 64–6, 69, 140–1
critical and inclusive discussion, 57, 119
academic freedom and, 85, 89–90, 94–6, 131, 138, 143–4
cases focusing on, 19–22, 77, 98–9, 122–3, 134–5
concept of, 24–5, 60, 125, 136
constitutional protections versus, 49, 52–4, 66–7, 71–2, 94–6, 131, 138–41
ideals of/requirements for, 17–18, 89–90, 96, 100, 139, 148
legislation affecting, 108, 114
as positive right, 17, 19, 60, 98
social media tensions with, 98–103, 108, 113, 117–24, 127–30

Dalhousie University, 80
Dalzell, Stewart, 97, 99
Dea, Shannon, 96, 163n26
on academic freedom versus free speech, 72, 79, 81, 85–6, 94
decolonial perspectives, 80, 144, 148
defamation, 9, 92–3, 107, 110, 140
Deibert, Ronald, 101
democracies, modern,
constitutional legitimation of, 53–4
curtailing government power in, 11, 51, 60, 67

free speech debates in, 8, 27–30, 41–4, 47
participation in, *see* critical and inclusive discussion
private companies versus, 8, 117, 125, 129
public sphere in, 114, 116–17, 119, 139
"reasonable limits" on free expression in, 54–6, 64–5, 74
democracy, 89
  Charter valuing of, 11, 13
  First Amendment and, 3, 82
  free speech presence in, 27, 41–4, 47, 130
  representative, 28–30, 34, 102, 156n41
  self-government and, 41–4, 119, 130
  social media/internet use and, 5, 99–101, 104, 116–19, 124, 127–9
  too much, 41, 43
  tyranny of the majority versus, 28–9, 34–6, 41–3, 130, 155n20
Dickson, Brian, 65
Digital Millennium Copyright Act, 111–13
disinformation,
  dissemination of, 21, 126, 128
  increasing, 5, 7
  online, 21, 101, 124, 176n92
Doctorow, Cory, 111, 121
D'Orazio, Dax, 74–5, 94
Douglas, William, 82

East Side White Pride, 3–4
Eldridge v. British Columbia, 64, 164n36
equality,
  academic freedom and, 72, 142
  constitutional protection of, 41, 64
  formal versus substantial, 17
  free expression and, 9–10, 13, 27, 42
  hate speech versus, 45, 90
  internet use and, 5, 126
  marketplace of ideas and, 58–60
  see also inequalities

Erasmus, 116–17

Facebook,
  business model, 106–10, 118–22
  court cases involving, 79–81, 102
  free speech presence on, 10–11, 62, 97–9, 102, 127
  legislation pertaining to, 107–8, 112, 122–3
  oversight adjudication, 8, 100, 110–11, 125
  Trump lawsuit against, 18, 52, 103–4
  see also Meta
fake news, 99, 101, 126, 169n9
Fairness Doctrine (FCC), 113
far right, the, 70, 99; *see also* right wing
Federal Communications Commission (FCC), 113, 122
Fifth Amendment, 41–2
Finckenstein, Konrad von, 122, 124, 172n37
First Amendment, 132
  absolute freedom of speech in, 18, 41–4, 49, 54, 62, 67
  Charter freedom of expression versus, 25, 54–5, 63
  curtailing government infringements, 16, 20, 22, 24, 52, 152n27
  as defining/protecting free speech, 3, 7, 15–16, 25, 41–4
  hate speech, protection of, 1, 4–5, 136, 138, 140, 165n48
  marketplace of ideas and, 58–60, 67
  misuse of, 18, 52–3
  social media and, 102–6
  speech versus action and, 9, 40–1, 55–7, 159n22
  universities, applicability to, 71, 74, 77–8, 81–2, 88–9, 92
Fish, Stanley, 14, 72, 77
Fishman, Aidan, 137
Ford, Doug, 8, 71, 90, 94
Foundation for Individual Rights and Expression (FIRE), 132
Fourteenth Amendment, 41, 54, 61, 82

Fraser, Nancy, 115
freedom(s), 47, 72, 83
　absolute versus relative, 41–2
　Charter, 3, 7, 24, 54, 67, 122, 157n3
　concept of, 24–5
　enlightenment and, 30–4, 42–4, 58, 77, 104, 119
　inclusive, 71, 88–91
　positive versus negative, 17–18, 49–52, 66–8, 76, 98, 128–9
freedom of expression,
　academic freedom versus, 2–3, 14–15, 74, 86–8, 100, 145
　cases of reasonable infringement, 54–6, 64–5, 74
　concept of, 49–51
　false dichotomy with, 1–2, 92
　freedom of speech versus, 25, 49, 54–5, 57
　government, role of, 49–51
　reasonable limits on, 54–5, 64–5, 67, 88
　Supreme Court cases on, 54–5, 63–5, 79–81
freedom of speech,
　academic freedom and, 74–5, 78, 81–2, 89
　Chicago Principles and, 89, 91–2
　concept of, 49–52, 54–5
　First Amendment on, 18–22, 41–4, 49, 54, 62–3, 67
　freedom of expression versus, 24–5, 49, 54–5, 57
　social media and, 103–6, 116, 128
　Supreme Court cases on, 54–7, 61, 65
　theorizing on, 2, 11, 48, 74–5, 132–3
free speech, 103
　academic freedom versus, see academic freedom
　concepts of, 11–14, 22–3, 47, 53, 95
　considerations on, 2, 8–13, 90, 101
　crisis of, 8, 70
　criticisms of, 2, 9–10, 13–14, 32–4, 104
　dimensions/questions of, 16–19, 21–3, 149
　domains of, 23–5
　fighting words versus, 56–7
　goals of, 15–16, 42–3, 46, 54, 119–21, 128–32
　as marketplace of ideas, see marketplace of ideas analogy
　regulating, 41, 48, 50–2, 101
　screwdriver metaphor for, 15, 96
　tools for, 15–17, 124, 131–3
　variability of lines drawn on, 8–13, 15–17, 49, 67, 130

Gabbert, Mark, 95
Gehl, Robert, 127
gender identity or expression, jurisprudence on, 2, 64, 69
genocide, 1–2, 100
GETTR, 10, 111
　terms of use, 103–4
Globe and Mail, 70, 87
Google, 118
　data collection/sale, 100, 107–9
　dominance of, 121, 123
　media outlets, impact on, 112
　Trump lawsuit against, 18, 52
　US legislation relating to, 107–8, 111
governments,
　academic freedom legislation, 8, 71–4
　Charter curtailing infringement by, 9, 16, 49, 63
　democracies' curtailing power of, 11, 51, 60, 67
　First Amendment curtailing infringement by, 16, 20, 22, 24, 52, 152n27
　functions of democratic, 49–52
　Kant on role of, 32–4, 38–9, 41, 47
　Mill on role of, 28, 35–9, 45
　restrictions on censorship by, 17, 49–50, 74, 89, 100, 123, 137
　self-, 41–4, 47–8, 92, 119, 130–1

Habermas, Jürgen, 32–3, 114–15, 127
Haidt, Jonathan, 99, 128
Hampton, Eber, 146
Hannan, Jason, 116
Haque, Eve, 75, 95–6
Harper, William Rainey, 92, 95
Harper's Magazine letter,
    cancel culture and, 35, 45
    "caustic counter-speech" support, 20, 38, 139, 148–9
    concepts of free speech in, 19, 21–2, 46–7, 50, 53
hate propaganda, 3, 52, 64–5
hate speech, 14, 90, 99–100
    Canadian law on, 2, 41, 52, 55, 88, 133–6
    Criminal Code on, 64–6, 69, 140–1
    Edwin Baker on, 44–6
    First Amendment protection of, 1, 4–5, 136, 138, 140, 165n48
    social media and, 99–101, 126
Haudenosaunee, 67, 146, 148
Hawley, Josh, 18, 52–3, 100
Heer, Jeet, 20
Helvétius, Claude-Adrien, 29–30
Heritage Front, 4
Holmes, Oliver Wendell, 5, 28, 97, 99
    clear-and-present-danger test, 9, 43, 55–6, 60–1, 92
    First Amendment Supreme Court case law, 54, 61–2
    free speech as marketplace of ideas, 37, 58, 60, 104, 132
Hrynyshyn, Derek, 125–6
Hughes, Chris, 122–4
Hutchins, Robert M., 28, 148

Independent Jewish Voices, 142–4
Indigenous peoples, 158n8
    Bill of Rights influenced by, 67–8, 148
    "complex understanding" of, 146–7
    hatred targeting, 5, 7, 31
    insights/values of, 6, 17, 28, 68, 90
    mino-bimaadiziwin, 68, 147

    on Western tradition scholarship, 19, 67
inequalities, 62, 115, 123
    free speech masking, 14, 59
Instagram, 98, 112, 119, 121
insurrection attempt (on US Capitol), 5, 18, 52–3
International Holocaust Remembrance Alliance (IHRA) antisemitism definition,
    examples of, 134, 137–8
    government/university adoption of, 135–8, 140–3
    as originally non-legally binding, 134–6, 140–2, 144–5
    public/organizational disputing of, 136–8, 140–2, 144
    see also Boycott, Divestment and Sanctions (BDS) movement; Jewish people
internet, the, 116
    attempts to structure/regulate, 16, 97–9, 101, 105, 121–4
    government involvement in development of, 18, 106–7, 118
    hate speech on, 5, 66, 101
    user data on, 109, 111–12, 121
    vehicle for expression/discussion, 5, 24, 26, 96–102, 119, 128
Irwin Toy Ltd. v. Quebec, 64
Israel,
    conflict with Palestine, 1, 7, 138
    criticism of, 7, 23, 133–8, 141–4
    see also antisemitism; International Holocaust Remembrance Alliance (IHRA) antisemitism definition

Jerusalem Declaration, 136
Jewish people, 143
    concerns for comfort of, 1, 135
    hatred targeting, 1, 5, 134
    recognition of BDS legitimacy, 136–7
    right-wing weaponizing of IHRA definition, 135, 142, 144
    see also antisemitism; International Holocaust Remembrance Alliance (IHRA) antisemitism definition

Jilani, Zaid, 21

Kant, Immanuel, 18–19, 27–8, 50, 97, 131, 145
    on autonomy and individualism, 30–1, 37
    debates on racism/sexism in, 31–2, 35, 154n12
    on enlightenment, 30–4, 42–5, 47, 58, 104, 119
    government, role of, 32–4, 38–9, 41, 47
    on im/maturity, 30–2, 34, 40
    on public use of reason, 32–4, 47, 77, 99, 114
Kenney, Jason, 8, 71, 90, 94
Khan, Masuma, 80
Khanna, Ro, 101, 106, 126–7
King, Jr., Martin Luther, 132–3, 139

language,
    free speech as part of, 12–13
    government determination of school, 51
    politics of use, 5–6, 12–13, 69, 90
    speech act theory, 40, 57
left wing, the, 123
    free speech advocacy, 1, 7, 152n24
legal system, regulation of free speech, 23–4, 50, 67
Leiter, Brian, 23–4, 50
Leong, Nancy, 59
libel, 9, 42, 75, 110, 117
Liberal Party of Canada,
    hate speech legislation, 66
    MPs' letter to university presidents, 1–2, 133
Little Sisters Books and Art Emporium v. Canada, 64
Lynk, Michael, 85

Macfarlane, Emmett, 49–50, 52, 157n3
MacLatchy, Deborah, 86–8, 90
marketplace of ideas analogy, 24, 37, 53, 132
    concept of, 23, 56–8, 60–1
    critiques of, 58–60, 65, 67

    social media versus, 103, 127
Marxist critique, 12, 82, 117
Mchangama, Jacob, 12, 99, 128, 132, 169n9
McKinney v. University of Guelph, 63–4, 79
McLachlin, Beverley, 65–6
McLuhan, Marshall, 115
media, traditional,
    free speech debates on, 7, 19, 25, 70–1, 78
    outcry on issues, 2, 23, 86
    outlets, 22–3, 105, 112–13
    public broadcasters, 101, 113, 121
    regulation of, 54, 101–2, 122–5
    revenue generation, 101–2, 124–5
    shaping of communication, 97, 115–16, 130, 141
    studies, 59
    traditional, 97, 105, 108, 115–16, 120
    see also CBC; social media
Meiklejohn, Alexander, 5, 139, 155n20
    on free speech and self-government, 41–3, 47–8, 92, 119, 131
    other Western political philosophers versus, 19, 33–5, 39, 43–4, 50, 156nn41,43
    on technological changes, 97, 116–17, 119
    on US constitutional freedoms, 41–3
Menzies, Peter, 122, 124, 172n37
Mercer, Rick, 70, 78, 96
Mesley, Wendy, 77–8
Meta, 8, 109–12, 121; *see also* Facebook
Metzger, Tom, 3–4
Mill, John Stuart, 5, 33, 59, 67, 145
    on democracy/tyranny of the majority, 28–9, 34–6, 41–3
    on free expression, 25–6, 36–41, 47–50, 54, 95, 131
    government, role of, 28, 35–9, 45
    harm principle, 35, 39, 44, 61, 92, 104
    liberty versus authority, 28, 35–7, 39–40

on social progress, 25–6, 37–8,
42–4, 47, 58, 119
on speech versus action, 9, 38–41,
45, 92
utilitarianism of, 36–8, 47, 139
Miller, Jason, 103–4
Mills, Charles W., 31
misogynist speech, 2, 5, 14, 127,
157n60
Mohawk, John, 67, 148
Mondal, Anshuman, 59, 98
Moon, Richard, 46, 62, 94, 105, 175n81
on right to free expression, 11, 49,
52, 65–6
"more speech" principle, 5, 100, 128,
132
counter-speech doctrine and, 5,
20, 53, 58, 61–3
Moskowitz, P.E., 13–14, 80, 145
Musk, Elon, 10, 99
Muthu, Sankar, 31

Nadeau, Mary-Jo, 134
Napoli, Philip, 60, 62, 105, 118
National Post, 70, 78
Newhouse, David, 90, 146–7
New York Times, 74
Northwest Territories, 63, 66

Oakmont, Inc. v. Prodigy Services Co.,
107
Online Harms Act (Bill C-63): 66
Online News Act (Bill C-18): 112
Onondaga, 90, 146–7
Ontario,
free speech case in, 69, 71, 80–1,
89
notions of free expression in, 8,
89–91, 94
open-source software, 126–7
Oregon, white-supremacist activity in,
3–5

Palestine, 2, 135
conflict with Israel, 133, 138
protests supporting, 1, 7, 136, 142,
144

test, 133–4
Parler, 10, 111
Penny, Laurie, 139
people of colour, hatred targeting, 5,
7, 31
Peters, John Durham, 29
Petersen, Jennifer, 102, 118, 159n23
Peterson, Jordan, 2, 69–71, 78, 86
Pimlott, Hillary, 70, 87
Plato, 32
polarization, 169n9
attempts to reduce, 22, 98–9, 130,
147
increasing, 5, 13, 87, 101, 110, 128
POPS (private owned public spaces),
117–18
post-colonial scholarship, 59, 76, 146
Postman, Neil, 115–16
Pridgen v. University of Calgary, 79–80,
102
public discussion, 14
academic freedom debates versus,
2–3, 84–5, 96
arenas for, 37–8, 45–6, 112
democratic participation in, *see*
critical and inclusive discussion
evaluating free speech in, 7–8, 11,
20–5, 119–20, 127–8, 135–40
freedom of expression rights in,
50, 53, 67, 129–31
Indigenous traditions of, 19, 147
internet/social media as site of, 5,
22, 98–105, 113, 116
Western political philosophies of,
18–19, 37–8, 45, 58, 67, 156n41
see also counter-speech; *Harper's
Magazine* letter
public sphere/realm, 29
democratic, 114, 116–17, 119, 139
digital, 97–9, 108, 114, 118, 121
Habermas' concept of, 32–3,
114–15, 127
media transformations in, 101–2,
110–12, 114–18, 121
reforming, 122, 125

Quebec, 64

notions of academic freedom in, 8, 71, 73–4
queer/LGBTQ+ people, 7, 8, 64, 76

racialized people, harm from white supremacy, 4, 59, 77–8, 148, 157n60
racism, 77, 118
    definitions of, 135–7
    freedom of speech versus, 132–3, 139, 145
    free speech masking, 4, 14, 59–60, 80, 96
    hate speech and, 44–6
    impacts on public participation, 28, 59–60, 78, 127, 157n60
    violent, 4–5, 28
    Western tradition and, 28, 31, 36, 59, 132–3
    see also anti-racism; white supremacy
radio, 24, 69, 101, 105–6, 113, 116
Rahman, K. Sabeel, 120, 124–5
Rambukkana, Nathan, 69–70, 87
Rangwala, Shama, 91, 93–4
Reddit, 98–9, 171n30
religion, 54
    freedom of, 12, 41, 67, 148
rights, 16
    free speech versus other, 9–10, 41, 64–7, 132, 144, 158n9
    human/individual, 26, 52, 62–3, 72, 135, 137
    positive versus negative, 17–18, 24, 50, 85, 89
    "reasonable limits" on, 54–6, 74–5, 134
    Western tradition philosophers on, 11, 23, 44–8, 49, 52, 119, 139
    women's, 36
    see also Charter of Rights and Freedoms; First Amendment; freedom of expression; freedom of speech
right wing, 122, 171n30
    governments, 73–4
    protests by, 7, 23
    social media, 10, 21, 103–4
    see also far right, the
Rogan, Joe,
    critiques of show, 21–3
    fake information, spreading, 21–2, 48
Rohingya population (Myanmar), 100
Rousseau, Jean Jacques, 38, 43, 156n43
Ruth, Jennifer, 72, 78, 100, 164n32
R. v. Keegstra, 64–5
R. v. Whatcott, 79
RWDSU v. Dolphin Delivery, 63

Sachs, Jeffrey, 83, 141–2
Said, Edward, 96
Sanders, Bernie, 123–4
Saskatchewan (Human Rights Commission) v. Whatcott, 66
Schauer, Frederick, 11–12
Schenck v. United States, 9, 43, 55–6, 61
Schroeder, Jared, 59–60
Scopes Monkey Trial, 81–2
Scott, Joan Wallach, 72, 75–6, 78, 87
Sears, Alan, 134
Seraw, Mulugeta, 3–5
Shepherd, Lindsay, 2–3, 23, 69–73, 78–80, 85–90, 96
Simon & Schuster, 18, 52–3
slander, 9, 42, 75
Smith, Stephen A., 8, 148
Snapchat, 11, 98, 102, 121
socialism, 56
    platform, 125–6
social media, 97
    ads, 10, 108–9, 112, 119–20, 123–6
    algorithms, 60, 108–10, 119–20, 124, 127, 159n23
    business model of, 11, 18, 24, 102–16, 124–6
    Charter rights and, 122, 131
    censorship, 103–5, 123, 126
    communication through, 2–3, 24–6, 98–9, 102, 114
    company profit motives, 9, 108–10, 114, 117–20, 126–9, 132
    content moderation on, 10–11, 98–9, 103–8, 110–11, 114
    cookies, 109, 112–13

data collection and analysis, 100, 108–13, 118–21, 124–7
decentralization of, 125, 127
democracy and, 5, 99–101, 104, 116–19, 124, 127–9
fediverse, 127
First Amendment and, 102–6, 116, 128
free expression considerations, 9–12, 50, 65, 99–104, 117–19, 145
free speech advocacy, 103–4, 110, 122–3
hate speech on, 99–101, 126
interoperability, 121, 125
issues raised by, 5, 7–9, 52, 98–104, 146–7
marketplace of ideas analogy for, 59–60, 62, 103, 127
non-profit, 121, 126
public utility model of, 122, 124–5
regulation/reform of, 100, 106–8, 110–14, 118–21, 129
right-wing, 10, 21, 103–4, 111
role of, 7, 96
as site of discussion, 5, 22, 98–105, 113, 116
surveillance, 109, 124–5, 127–8
tensions regarding inclusivity, 98–103, 108, 113, 117–24, 127–30
see also media, traditional
social media responsibility act, 122
speech/action distinction,
Charter of Rights and Freedoms on, 40–1, 67
First Amendment on, 4, 40–1, 55–7, 90–2, 104
philosophical arguments on, 9, 33–5, 38–41, 43–7, 57
public cases of, 20–1, 55–7, 159n22
Supreme Court decisions, 9, 55–7, 67, 159n22
see also clear-and-present-danger test
Spinoza, Baruch de, 30
Spotify, 21–2, 48, 50, 98, 153n31
Srnicek, Nick, 110, 117, 125
Stern, Kenneth, 135–6, 140, 143

Supreme Court of Canada,
constitutional interpretation, 53–5, 63–5, 79–81, 88
on free expression, 50, 54–5, 63–7, 79–81, 102
see also Charter of Rights and Freedoms
Supreme Court, US, 8, 107
clear-and-present-danger test, 9, 43, 55–6, 60–1, 92
constitutional interpretation, 53–4, 81–2
on free speech, 54–7, 61, 65
speech/action distinction, 9, 55–7, 67, 159n22
see also First Amendment
Sweezy v. New Hampshire, 82

Taylor, Charles, 46
teaching assistants (TAs), 81
academic freedom case, 2, 69, 85–6
Teachout, Zephyr, 120, 124–5
Telecommunications Act, 106–7
television, 24, 69, 101, 106, 113–16
TikTok, 98, 107
Titley, Gavan, 59
trans people, hatred targeting, 5, 136, 157n60
transphobia, increasing, 5, 7, 14
trolling, 8, 99, 105, 116
Trump, Donald, 107, 135
banned from social media, 10, 104
social media lawsuit, 18, 52, 100
Truth Social platform, 10, 104, 111, 171n28
white-supremacist followers, 5, 38, 52–3, 103
Truth Social, 10, 104, 111
Turk, James, 79, 81, 94
Twitter/X, 80
business model, 18, 104, 107–10, 172n37
"cancelling" on, 22, 103
as forum for expression, 62, 98–100, 104, 127
name change, 10, 99

regulation/reform of, 107–8, 110–11, 121
Trump lawsuit against, 18, 52
tyranny of the majority, 28–9, 34–6, 41–3, 130, 155n20

UAlberta Pro-Life v. Governors of the University of Alberta, 80–1
United Jewish People's Order, 142–3
United States,
absolute freedom of speech in, 18, 41–4, 49, 54, 62, 67
academic freedom in, 23, 71, 79, 81–2, 88–95, 134
Chicago Principles, 8, 25, 71, 89, 91–2
clear-and-present-danger test, 9, 43, 55–6, 60–1, 92
constitution, 53–4
court decision-making in, 4–5, 51–4, 67, 82
curtailing government infringement, 16, 20, 22, 24, 52, 152n27
hate speech, protection of, 1, 4–5, 136, 138, 140, 165n48
social media regulation, 107–8, 111
Supreme Court, *see* Supreme Court, US
United States v. Alvarez, 61–2
universities, 2
academic freedom in, *see* academic freedom
adoption of IHRA antisemitism definition, 140–3
censorship in, 74, 78, 137
Charter non-applicability in, 15, 63–4, 71–6, 79–81, 94, 143
collective agreements with faculty/unions in, 74, 79, 81–5
decision-making versus courts, 93–4, 102
First Amendment applicability to, 71, 74, 77–8, 81–2, 88–9, 92
free speech limits created by, 9, 24–5, 72–6
goals of, 9, 11–12, 14, 85
as workplaces, 73–9, 84

see also Canadian Association of University Teachers (CAUT); Wilfrid Laurier University
University of Winnipeg, 79, 83, 86
university panel "My Jerusalem," 142

vaccines, debates on, 7–8, 21–2, 31, 48
violence, 138
antisemitic, 136, 140
factors that reduce, 10, 45, 104
freedom of speech and, 38–9, 100, 126, 140
language and, 12, 70, 123
social media and, 100, 103–4
white-supremacist, 3–5
Voltaire, 29–30, 39, 71

Warren, Elizabeth, 123–4
Weinrib, Laura, 62, 158n9
Western tradition,
colonialism and, 19, 28, 36
on free speech, 25–7, 32–48, 50, 54, 92, 131
Indigenous critiques of, 19, 67
on public discussion, 18–19, 37–8, 45, 58, 67, 156n41
racism and, 28, 31, 36, 59, 132–3
on rights, 11, 23, 44–8, 49, 52, 119, 139
White Aryan Resistance (WAR), 3–4
white supremacy,
Canadian versus US legislation on, 5
harmful speech, 2, 14, 56, 31
local organizing, 3–5, 56
struggles against, 133, 139
Whitfield, Kevin, 59
Whitney v. California, 56, 61–2
Wilfrid Laurier University, 2, 23, 69, 71, 83, 85–90
Wilson v. University of Calgary, 79
Winnipeg, 6, 149; *see also* University of Winnipeg
Wittgenstein, Ludwig, 40, 57, 152n20
women, 114
hatred targeting, 5, 7

marginalization/denigration of, 30–2, 76, 115, 154n12
rights for, 28, 36, 42–3
Wu, Timothy, 105–6

X, *see* Twitter/X

Young, Neil, 21–2, 48, 51
YouTube, 86, 98, 104, 107, 109, 121

Zuboff, Shoshana, 108–10, 113, 117, 119–20
Zuckerberg, Mark, 110, 122, 173n45